ANIMAL CAPITAL

CARY WOLFE, SERIES EDITOR

ANIMAL CAPITAL
Rendering Life in Biopolitical Times

NICOLE SHUKIN

posthumanities 6

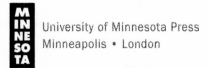

University of Minnesota Press
Minneapolis • London

Portions of chapters 2 and 3 were previously published as "The Mimetics of Mobile Capital," in *Against Automobility*, ed. Steffen Bohm, Campbell Jones, Chris Land, and Matthew Paterson (Oxford: Blackwell Publishing / Sociological Review, 2006), 150–74. Reprinted with permission of Sociological Review.

Published by the University of Minnesota Press
111 Third Avenue South, Suite 290
Minneapolis, MN 55401-2520
http://www.upress.umn.edu

Library of Congress Cataloging-in-Publication Data

Shukin, Nicole.
   Animal capital : rendering life in biopolitical times / Nicole Shukin.
      p.   cm. — (Posthumanities ; 6)
   Includes bibliographical references and index.
   ISBN 978-0-8166-5341-6 (hc : alk. paper) — ISBN 978-0-8166-5342-3 (pb : alk. paper)
      1. Animals—Symbolic aspects.   2. Animals—Economic aspects.
   3. Animals—Political aspects.   4. Human–animal relationships.
   5. Wildlife utilization.   I. Title.
   GR705.S48 2009
   304.2—dc22   2008048773

Printed in the United States of America on acid-free paper

The University of Minnesota is an equal-opportunity educator and employer.

18 17 16 15 14 13   10 9 8 7 6 5 4 3

Contents

Acknowledgments

The research and writing of this book were made possible by fellowships and grants from the Social Sciences and Research Council of Canada, the University of Alberta, and the Province of Alberta. I am grateful to members of the Department of English at the University of Victoria, who granted me a year to complete my postdoctoral fellowship prior to taking up a position there. Without that period of grace, this book would have been several more years in the works.

This book is indebted to and inspired by conversations with numerous scholars and friends. At the University of Alberta, Heather Zwicker, Mark Simpson, and Julie Rak braced my research with unflagging support and careful readings of chapters. They have been models of engaged intellectuals and generous individuals. Dianne Chisholm never failed to support my interest in the cultural politics of nature. Imre Szeman and Anne Whitelaw offered thoughtful feedback on the dissertation out of which this book has evolved. At the University of Western Ontario, Colette Urban inspired me with her installation piece *Recalling Belvedere* and its collection of elephant paraphernalia, as well as with her kindness. I am also grateful for the guidance of Julia

Emberley at the University of Western Ontario and for the wonderful students in the Animal Signs in Literature, Film, and Theory course that I taught there in 2006. At the University of Victoria, Warren Magnusson in the Department of Political Science generously read and commented on chapter 1. In the company of someone so fluent in political theory, I recognized my disciplinary limitations in attempting to theorize animal capital but at the same time grew in my commitment to interdisciplinary risk taking. My new colleagues in the Department of English enthusiastically engaged with a version of chapter 4 at a faculty colloquium organized by Chris Douglas, and I deeply appreciate their collegiality.

I am fortunate to have had Richard Morrison as editor at the University of Minnesota Press, and I am grateful to Adam Brunner for his help and advice. Two anonymous readers offered valuable feedback that helped make this a much stronger book. Many thanks to Tara Thompson, a graduate student at the University of Victoria, who painstakingly formatted the manuscript.

My parents and siblings are among the most exceptional people I know; I've been blessed with a surplus of familial love and support. Pauline Wakeham has never failed to awaken the best in me through her unparalleled combination of intellectual commitment, personal integrity, and quirky humor; she is brilliant not only as a scholar but as a friend. Finally, to Jay and John, who patiently weathered the everyday of this book with me, thank you.

New Life Forms and Functions of Animal Fetishism

Animal Nation

In 2002, *Maclean's* magazine, one of Canada's oldest national newsweeklies, ran an advertisement configuring the nation as a beaver spread out across the page like a dissection specimen.[1] The beaver's internal organization is bared to encyclopedic view, with lines spoking out from its interior to labels biologically identifying blood organs and body parts (see Figure 1). The ad caption consists of a few pithy words tacked beneath the splayed sign of the animal: *"Maclean's.* Canada. In depth." The equivalent standing of the two proper names in the caption, *"Maclean's"* and "Canada," positions the media and the nation as virtually synonymous powers; the sober black print of "Canada" is, if anything, overshadowed by the larger, bolder *"Maclean's,"* whose blood-red typography chromatically resonates with the red tissues and organs of the beaver. A third proper name and trademark appear in more discrete red type at the top right-hand corner of the advertisement: "Rogers," short for Rogers Communications Inc. The Rogers conglomerate owns *Maclean's* as well as numerous other print, television, and telecommunications media. The placement of its name in the ad is suggestive of the

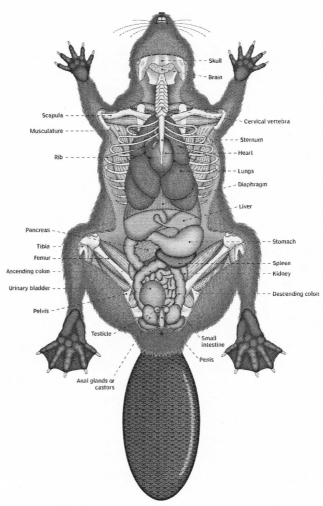

Figure 1. "*Maclean's. Canada. In depth.*" *The visceral figure of the nation in a 2002 advertisement for* Maclean's, *Canada's only national weekly current affairs magazine.*

superordinate power of capital over both the press and the nation in our current era.

Taxonomically tacking a powerful network of proper names onto an animal anatomy is generative of fetishistic effects that Marx first theorized in relation to the commodity form, in this case effecting a reification of the nation form by associating "*Maclean's*," "Canada," and "Rogers" with the raw facticity of the specimen. Yet it is not just any specimen to which the trinity of powers has been attached. The beaver is already an iconic symbol, a fetishized sign of the nation whose familiarity and recognition are presupposed by the ad's "inside" joke. If the beaver has furnished one species of animal capital for the nation as colonial pelt, it has furnished another as postcolonial brand. Instated as Canada's official emblem in 1975, the sign of the beaver was deployed as a tool of affective governance to involve Canadians in a project of national identity building and unity. The move consolidated the economic and symbolic capital accumulated in the sign of the beaver over three centuries of Euro-Canadian traffic in North America, presenting it as a natural, self-evident sign of the nation.[2]

Yet, as this book sets out to show, animal signs are anything but self-evident. Confronting their fetishistic functions in cultural discourses of the twentieth and twenty-first centuries begins with a determination to excavate for the material histories of economic and symbolic power that are cunningly reified in them. Animal signs function fetishistically in both Marxian and psychoanalytic senses; that is, they endow the historical products of social labor to which they are articulated with an appearance of innate, spontaneous being, and they serve as powerful substitutes or "partial objects" filling in for a lost object of desire or originary wholeness that never did or can exist, save phantasmatically. The beaver is Canada's fetish insofar as it configures the nation as a life form that is born rather than made (obscuring recognition of the ongoing cultural and material history of its construction) and insofar as it stands in for an organic national unity that in actuality does not exist.

Contrary to its fetishistic effects, then, there is nothing natural about the beaver sign institutionally minted in the 1970s as a means of affectively interpellating citizens into an ideal of national unity through the "innocent" appeal of the animal and of construing the nation as an

indigenous organism. Nor is the normative chain of associations triggered by the symbol of the Canadian beaver—moth-eaten stereotypes
of the fur trade nostalgically evoking a bygone era of colonial contact
and commerce, an era of imagined authenticity and fullness of nature
prior to the ostensible "vanishing" of aboriginal and animal populations[3]—natural. In the 1970s, the institutionalization of the sign of
the beaver mustered this nostalgic web of associations into the political service of a dominantly white, Euro-Canadian discourse of national
culture, one pivoting on an assertion of its *own* indigeneity. Through
the animal capital of the national symbol, a postcolonial project of
national culture deeply structured by the logics of capital and "White
normativity" has become the privileged content of a discursive struggle
for "native space," displacing the ongoing machinations of internal colonialism and white supremacy, as well as infranational struggles for
First Nations' self-determination.[4]

The Canadian beaver constitutes a powerful nodal point within a
national narrative that nostalgically *remembers* the material history of
the fur trade as a primal scene in which Native trappers, French coureurs
de bois, and English traders collaboratively trafficked in animal capital,
at the same time as it advantageously *forgets*, through the symbolic violence of occupying the semiotic slot of indigeneity, the cultural and
ecological genocides of the settler-colonial nation form mediating capital's expansion. Ostensibly free of any (human) linguistic, ethnic, racial,
class, or gender traits, the indigenous species is put into symbolic circulation as a neutral signifier incapable, it would seem, of communicating
political bias against any individual or constituency in Canada. Yet as
feminist, critical race, poststructuralist, and postcolonial theorists have
labored to show, the "privileged empty point of universality" slyly enciphers the dominant subject position in a social order, enabling that
subject position to pass as the unmarked social standard.[5] That "tes-
ticle" and "penis" are pointed to in *Maclean's* somatic diagram of the
beaver (alongside "spleen" and "stomach") inadvertently reveals the de-
fault, or universal, gender of the national ontology. Enciphering white
masculine English embodiment as a national and natural standard, the
Canadian symbol also tacitly racializes the difference of ethnic and
diasporic citizenship. Under the universal alibi of species life, prover-

bially innocent of political designs, the Canadian beaver subtly counter-indicates the relinquishment of white English cultural and economic privilege pronounced by official state multiculturalism.

Heavily burdened with a historical complex of economic and libidi-nal investments, the sign of the beaver rematerialized in a national magazine in 2002 to reify a new nexus of knowledge, nation, and capi-tal at the dawn of the twenty-first century: *Maclean's,* Canada, Rogers.[6] The wit and ostensible difference of the *Maclean's* discourse lies in its *literal* cross-sectioning of the nation's animal fetish. The magazine's deliberately literal treatment holds the defamiliarizing potential of open-ing the organic ideology of the nation to an ironic gaze and of bring-ing a "wry" self-reflexivity to bear on the stock image of the nation.[7] Yet the biological schema of the nation's organic constitution serves to repress rather than open those "recesses of the national culture from which alternative constituencies of peoples and oppositional analytic capacities may emerge."[8] Granting less an ironic analysis of the nation-fetish and more a medicalized scopophilia arousing fascination cum revulsion around its mock vivisection, the ad paradoxically manages to *revive* a tired cliché at risk of ending up on the scrap heap of history as global capitalism threatens to render the distinct "life" of the nation passé.

What makes animal signs unusually potent discursive alibis of power is not only that particularist political ideologies, by ventriloquizing them, appear to speak from the universal and disinterested place of nature. It is also that "the animal," arguably more than any other sig-nifier by virtue of its singular mimetic capaciousness (a notion that will be further elaborated over the course of this book), functions as a hinge allowing powerful discourses to flip or vacillate between literal and figurative economies of sense. Even in its rendering as a vivisection—or perhaps, especially in *Maclean's* raw rendering—the national fetish hinges on the double sense of animals' material and metaphorical cur-rency. Here the tools of colonial discourse analysis can be brought to bear on animal capital inasmuch as the animal sign, not unlike the racial stereotype theorized by Homi Bhabha, is a site of "*productive* ambiva-lence" enabling vacillations between economic and symbolic logics of power.[9] For Bhabha, ambivalence constitutes the discursive structure of fetishism. "Within discourse," he writes, "the fetish represents the simultaneous play between metaphor as substitution (masking absence and difference) and metonymy (which contiguously registers the perceived lack)."[10] As William Pietz suggests, however, couching the problem of fetishism *rhetorically*, as Bhabha does, risks textualizing it and detaching it from a material field of relationships that are not reducible to linguistic-discursive structures.[11] By the end of this book it should be clear that animal capital resists both culturalist tendencies to reduce capitalism to an economy and fetishism of signs and materialist tendencies to reduce capitalism to an economy and fetishism of substances.

Much more could be done to comparatively evaluate the productive ambivalence of the colonial stereotype and that of the animal sign. For now, suffice it to say that it is the capacity of animal life to be taken both literally and figuratively, as a material and symbolic resource of the nation, that constitutes its fetishistic potency. As will be elaborated over the course of this book, the ambivalence of animal signs is for this reason a pivotal means of depoliticizing volatile contradictions between species and speculative currencies of capital and between capitalism's material and symbolic modes of production. In the particular case of the *Maclean's* ad, the productive ambivalence of the beaver mediates a national discourse that vacillates between a traumatic remembering and a willful forgetting of Canada's forced birth. While the image of a dead specimen *potentially* yields a grisly reminder of the material exercise of power upon which the birth of the nation is historically contingent, it *actually* works to render the material violence of the nation merely metaphorical for our times.

Animal Capital

The *Maclean's* text helps to introduce a book intent on theorizing a biopolitical terrain and time of animal capital that includes, but invariably exceeds, the cultural discourses of the specific nation from which I write. The juxtaposition of two terms rarely theorized in conjunction— "animal" and "capital"—signals a double-edged intervention into two subjects whose dangerously universal appeal necessarily situates this study within the broader field of transnational cultural studies. On the one hand, *Animal Capital* constitutes a resolutely materialist engagement with the emergent "question of the animal," in Cary Wolfe's words, challenging its predominantly idealist treatments in critical theory and animal studies by theorizing the ways that animal life gets culturally and carnally rendered as capital at specific historical junctures.[12] On the other hand, by developing a series of unorthodox genealogies of animal capital across Fordist and post-Fordist eras, the book seeks to rectify a critical blind spot in Marxist and post-Marxist theory around the nodal role of animals, ideologically and materially, in the reproduction of capital's hegemony. While theorists of biopower have interrogated the increasingly total subsumption of the social and biological life of the *anthropos* to market logics, little attention has been given to what I am calling animal capital. This book's double-edged intervention suggests a critical need within the field of cultural studies for work that explores how questions of "the animal" and of capital impinge on one another within abysmal histories of contingency.

Against a mythopoetic invocation of animal signs as a universal lingua franca transcending time and space, then, I seek to historicize the specific cultural logics and material logistics that have produced animals as "forms of capital" (in the words of Pierre Bourdieu) across the twentieth and early twenty-first centuries. "Animal capital" simultaneously notates the semiotic currency of animal signs *and* the carnal traffic in animal substances across this period. More accurately, it signals a tangle of biopolitical relations within which the economic and symbolic capital of animal life can no longer be sorted into binary distinction. This book argues that animal memes and animal matter are mutually overdetermined as forms of capital, and its aim is to track what Bourdieu terms the "interconvertibility" of symbolic and economic forms of capital via the fetishistic currency of animal life.[13]

A conjugated inquiry into the historical entanglements of "animal" and "capital" not only is long overdue within the variegated field of transnational cultural studies but arguably is pivotal to an analysis of biopower, or what Michel Foucault describes as a "technology of power centered on life."[14] At stake in biopower is nothing less than an ontological contest over what Michael Hardt and Antonio Negri refer to as the "production and reproduction of life itself."[15] Foucault was the first to remark on how the sign of the animal emerged at the "threshold of biological modernity," marking a shift to "untamed ontology" or "life itself" as the new object of power.[16] The fascination in the *Maclean's* ad with the internal organs of the beaver—rather than with bodily extremities such as teeth, fur, tail, and feet—would seem to dramatize Foucault's claim that when life becomes the "sovereign vanishing-point" in relation to which power is oriented, it is the "hidden structures" of the animal, its "buried organs" and "invisible functions," that emerge as its biological cipher.[17]

The role of biopower in the globalization of market life has compelled a growing body of theory devoted to illuminating its diverse means and effects. Many recent theories of biopower have migrated away from Foucault's focus on the discourses and technologies of the state to scan instead networks and technologies of global capitalism. Hardt and Negri draw on Foucault to theorize "the biopolitical nature of the new paradigm of power" in the context of a transnational empire of capital that, they claim, has superseded the sovereignty of the nation-state.[18] Empire, they argue, operates as a "society of control," a diffuse network of power in which "mechanisms of command become ever more 'democratic,' ever more immanent to the social field, distributed throughout the brains and bodies of the citizens" (23). In this paradigm of power, hegemonic consent and participation in market life is solicited by means of semiotic and affective technologies increasingly inseparable from the economic and material conditions of capital's reproduction. As Hardt and Negri describe it, "Biopower is a form of power that regulates social life from its interior, following it, interpreting it, absorbing it, and rearticulating it. Power can achieve an effective command over the entire life of the population only when it becomes an integral, vital function that every individual embraces and reactivates of his or her own accord. As Foucault says, 'Life has now become . . . an object of power'" (23–24).

Hardt and Negri reiterate another seminal remark of Foucault's: "The control of society over individuals is not conducted only through consciousness or ideology, but also in the body and with the body. For capitalist society biopolitics is what is most important, the biological, the somatic, the corporeal."[19] However, their analysis immediately gravitates away from the body and toward the figure of a "social *bios*" in which "immaterial" modes of intellectual-symbolic labor, they argue, now predominate.[20] Hardt and Negri do carefully qualify that to claim that immaterial production is now dominant is not to say that material labor has disappeared as a condition of capital.[21] Nevertheless, by theoretically privileging the intellectual-linguistic conditions of capital in their own analysis, they risk reinforcing empire's ether effects, which is to say the effacement of the material-ecological platforms supporting capitalism's symbolic, informational, and financial networks. In privileging *bios* over *zoē* in their analysis—two Greek terms for life that, according to Giorgio Agamben, respectively signify "the form or way of living proper to an individual or group" and "the simple fact of living common to all living beings (animals, men, or gods)"[22]—Hardt and Negri suggest that somehow human social life (as the subject of biopolitics) can be abstracted from the lives of nonhuman others (the domain of zoopolitics). Zoopolitics, instead, suggests an inescapable contiguity or bleed between *bios* and *zoē*, between a politics of human social life and a politics of animality that extends to other species. However, what Hardt and Negri term "the ontology of production"[23]— namely, the immanent power of the multitude to constitute the substance of its life world—takes on an unexpectedly metaphysical quality in its association with forms of "immaterial [social] labour" that no longer appear contingent on animal bodies.[24] Indeed, the "social flesh" of the multitude is conceived in Deleuzian fashion as "pure potential" or virtuality.[25] Despite Hardt and Negri's attempt to move beyond the "horizon of language and communication" that contours the concept of immaterial labor in the work of contemporary Italian Marxists (something they do by theorizing affect as the missing biopolitical link to the animal body), there are few signs that the social flesh eats, in other words, few signs that the social *bios* is materially contingent upon and continuous with the lives of nonhuman others.[26]

This book initiates a different trajectory of biopolitical—or, we might say, zoopolitical—critique, one beginning with a challenge to the assumption that the social flesh and "species body" at stake in the logic of biopower is predominantly human.[27] Actual animals have already been subtly displaced from the category of "species" in Foucault's early remarks on biopower, as well as in the work of subsequent theorists of biopower, for whom animality functions predominantly as a metaphor for that corporeal part of "man" that becomes subject to biopolitical calculation. In Agamben's influential theorization of "bare life," for instance, animals' relation to capitalist biopower is occluded by his species-specific conflation of *zoē* with a socially stripped-down figure of *Homo sacer* that he traces back to antiquity.[28] However, the theorization of bare life as "that [which] may be killed and yet not sacrificed"[29]—a state of exception whose paradigmatic scenario in modernity is, for Agamben, the concentration camp—finds its zoopolitical supplement in Derrida's theorization of the "non-criminal putting to death" of animals, a related state of exception whose paradigmatic scenario is arguably the modern industrial slaughterhouse.[30] Indeed, the power to reduce humans to the bare life of their species body arguably presupposes the prior power to suspend other species in a state of exception within which they can be noncriminally put to death. As Cary Wolfe writes, "as long as it is institutionally taken for granted that it is all right to systematically exploit and kill nonhuman animals simply because of their species, then the humanist discourse of species will always be available for use by some humans against other humans as well, to countenance violence against the social other of *whatever* species—or gender, or race, or class, or sexual difference."[31] Trophy photos of U.S. military personnel terrorizing Iraqi prisoners in Abu Ghraib prison in 2004 showed, among other things, a naked Iraqi man on all fours, with a leash around his neck, and prisoners cowering before German shepherd dogs. Cruelly, the dog is made to function as a racist prosthetic of the U.S. military's power to animalize "the other," *a power that applies in the first instance to the animal itself.*[32]

The biopolitical production of the bare life of the animal other subtends, then, the biopolitical production of the bare life of the racialized other. Returning to Foucault's ruminations on biopower, it becomes apparent that within "the biological continuum addressed by biopower" there is a line drawn within the living prior to the one inscribed by racism, a species line occluded and at the same time inadvertently revealed by Foucault's use of the term "subspecies" to describe the effects of racialization:

What in fact is racism? It is primarily a way of introducing a break into
the domain of life that is under power's control: the break between what
must live and what must die. The appearance within the biological continuum of the human race of races, the distinction among races, the hierarchy of races, the fact that certain races are described as good and that
others, in contrast, are described as inferior: all this is a way of fragment-
ing the field of the biological that power controls.... This will allow
power... to subdivide the species it controls, into the *subspecies* known,
precisely, as races.[33]

The pivotal insight enabled by Foucault—that biopower augurs "nothing less than the entry of life into history, that is, the entry of phenom-
ena peculiar to the life of the human species into the order of knowledge
and power"[34]—bumps up against its own internal limit at the species
line. The biopolitical analyses he has inspired, in turn, are constrained
by their reluctance to pursue power's effects beyond the production
of human social and/or species life and into the zoopolitics of animal
capital.[35]

　　The crux of this book's argument is that discourses and technologies
of biopower hinge on the species divide. That is, they hinge on the
zoo-ontological production of species difference as a strategically
ambivalent rather than absolute line, allowing for the contradictory
power to both dissolve and reinscribe borders between humans and
animals. The phrase *animal capital* points, among other things, to the
paradox of an anthropocentric order of capitalism whose means and
effects can be all too posthuman, that is, one that ideologically grants
and materially invests in a world in which species boundaries can be
radically crossed (as well as reinscribed) in the genetic and aesthetic
pursuit of new markets.

　　The "question of the animal" exerts pressure on theorists of biopower and capital to engage not only with the ideological and affective
functions of animal signs but with material institutions and technologies of speciesism. The material dimensions of the question are once
again raised by Derrida, who writes in unmistakably Foucauldian terms:

It is all too evident that in the course of the last two centuries these
traditional forms of treatment of the animal have been turned upside

down by the joint developments of zoological, ethological, biological, and genetic *forms of knowledge* and the always inseparable *techniques* of intervention with respect to their object, the transformation of the actual object, its milieu, its world, namely, the living animal. This has occurred by means of farming and regimentalization at a demographic level unknown in the past, by means of genetic experimentation, the industrialization of what can be called the production for consumption of animal meat, artificial insemination on a massive scale, more and more audacious manipulations of the genome, the reduction of the animal not only to production and over-active production (hormones, genetic crossbreeding, cloning, and so on) of meat for consumption but also of all sorts of other end products, and all of that in the service of a certain being and the so-called human well-being of man.[36]

Derrida's words intimate that it is not enough to theorize biopower in relation to human life alone and that the reproductive lives and labors of other species (sexually differentiated labors, let us not forget) also become a matter of biopolitical calculation. Yet the reproductive value of animals is by no means only biological, as the preceding passage might suggest; animal signs and metaphors are also key symbolic resources of capital's reproduction. Given the soaring speculation in animal signs as a semiotic currency of market culture at the same time that animals are reproductively managed as protein and gene breeders under chilling conditions of control, an interrogation of animal capital in this double sense—as simultaneously sign and substance of market life—emerges as a pressing task of cultural studies.

If biopolitical critique has largely bracketed the question of the animal, critical theory and the emergent field of animal studies have, apart from a few significant exceptions, tended to sidestep materialist critique in favor of philosophical, psychoanalytical, and aesthetic formulations of animal alterity. Ironically, in contradiction to the passage cited earlier in which Derrida links the "over-active production" of animal life to the machinery of capitalism, the importance of the figure of the animal to deconstruction, which becomes explicit in Derrida's later work, is a key force to be contended with in countering the idealism surrounding the question of the animal. The Derridean text that will serve throughout this book as a foil against which I elaborate a politics of animal capital is Akira Mizuta Lippit's *Electric Animal: Toward a Rhetoric of Wildlife* (2000). If I obsessively return to it throughout, it is because Lippit's aesthetic theory of animal affect and cinematic transference is at once riveting *and* profoundly idealizing, inasmuch as it allows capital to largely go missing as motive force and mediating material history. I will return to the work of Derrida and Lippit in a later section of this Introduction.

Glancing briefly back at the *Maclean's* ad, I want to tease out one last implication of the injunction it makes against the naïveté of taking the animal sign literally. Does not this injunction enable a kind of temporal transcoding whereby the naïveté of reading literally—and the economic violence of literally trapping an animal specimen—gets mapped onto the past, while the ironic stance of taking the animal figuratively effectively establishes the current era's distance and difference from that past? In the magazine's positioning of its readers in a relation of postmodern ironic distance from a past colonial traffic in beaver pelts, there is a hint of an underlying narrative of historical progress from economic to symbolic forms of animal capital (linked to larger narratives of progress from colonial violence to postcolonial reconciliation and from industrial to postindustrial modes of production). There is a suggestion, in other words, that through the progress of history Canadians have left behind not only a colonial past (metonymized by the violence of taking animals literally) but the messy necessity of any "real," material exploitation of nature altogether. Pheng Cheah argues that "the canonical understanding of culture in philosophical modernity" consists in the idealism of imagining that culture can transcend its "condition of miredness" in the political-economic field, which in the context of his argument is that of the nation-state.[37] While Cheah discerns a "closet idealism" in postcolonial discourses of migration and hybridity that valorize transnational mobility over national bondage, the hegemonic expression of the idea that culture can achieve "physical freedom from being tied to the earth" is, as Cheah is aware, that of neoliberal globalization.[38] It is this liberal fantasy of culturally transcending the materiality of nature that can be glimpsed, finally, in the mock biology of the *Maclean's* ad.

In his theorization of intangible or symbolic forms of capital accruing to signs of social status such as good taste and education, Pierre
Bourdieu contends that "the fact that symbolic capital is less easily
measured and counted than livestock" only makes its violence harder
to discern.[39] For Bourdieu, symbolic capital is ultimately "a disguised
form of physical, 'economic' capital."[40] The distribution of forms of
animal capital according to a narrative of historical progress—encouraging the sense that economic and symbolic orders of capital are succes-
sive rather than coeval—is a temporizing maneuver that works against
recognition of their simultaneity, "disguising" the interconvertibility
or supplementarity of their violence. Although a study of animal capital
would seem to reinforce Hardt and Negri's claim that immaterial
forms of intellectual and symbolic production have achieved historical
hegemony over material modes of production—a shift traceable, among
other places, in the etymology of "branding," which no longer predominantly signifies the literal act of searing signs of ownership onto biological property but rather signifies the symbolic production of affective
trademarks—this book continuously strives to locate the economic or
material exercise of power with which symbolic capital is coeval. While
the postindustrial idioms of "branding" and "stock" have successfully
dissociated capital from its material conditions and effects (*stock*, like
branding, increasingly signifies a field of virtual speculation freed from
capitalism's roots in biological property), one of the aims of this book
is to restore a sense of capital's terrestrial costs.

The Ring of Tautology

To this end, this book struggles, unfortunately with no guarantee of
success, against the abstract and universal appeal of *animal* and *capital,*
both of which fetishistically repel recognition as shifting signifiers
whose meaning and matter are historically contingent. Against his con-
temporaries, Marx argued that rather than having instrinsic properties,
capital was the reified expression of historically specific relationships
of labor and exchange. He dared to pose a simple question—What is
a commodity?—and to unravel from this seemingly "obvious, trivial
thing" the social relations between "men" that are occulted in the

apparent autonomy of the products of their labor.[41] "The animal," likewise, has circulated in cultural discourses of Western modernity as a
generic universal—a "general singular"[42]—whose meaning is ostensibly
self-evident. Yet asking the simple question "What is an animal?" (as
Tim Ingold does in an edited volume of that title) can similarly reveal
that the meaning of *the animal* fluctuates with the vicissitudes of
culture and history and, more particularly, with the vicissitudes of a
species line that can be made either more porous or impregnable to
suit the means and ends of power. That *the animal* has regularly been
distended in the West to encompass racialized members of *Homo sapiens,*
as the recent example of Abu Ghraib demonstrates, belies the essentialist tenet that *the animal* has fixed or universal referents.

David Harvey rues the "tendency in discursive debates to homoge-
nize the category 'nature'...when it should be regarded as intensely
internally variegated—an unparalleled field of difference."[43] This book
attempts to intervene into the homogenized category of nature by way
of the more specific but equally generic category of "the animal." Derrida
has eloquently declaimed the asininity of corralling "a heterogeneous
multiplicity of the living" into "the strict enclosure of this definite article."[44] My hope is that if *animal* and *capital* are read in genealogical
relation to one another they will break down as monolithic essences
and reveal their historical contingencies.

Yet even as the chapters in this book pit genealogical specificity
against the generic force of their intertwined subjects, in the ring of
animal capital can be heard a real threat of totality posed by the global
hegemony of capital. There is meant to be a tautological ring to *animal
capital;* the two words are supposed to sound almost, but not quite, the
same. Indeed, much of this book is devoted to analyzing market discourses that seek to effect a perfect mimicry of animal and capital,
including advertising campaigns depicting mobile phones and cars
morphing into the instinctive species-life of monkeys or rabbits. A
recent example of this mimicry appeared in "Nissan Animals," an ad
campaign promoting the automaker's 4 x 4 vehicles. One fifty-second
television ad in the campaign, aired in North America during the premier time slot of the 2007 Super Bowl, showed a series of Nissan 4 x 4s
changing into and out of species shapes (a computer-generated puma,

spider, crocodile, and snake) as they traversed rugged off-road terrain. As the ad's tagline spelled out, Nissan animals are "naturally capable" of navigating a landscape that requires them to "shift capabilities."[45]

The tautological ring of *animal capital* purposefully conjures Bhabha's theory of colonial mimicry as "the desire for a reformed, recognizable Other, *as a subject of a difference that is almost the same, but not quite.*"[46] Similar examples of market mimicry engaged in detail in later chapters will be seen to be as productively ambivalent in their rendering of species sameness-difference as Bhabha argues colonial discourses are in their rendering of race (race and species often function as substitutes, moreover, in the discursive repertoires of biopower). Yet the partial rather than perfect symmetry of *animal* and *capital* is meant to suggest something else, as well: the final inability of capitalist biopower to fully realize a perfect tautology of nature and capital. The near-sameness of the two sounded by the title will take on greater theoretical substance as I historicize the powerful mimicry of *animal capital* in relation to Antonio Negri's formulation of "tautological time," a time of real subsumption that corresponds, for Negri, to the penetration of biopower into the entire fabric of social life in capitalist postmodernity.[47] The ring in this book's title intimates, with simultaneously ominous and hopeful repercussions, that animal and capital are increasingly produced as a semiotic and material closed loop, such that the meaning and matter of the one feeds seamlessly back into the meaning and matter of the other. In the nauseating recursivity of this logic, capital becomes animal, and animals become capital. While the balance of power seems, ominously, to be all on the side of capital, it is crucial to also recognize the amplified vulnerability of capitalism in tautological times. Indeed, novel diseases erupting out of the closed loop of animal capital—mad cow disease, avian influenza—are one material sign of how the immanent terrain of market life becomes susceptible, paradoxically, to the pandemic potential of "nature" that early modern discourses of biopower originally sought to circumscribe (see chapter 4 and the book's postscript).[48]

Unlike Negri, however, I do not equate tautological time with postmodernity alone, and I will trace different biopolitical *times* of animal capital across Fordist and post-Fordist economies of power. As Fredric

Jameson notes in *The Seeds of Time*, the analysis of capitalism requires "the realization (strongly insisted on by Althusser and his disciples) that each system—better still, each 'mode of production'—produces a temporality that is specific to it."[49] For Jameson, "mode of production" is here broadly conceived in relation to late capitalism, a period whose accelerated logic of "perpetual change" paradoxically produces an effect of profound stasis within which actual change (i.e., alternatives to capitalism) appears increasingly impossible.[50] The temporal effect of capitalist postmodernity is, in other words, that of the "end of History."[51] The more specific temporal effect linked to the production of animal capital, I am suggesting, is that of tautological time. The time of animal capital recurs across Fordist and post-Fordist eras, exceeding historical containment within either one or the other and troubling many of their periodizing criteria. Yet this is not to say that animal capital is not rearticulated in relation to the shifting modes of production and technologies earmarked by the neologisms of Fordism and post-Fordism or that it remains a historical constant. It is precisely the trajectory of its proliferation from a partial to a more totalizing time that I am exploring here.

What appears in the tautological time of real subsumption, according to Negri, is a profound *indifference* between the time of capital's production and the surplus time of social life itself, or that life time left over after the so-called working day. In an era of real as opposed to formal subsumption, contends Negri, there is no longer any life time extrinsic to the time of capitalist production (an argument taken up in more detail in chapter 1). The tautological ring of this book's title seeks to make audible a related time of real subsumption effected by material and metaphorical technologies pursuing the ontological indifference of capital and animal life. The ecological Marxist James O'Connor holds that, in our current era, the reproduction of capital's conditions of production and the very biophysical conditions of *"life itself"* have become one and the same thing.[52] The use of the sign of "the animal" is increasingly expedient in promoting a social fantasy of "natural capitalism."[53] Concurrently, the *substance* of animal life materially mediates actual incarnations of this fantasy, as "more and more audacious manipulations of the genome"[54] and as agri-, bio-, and genetic technologies of farming, cloning, and "pharming" implant the logic of capital into the reproductive germ plasm and micromatter of life itself.[55] Whereas Negri initiates an "ontological turn" to joyously affirm the constituent power and collective substance of a counterhegemonic multitude, in what follows "the ontological" more pessimistically connotes the hegemonic effects of capital seeking to realize itself through animal figures and flesh.

If on the one hand *Animal Capital* presents the task of developing alternative genealogies not accounted for in the history of capitalism, then it also supplies a trope for a time of subsumption threatening a total mimicry of capital and nature, one well underway in a Fordist era of capitalism if not yet endemic in its effects. I am conscious, however, that the heuristic value of supplying a metaphor for capital as a biopolitical hegemon is potentially counteracted by the danger that it could reinforce the fetishistic effect of a coordinated global body of capitalism that in actuality does not exist. A perfect tautology of market and species life is never seamlessly or fully secured but is continuously pursued through multiple, often competing, and deeply contradictory exercises of representational and economic power. In actuality, the mimicry of animal capital is a "messy," contested, and unstable assemblage of uncoordinated wills to power, as well as immanent resistances to that power.[56] David Harvey argues that the triumphalist effect of end-of-history global capitalism and oppositional discourses that inadvertently reify a capitalist totality are equally agents of the thinking that positions culture and nature in binary opposition and imagines that the former could possibly exercise a sovereign power of death over the latter.[57] It is therefore crucial that "animal capital" remain tensed between its alternate gestures, at once a *metaphor* that strategically amplifies the totalizing repercussions of capital's mimicry of nature in tautological times and a *material history* that tracks the contradictory discourses and technologies that can never perfectly render capital animal.

"In his mature thought," writes William Pietz, "Marx understood 'capital' to be a species of fetish."[58] In the tautological time of animal capital, finally, a redoubled species of fetishism, or a metafetishistic species of capital, is at stake. The analogy of commodity fetishism becomes powerfully literal, and in this sense metafetishistic, when commodities are explicitly produced or worshiped as animal. This becomes clearer when one recalls, as William Pietz does, the Enlightenment discourse of primitive religion informing Marx's concept of commodity fetishism.[59] "Fetishism was defined as the worship of 'inanimate' things even though its paradigmatic historical exemplifications were cults of animate beings, such as snakes," notes Pietz.[60] "The special fascination that Egyptian zoolatry and African fetishism exerted on eighteenth-century intellectuals," he adds, "derived not just from the moral scandal of humans kneeling in abject worship before animals lower down on the 'great chain of being,' but from the inconceivable mystery (within Enlightenment categories) of any direct sensuous perception of animateness in material beings."[61] Marx's great insight, expressed in the analogy of commodity fetishism, is that the commodity is similarly charismatic in its lifelike effects, because in it "the social characteristics of men's own labour" appears "as objective characteristics of the products of labour themselves."[62]

Yet Marx's concept of commodity fetishism "bears an eighteenth-century pedigree" inasmuch as it also endorses the enlightenment teleology embedded in a Eurocentric discourse of fetishism.[63] Indeed, Marx's genius in bringing European political economy and "primitive" religion together in the phrase *commodity fetishism*—a phrase calculated to break the irrational spell of both capitalism and religion and to jolt Europeans to their rational senses—has risked reinforcing a master narrative of European reason. The point I want to make here, however, is that what was for Marx an *analogy* is *literalized* in the mimicry of animal capital.[64] Recall the "Nissan Animals" advertisement I referred to earlier in which 4 x 4 vehicles are depicted digitally morphing into animal signs (a snake, a spider, etc.) on their off-road trek. The suggestion is that the inner essence of the automobile becomes, for an instant, visible on the outside, revealing the machine's animating force to be, well, animal. In the currency of animal life, capital becomes most potently literal and self-conscious in its fetishistic effects.

Yet it is because animal capital constitutes such a literal or tautologous species of fetish that it is at the same time unusually visible and vulnerable in its discursive operations. For this reason, it suggests a privileged site from which to critically grapple with the naturalizing forces of capitalism.

The Double Entendre of Rendering

The tautological ring of animal capital finds echo in the double entendre of another word in this book's title: *rendering*. *Rendering* signifies both the mimetic act of making a copy, that is, reproducing or interpreting an object in linguistic, painterly, musical, filmic, or other media (new technologies of 3-D digital animation are, for instance, called "renderers") *and* the industrial boiling down and recycling of animal remains. The double sense of *rendering*—the seemingly incommensurable (yet arguably supplementary) practices that the word evokes—provides a peculiarly apt rubric for beginning to more concretely historicize animal capital's modes of production.

The double entendre of *rendering* is deeply suggestive of the complicity of "the arts" and "industry" in the conditions of possibility of capitalism. It suggests a rubric for critically tracking the production of animal capital, more specifically, across the spaces of culture and economy and for illuminating the supplementarity of discourses and technologies normally held to be unrelated. Such an interimplication of representational and economic logics is pivotal to biopolitical critique, since biopower never operates solely through the power to reproduce life literally, via the biological capital of the specimen or species, nor does it operate solely through the power to reproduce it figuratively via the symbolic capital of the animal sign, but instead operates through the power to hegemonize both the meaning and matter of life.

The rubric of rendering makes it possible, moreover, to begin elaborating a biopolitical, as opposed to simply an aesthetic, theory of mimesis. In contrast to the literary-aesthetic approach modeled, for instance, by Erich Auerbach's seminal *Mimesis: The Representation of Reality in Western Literature* (1968), a biopolitical approach to mimesis suggests that textual logics of reproduction can no longer be treated in isolation from economic logics of (capitalist) reproduction.[65] In the double entendre of *rendering*, there is a provocation to analyze the discomfiting complicity of symbolic and carnal technologies of reproduction. *Rendering* thus also redefines mimesis beyond its semiotic association with textual or visual "reality effect[s]," as Roland Barthes puts it, by compelling examination of the economic concurrencies of signifying effects.[66] Although *rendering* expands the sense of mimesis beyond its canonical associations with *realist* rendition, market cultures' hot pursuit of the representational goal of realism via new technological fidelities will remain vital to its logic. So will other representational objectives and histories of mimesis, such as those accruing to biological tropes of "aping" and "parroting" mobilized by the racializing discourses of European imperialism and colonialism. Yet enlarging mimesis to include multiple representational objectives and histories is not in itself sufficient to counter its overdetermination by aesthetic ideologies invested in distinguishing culture and economy. Even Theodor Adorno and Max Horkheimer's concept of "the culture industry," which radically pronounces culture's imbrication in economy, is qualified by Adorno's remark that "the expression 'industry' is not to be taken too literally."[67]

A biopolitical theory of mimesis, by contrast, encompasses the economic modes of production evoked by the "literal" scene of rendering. The double sense of *rendering* implicates mimesis in the *ontological politics* of literally as well as figuratively reproducing capitalism's "social flesh" (in the words of Hardt and Negri). As I show in later chapters, the rendering of animal figures and animal flesh can result in profoundly contradictory semiotic and material currencies. Yet, rather than undercutting the hegemony of market life, the contradictions of animal rendering are productive so long as they are discursively managed under the separate domains of culture and economy. That said, the productive contradiction of animal capital's metaphorical and material currencies is constantly at risk of igniting into "real" social antagonism should their separate logics brush too closely up against one another. This is the volatile potential latent in the rubric of rendering.

Again, *rendering* indexes both economies of representation (the "rendering" of an object on page, canvas, screen, etc.) and resource economies trafficking in animal remains (the business of recycling animal trimmings, bones, offal, and blood back into market metabolisms). Later chapters elaborate the double sense of *rendering* in the more affective terms of "sympathetic" and "pathological" economies of power. This terminology is indebted to Michael Taussig's formulation of "the magic of mimesis," the mysterious power of a reproduction to materially affect the thing it copies.[68] Taussig recalls James George Frazer's anthropological study of sympathetic magic in *The Golden Bough: A Study of Magic and Religion* (1911), where Frazer describes, among other things, how sorcerers of Jervis Island in the South Pacific Ocean manipulate effigies in order to affect the subjects they resemble. As Taussig relates, "If the sorcerer pulled an arm or a leg off the image, the human victim felt pain in the corresponding limb, but if the sorcerer restored the severed arm or leg to the effigy, the human victim recovered" (49). Building on the two types of sympathetic magic distinguished by Frazer, "the magic of *contact*, and that of *imitation*," Taussig emphasizes "the two-layered notion of mimesis that is involved—a copying or imitation and a palpable, sensuous, connection between the very body of the perceiver and the perceived" (21–22). Rendering an object's likeness, in other words, is not sufficient to gain power over it; the power to affect the other also requires stealing a tangible piece of its body in order to establish a pathological line of communication between "original" and "copy." As Taussig suggests, mimetic power in this sense involves the magic of "the visual likeness" *and* the "magic of substances" (50).

In a similar vein, the rubric of rendering brings mimesis into sight as a "two-layered" logic of reproduction involving "sympathetic" technologies of representation and "pathological" technologies of material control. Taussig's notion of a two-layered economy of mimesis helps to counter aesthetic theories that reserve mimesis for representational practices tacitly held at a distance from the material exploits of a capitalist economy. However, there is also cause to be wary both of the ethnographic language of sympathetic magic that Taussig resuscitates and of his stated desire to reawaken appreciation for the "mimetic mysteries" in order to break the "suffocating hold of 'constructionism'" in the academy (xix). Such a desire suggests that exoticizations of the Other that the discipline of anthropology sought to purge, under the pressure of poststructuralist and postcolonial theory, have the potential to reappear in sublimated form as a fascination with the alterity of mimesis itself. In contrast to the language of magic favored by Taussig, the language of "rendering" makes it harder to re-enchant mimesis.

A glance at the dictionary reveals that *rendering* encompasses a multiplicity of additional meanings and ranges in reference from the building arts (applying plaster onto brick or stone) to interpretive performance (rendering a musical score) to surrendering or paying one's earthly dues ("render unto Caesar what is Caesar's"). The rubric of rendering encompasses a cacophony of logics that exceed the "double entendre" this book explores. Consider, for instance, the case of "extraordinary rendition," otherwise known as "extreme rendering." Taking the 2001 attacks on New York's Twin Towers as license to use state-of-emergency measures in its war against terrorism, the U.S. Central Intelligence Agency justifies its extrajudicial transfers of suspected terrorists to third-party states known to inflict torture on detainees.[69] The racialized terrorist suspect is subject to a relay of power, facilitated by the rhetoric of rendering or rendition, in which hints of animal rendering insidiously blend with other political economies of sense. The physical work of pulverizing an animal body bleeds into the sense of rendering as a delivery of retributive justice, couched as the "return" of purported terrorists to torture cells in the lawless states from whence they supposedly sprang. Both of these connotations further bleed into the sense of "rendition" as an interpretive work of art to ultimately link the turning over of detainees with the production of culture, exciting an aesthetics of torture. Here *rendering* appears to signify the creative license of the powerful to interpret the law in (permanently) exceptional times. At the same time, *extreme rendering* circulates as code, in the techno-speak of 3-D computer animation, for the cutting edge of high-speed image processing. Biopower arguably hails from the cacophony of incommensurable carnal and cultural sense that *rendition* accommodates.

If every act of writing, every critique, produces a remainder, it is the excessive sense of rendition that is the remainder of this book's necessarily partial theorization of the double entendre of *rendering*. I inevitably boil down the politics of rendering itself by theorizing its doubleness, given that it comprises much more than the logics of representation and recycling that I have singled out. However, these two logics are peculiarly apt, as I have noted, to the cultural and material politics of animal capital. Unlike critical race, feminist, postcolonial, and globalization theories, which variously engage with technologies of animalization in relation to racialized human subjects but rarely with reductions of animals themselves, the double entendre of *rendering* I evoke is designed to make "the question of the animal" focal. Again, Cary Wolfe makes a helpful distinction between the *discourse* of speciesism — a "constellation of signifiers [used] to structure how we address others of whatever sort (not just nonhuman animals)" — and the *institution* of speciesism.[70] "Even though the *discourse* of animality and species difference may theoretically be applied to an other of whatever type," writes Wolfe, "the consequences of that discourse, in *institutional* terms, fall overwhelmingly on nonhuman animals."[71] Similarly, while the practice of extraordinary rendition illustrates that the politics of rendering is not reducible to that of animal capital, like the "asymmetrical material effects" of speciesist discourse, the material violence of rendering arguably falls most heavily on animal life.[72]

Rendering As Critical Practice: Discourse Analysis, Distortion, Articulation

Biological and genetic "stock" rendered from animals materially and speculatively circulates as capital even as animals appreciate in value as metaphors and brands mediating new technologies, commodities, and markets. Yet the market's double stock in animal life has persistently eluded politicization, possibly because so much is at stake. For the biopolitical interpenetrations with substances and signs of animal life that help to secure capitalism's economic and cultural hegemony also betray its profound contingency on nonhuman nature. If animal life is violently subject to capital, capital is inescapably contingent on animal life, such that disruptions in animal capital have the potential to percuss through the biopolitical chains of market life. One task of the critic of animal capital, then, is to *make their contingency visible*. This involves pressuring the supplementary economies of rendering into incommensurability and antagonizing animal capital's productive contradictions.

Whereas the previous section introduced rendering as hegemonic logic, this section examines how rendering might also serve as a generative trope for counterhegemonic forms of critical practice that strive to illuminate the contingency of animal capital to political effect.

Given that I have sketched rendering as a logic of biopower or discursive power, its counterhegemonic deployment can be most broadly identified with critical discourse analysis and immanent critique, albeit with some qualifications. Postcolonial theorists such as Edward Said, Gayatri Spivak, and Homi Bhabha and post-Marxist theorists such as Ernesto Laclau and Chantal Mouffe have been influential in expanding Foucault's insights to an analysis of the *discursive* conditions of imperialism and colonialism and the constitutively discursive character of the social field, respectively. Like the many efforts of discourse analysis inspired by them, rendering draws attention to the role that symbolic power plays in the reproduction of market life, resisting the Marxian tendency to privilege economic relations of production as the empirical "truth" underlying the cultural superstructure. Post-Marxist discourse analysis emerged, after all, in resistance to the perceived economic essentialism of Marxist critique and to the conception of ideology as false consciousness accompanying it. Foucault's remark that the "control of society over individuals is not conducted only through consciousness or ideology, but also in the body and with the body"[73] challenges a Marxist paradigm of critique by locating ideology not in the so-called cultural superstructure of ideas but in the body, that is, in a biological substrate of desires and life drives previously held to be "beneath" ideology, or pre-ideological. The rethinking of ideology as constitutive of social-bodily existence is crucial to the study of animal capital, particularly in light of the conflation of "the animal" with the ostensibly pre-ideological realm of the body, instinctual drives, and affect in cultural discourses of the West (something I will return to shortly).

However, rendering also suggests a critical practice alert to the risk of "semiological reduction" run by overly culturalist strains of discourse analysis.[74] It provides a trope for a cultural-materialist analysis that navigates a fine line between reductively materialist *and* reductively culturalist approaches to the field of capital. Rendering's evocation of a literal scene of industrial capitalism is constantly at risk of implying recourse to an economic reality underlying the ideological smokescreen of animal signs; that is, it is at risk of sliding back into an essentialist Marxist materialism. Yet it is a risk that I hazard in order to avoid the alternate pitfall of overcompensating for the economic essentialism of Marxist criticism by describing all of social space in terms of a linguistic model of discourse. Following from Saussure's claim that *language is a form and not a substance*," semiological approaches that read capitalism strictly as an economy of signifiers conflate an economic logic of exchange value with a logic of linguistic value conceived as empty and formal, one in which the contingent "substance" of the sign is reduced to irrelevance.[75]

For this reason, argues Régis Debray, the semiotic turn instigated by Saussure frees thought from the *"referential illusion"* only to itself fall prey to a fantasy of pure code.[76] Debray contends that a "mediology" is needed to remedy the *"semiotic illusion,* in order to again find a strong reference to the world, its materials, its vectors and its procedures."[77] In his biopolitical approach to naturalist discourses in turn-of-the-century North America, Mark Seltzer likewise cautions against the "sheer culturalism" of "proceed[ing] as if the deconstruction of the traditional dichotomy of the natural and the cultural indicated merely the elimination of the first term and the inflation of the second."[78] "Rather than mapping how the relays between what counts as natural and what counts as cultural are differentially articulated, invested, and regulated," notes Seltzer, "the tendency has been to discover again and again that what seemed to be natural is in fact cultural."[79] Rendering resists both the "sheer culturalism" of reading animals as empty signifiers *and* the converse essentialism of reifying them as natural signs, following Seltzer's insight that biopower cannot be grasped by approaches that reduce the natural to the cultural, or vice versa.

If there is still critical mileage to be coaxed out of the audio effects I have been sounding in this Introduction, I would like to propose "distortion" as the form that a dialectical practice inspired by the double entendre of rendering might take once it recasts itself in the mode of immanent critique, relinquishing the possibility of a clear oppositional vantage point. Distortion, according to the *Oxford English Dictionary*, involves "a change in the form of (an electrical signal) during transmission, amplification, etc."[80] Distortion disrupts what Debray calls a telecom model of *"painless transmission"*[81] by routing the semiotic vector of an animal sign through a material site of rendering, for example, diverting film's time-motion mimicry of animal physiology through the carnal space of the abattoir (see chapter 2), or the animal signs in a Canadian telecommunications ad campaign through neocolonial bushmeat and war economies (see chapter 3). Like Mary Louise Pratt's notion of *"code-switching," distortion* connotes a strategic switching back and forth between rhetorical and carnal modes of production of animal capital with the aim of interimplicating and crossing their signals.[82]

As a model of immanent critique, distortion resists privileging either literal or rhetorical sites of rendering as truer vantage points from which to reckon with animal capital, emphasizing instead that both are effects of power. Like straws in water, there is no point from inside an immanent field of power at which the transmission or reception of animal signs can ever be transparent, or "straight." Literality is only an *effect* of transparency, or, as Laclau and Mouffe put it, "Literality is, in actual fact, the first of metaphors."[83] Conversely, while rhetorical power can efface its material conditions, it can never actually transcend them. By continuously interimplicating the double senses of rendering, ostensibly literal currencies of animal life, such as meat, can be shown to be veined through and through with symbolic sense, while the mimetic effects of filmic or digital animations, for example, can be pressured to reveal their carnal contingencies.

This leads to a final term crucial to conceptualizing rendering as a counterhegemonic critical practice: *articulation.* Laclau and Mouffe's theorization of articulation remains one of the most compelling contemporary efforts to think contingency. Write Laclau and Mouffe, "We will call articulation any practice establishing a relation among elements such that their identity is modified as a result of the articulatory practice."[84] In contrast to identity politics, which spawn the sense that subjects are pre-given to representation, "politico-hegemonic articulations" acknowledge that they "retroactively create the interests they claim to represent" (xi). Laclau and Mouffe begin from the antiessentialist premise that social identities do not preexist their social articulations.

The problem with dialectical thinking, in their view, is that it has historically sought to reduce social life to one essential, underlying logic (for Hegel, the historical unfolding of Spirit, for Marx, class consciousness as the motor of material history) and to reconcile antagonistic social elements within the telos of a unified social whole. By contrast, in the radical "logic of the social" that they theorize, "there is no single underlying principle fixing—and hence constituting—the whole field of differences" (3, 111). The social field is constituted, rather, by competing articulations vying for hegemony and is irreducibly antagonistic, or "pierced by contingency" (110).

All that distinguishes rendering as hegemonic discourse from rendering as critical practice, ultimately, is its self-recognition as a politically motivated articulatory practice. Without this self-reflexivity, the act of bringing disparate, unlikely things together under its rubric risks becoming a metaphorical exercise in suggesting that they share an underlying, unifying likeness rather than an effort to make their contingent character visible. As Seltzer writes, the "generalized capacity of 'combining together' dissimilar powers and objects, drawing into relation and into equivalence 'distant' orders of things such as bodies, capital, and artifacts: this *logic of equivalence* is the 'classic' logic of the market and of market culture."[85] Against the metaphorical temptation to reduce difference to sameness and against, too, the temptation to empirically justify the connections rendering makes, the critical practice of rendering needs to self-critically foreground that it also rhetorically *renders* relationships. Rendering as critical practice, no less than rendering as hegemonic logic, is a discursive mode of production, with the difference that it seeks to produce counterhegemonic rather than hegemonic relationships and effects. Lest its own motivated labor of *making* connections between symbolic and carnal economies of capital be fetishistically erased by the appearance that they are simply *revealed,* the critical practice of rendering needs to vigilantly foreground its own articulatory power.

This is not to say that there is no historical basis for the linkages rendered in later chapters between cinematic culture and animal gelatin or between animal ads and resource politics in the Eastern Congo; the actual metaphorical glue that binds them within a shared logic is the "concrete universal" of capital.[86]

Animals in Theory

Two rich veins of poststructuralist thought have played a particularly influential role in the proliferation of theoretical engagements with "the animal" in the late twentieth and early twenty-first centuries. The first vein is Derridean, the second Deleuzian. In both, animals appear as focal figures of immanent life (in contrast to metaphysical Being), and thus to a large extent tracking the figure of the animal through each vein of thought amounts to tracking two intellectual genealogies of the idea of immanence.

In the first vein, we encounter Derrida's concept of "animot" as the animal trace of the text; in the second we encounter Gilles Deleuze and Felix Guattari's concept of "becoming-animal" as a figure of deterritorialization and multiplicity. Rather than attempting a thorough comparative review of the role that these and other animal figures play in Derridean and Deleuzian critique, I want to briefly examine some of the critical ramifications—in relation to this book's concerns with animal capital—of articulating animal life to the concept of "hauntology" (Derrida) and to the idea of "becoming" as pure potential or virtuality (Deleuze and Guattari). The concepts of hauntology and becoming purportedly unsettle the ontological premises and power structures of Western culture. Yet articulating the alternative ontologies they name to and through animal signs has profound implications for their effectiveness in this regard. For starters, the figures of animal immanence posed by each are politically unsettling only to the extent that the dominant means and ends of power indeed correspond to a "metaphysics of presence" (Derrida) and to "molar" states of Being (Deleuze and Guattari). As Slavoj Žižek contends, however, the contemporary terrain of capitalism throws these assumptions into question inasmuch as it resembles what Deleuze and Guattari refer to as a deterritorializing "plane of immanence" and traffics in spectral currencies that in effect "deconstruct" distinctions between the living and the dead.[87] Is not "the impersonal circulation of affects," asks Žižek, "the very logic of publicity, of video clips, and so forth in which what matters is not the message about the product but the intensity of the transmitted affects and perceptions?"[88] Žižek goes so far as to argue that there are "features that justify calling Deleuze the ideologist of late capitalism."[89] Whether the same dare be said of Derrida depends, in the context of this discussion, on the *différance* (or lack thereof) that a logic of spectrality poses to animal capital.

Let me backtrack to the philosophical discourse of immanence announced in the West by Nietzsche's radical proclamation of the death of God, one carrying a note of joyous affirmation that peals through the Deleuzian lineage (from the pre-Nietzschian writings of Spinoza to the work of Hardt and Negri). Nietzsche sought the earthly repatriation of powers of creation that had been ceded to a metaphysical Being, not only the Being of God but also that of his earthly representative, Man. Zarathustra is able to converse with animals, whose immanent existence is iconic in the work of Nietzsche, because he represents the overcoming of the transcendental authority of both God and Man, that is, he represents the Overman.[90] In the work of Foucault, the refusal of the metaphysical foundations of Truth, History, and Subjectivity and the proclamation of the death of Man by virtue of his recognition as a historically contingent "invention of recent date" rearticulate a Nietzschian discourse of immanence.[91] It is in the writings of Deleuze and Guattari, however, that resistance to metaphysical paradigms of Being is formulated as an involuntary force of becoming-animal.

For Deleuze and Guattari, becomings constitute states of pure potentiality occurring in between those fixed, identifiable states of Being they call "molar."[92] Becoming-animal is not to be confused with actual animals, then, and certainly not with those "Oedipal pets" that represent for Deleuze and Guattari the most contemptible breed of molar, domesticated animal. Nor can becoming-animal be understood without understanding the role that affect plays in the work of Deleuze and Guattari. Affects are the prime movers on the "plane of immanence," the "pure intensities" that, like free radicals, are never permanently attached to molar organisms but are rather the virtual attractors of their potential becomings: becoming-woman, becoming-animal, becoming-molecular. (43). Unlike emotion, affect "is not a personal feeling, nor is it a characteristic; it is the effectuation of a power of the pack that throws the self into upheaval and makes it reel" (240). Affect, for Deleuze and Guattari, is contagious; it congregates into multiplicities that travel in "packs" (swarms of bees, rat packs, bands of werewolves), and it crosses species boundaries that are normally ontologically policed. The state, the family, and other "apparat[i] of capture" seek to domesticate the disorganizing power of impersonal affect by reducing it to personal emotion working in the service of normative social relations and identities (444).

For Deleuze and Guattari, affect is especially, quixotically, configured as an "animal rhizome"—a brush of fur, a scent, or spoor triggering the "nonvoluntary transmutation" of being into becoming and opening a "line of flight" out of fixed ontologies (47, 269, 277). Far from being politically motivated, the micropolitical force of affect described by Deleuze and Guattari—who in their writings are as fascinated with its feral carriers as they are contemptuous of the domesticated "house dogs" that guard against it (244)—is cast as a "nonvoluntary" force springing from the irrepressible multiplicity of heterogeneous nature. In other words, the concept of becoming-animal arguably fetishizes affect as an animal alterity that eludes rather than enters into the calculations of power. More problematically, because becomings signify for Deleuze and Guattari a virtual state of pure potential as opposed to a state of historical actuality, the figure of animality to which affect is attached is rendered profoundly abstract.[93] Brian Massumi reminds us that, for Deleuze, the virtual and the abstract are "real" and not to be confused with popular notions of virtual reality.[94] Yet Massumi's own rearticulation of the "*incorporeal materialism*" of the body in a virtual state of becoming similarly hinges on a distinction between the body as a form of energy (affect) and the body as matter.[95]

In the context of animal capital, there is a great deal at stake in romanticizing affect as a rogue portion of pure energy linked to animality as a state of virtual rather than actual embodiment. This is not because one could argue that affects and becomings have been successfully captured and reduced "to relations of totemic or symbolic correspondence" in the service of capitalism, since such an argument assumes, along with Deleuze and Guattari, that the primary aim of power is to "break" becomings.[96] Rather, it is because the field of power can no longer be clearly identified with a restriction on becomings. In other

words, forces of capital—especially those transnational forces delinked
from the mediating form of the nation-state—no longer achieve hegemony solely by means of breaking the "unnatural participations" and
"unholy alliances" across heterogeneous series that Deleuze and Guattari cherish as transgressive but also by inducing them (241–42).

At the very least, affect as an authentic animal alterity is impossible
to distinguish from the intensities unleashed by capitalism. On what
grounds, after all, does one definitively distinguish "real" becomings
from the pseudo- or simulated becomings spawned through the sorcery
of market culture? As Žižek asks:

> And what about the so-called Transformer or Animorph toys, a car or a
> plane that can be transformed into a humanoid robot, an animal that can
> be morphed into a human or robot—is this not Deleuzian? There are no
> "metaphorics" here: the point is not that the machinic or animal form is
> revealed as a mask containing a human shape but, rather, as the "becoming-
> machine" or "becoming-animal" of the human.[97]

Equating cultural and economic hegemony with the repression of becomings thus risks, as Hardt and Negri suggest, missing "the contemporary object of critique": capitalism as an empire that also achieves
hegemony through rhizomatic means.[98] The ineffectiveness of which
Hardt and Negri accuse postmodernist theory in this sense also extends to the "radicle-system" of becomings theorized by Deleuze and
Guattari,[99] which may not be as undermining of power as it appears to
be: "Postmodernists are still waging battle against the shadows of old
enemies: the Enlightenment, or really modern forms of sovereignty
and its binary reductions of difference and multiplicity to a single alternative between Same and Other. . . . In fact, Empire too is bent on doing
away with those modern forms of sovereignty and on setting differences
to play across boundaries."[100]

On this note, let me turn to the other, Derridean, lineage that has
also exerted tremendous influence upon late twentieth and early twenty-
first-century engagements with "the animal." While there are any number of potential entry points into the discourse of immanence it poses,
I will begin with Martin Heidegger's thesis that "the animal is poor in
world" and with Derrida's confrontation of that thesis.[101] Heidegger's

own critique, or "destruction," of an ontotheological idea of Being through his formulation of human *Dasein* ("being-there") as an indwelling in the house of language is a crucial forerunner of deconstruction and seminal to efforts to think immanence in the West.[102] Nevertheless, Derrida takes Heidegger to task for still seeking to demarcate "an absolute limit between the living creature and the human *Dasein*" based on the animal's lack of language.[103] The "poverty" in world of the animal is, for Heidegger, that of a being-in-the-world incapable of objectively apprehending world *as* world, one strictly differentiated from the *Dasein* of the human, who, as a language-being, is "world-forming."[104] According to Michael Haar, for Heidegger "the leap from the animal that lives to man that speaks is as great, if not greater, than that from the lifeless stone to the living being."[105] The idea of animal immanence as an unreflective or unconscious rather than conscious being-in-the-world is echoed in Georges Bataille's statement that animals are *"in the world like water in water."*[106]

Derrida's resistance to the philosophical doxa that language constitutes an absolute boundary between animal and human involves identifying animals with the immanent otherness of logos, something he achieves by suggesting that tropological sites of language, specifically metaphor, are animal. In an essay written over a decade after *Of Spirit: Heidegger and the Question* (1987), Derrida devises the neologism "animot" to capture the identity of animality and metaphoricity.[107] Derrida is not alone in his fascination with the (ostensible) animal alterity of metaphor, that is, with seeing in figurative language an affective trace of animality that undermines Western logocentrisms. John Berger, in his famous essay "Why Look at Animals," critiques the marginalization of animals in capitalist modernity by invoking a precapitalist relation of human and animal mediated in the first instance by metaphor. Writes Berger: "The first subject matter for painting was animal. Probably the first paint was animal blood. Prior to that, it is not unreasonable to suppose that the first metaphor was animal."[108] By tracing an ancient bloodline between metaphor and animal life, however, Berger risks obscuring how the rendering of animals, both metaphorically and materially, constitutes a politically and historically contingent, rather than

a primal or universal, relationship. Perhaps it is apt, then, to borrow
from Berger to suggest that the animal figures in Derrida's corpus also
come dangerously close to functioning as "first metaphors" for the ineluctable traits of deconstruction, primalizing the tracings, spacings, and
supplements deigned to estrange every claim of presence.[109]

Consider the covert figure of animality lurking in what had been
Derrida's long-awaited reading of Marx, *Specters of Marx: The State of
the Debt, the Work of Mourning, and the New International* (1994). There,
slippage between signs of spectrality and animality risks annulling
Derrida's efforts in a later text—"The Animal That Therefore I Am
(More to Follow)" (2002)—to deconstruct the reductive category of
"the animal" in favor of "an irreducible living multiplicity of mortals."[110]
Contrary to his invocation of the "unprecedented" and "monstrous"
conditions facing animals in the zoos, feedlots, abattoirs, holding pens,
corrals, and laboratories of Western culture,[111] Derrida's deconstruction
of commodity fetishism in *Specters of Marx* risks putting a materialist
critique of life in biopolitical times under suspension by virtue of formulating the "bodiless body" of the specter and animal life under the
same logic.[112]

In *Specters of Marx,* Derrida contends that the fetishism of commodities is not a false effect that can be exorcised by uncovering the
underlying "truth" of capital, as Marx suggested, but is rather an effect
haunting every presence, every use value, and every mode of production. There is *no* production, Derrida contends, that is not riddled with
a fetish or *"spectrality effect."*[113] "As soon as there is production," he
writes, "there is fetishism" (166). If there is an end to spectral special
effects, declares Derrida, it is "only beyond value itself" (166). It is
against a "Marxist ontology" that has sought to conjure away the spectral illusions of capital "in the name of living presence as material actuality" that Derrida proposes the notion of an always-already haunted
ontology, or hauntology (105). One of the potential dangers of Derrida's deconstruction of fetishism as a spectrality effect specific to market
culture, however, is a dilution of the historical contingency of capitalism
within an a priori, transhistorical order of inevitably haunted production. Troubling, too, is how Derrida covertly articulates now universal
and inevitable spectrality effects to the figure of a compulsive animality.

Signs of animality steep Derrida's close engagement with the famous passage in the first volume of *Capital*, in which Marx describes the transformation of use values into exchange values (a transformation that in many translations is likened to a table-turning séance). The fabulous table appears in the section titled "The Fetishism of Commodities and the Secret Thereof," where Marx writes: "As soon as it [the table] emerges as a commodity, it changes into a thing which transcends sensuousness. It not only stands with its feet on the ground, but, in relation to all other commodities, it stands on its head, and evolves out of its wooden brain grotesque ideas, far more wonderful than if it were to begin dancing of its own free will."[114] Purportedly paraphrasing "as literally as possible" the scene in which the commodity assumes life, Derrida writes that the table "seems to loom up of *itself* and to stand all at once on its paws."[115] Paws? The table "has become a kind of headstrong, pigheaded, obstinate animal that, standing, faces other commodities," writes Derrida (152). Again, "Become like a living being, the table resembles a prophetic dog that gets up on its four paws" (153).[116] In arguing against fetishism as a historically particular effect of capitalist production, Derrida insinuates tropes of animal life to raise spectrality as a primal *différance* immanent to all earthly existence. Derrida particularly favors the figure of a "headstrong dog," possibly because *dog*, a semordnilap for *god*, helps him to configure an immanent versus transcendent ontology (155).

Derrida thus insinuates the image of a compulsive becoming-animal into Marx's passage under the guise of a "literal" paraphrase. Yet it is widely held that Marx inscribed the fetishizing movement as an impersonation, or anthropomorphization, of the commodity. The sensuous use value that at first stands on all fours (the quadruped posture of the table in Marx's passage is at least, if not more, suggestive of animal life than the imposture of exchange that Derrida metaphorizes as animal) is overruled by the "grotesque" hegemony of abstract exchange.[117] Inverting the usual sense of the passage, however, Derrida *animalizes* the spectral ontology of the commodity. He identifies animal life not with the four-legged figure of use value that is hamstrung and drained by an abstract logic of exchange but with the "pigheaded" apparition, with exchangeability as a pugnacious potentiality immanent to value

itself. It is by configuring exchange as an animal alterity that precedes
and exceeds the historical hegemony of capital that Derrida decon-
structs the specific critique of commodity fetishism and develops a
global logic of spectrality in its place.

The draining of historical materiality out of the sign of animal life
risked by Derrida's conflation of animality and spectrality also threatens the animal autobiography he initiates in "The Animal That Therefore I Am (More to Follow)." Although Derrida starts this essay with
a striking encounter between himself as he emerges from the shower
and his cat—"a real cat," he insists, not "the *figure* of a cat"[118]—she
quickly dissipates into spiritualistic terms deeply resonant with those
Derrida deploys to describe both the becoming-animal of the commodity *and* the visitation of the ghost of Hamlet's father in Shake-
speare's play. *Specters of Marx* opens, after all, with a meditation on the
ghost of Hamlet's father, in which Derrida describes him in commodity terms as a sensuous non-sensuous "Thing that is not a thing."[119]
The ghost of Hamlet's father is able to appear on the phenomenal stage,
claims Derrida, only by donning a body "armor" or "costume," a "kind
of technical prosthesis" that constitutes "a body foreign to the spectral
body that it dresses" (8). Focal to the prosthetic appearance of the
specter, moreover, is what Derrida terms its "visor effect," its unsettling
gaze through slitted head armor (7). Pivotal to the spectral visitation,
in other words, is the visual sense that "this spectral *someone other looks
at us,* [and] we feel ourselves being looked at by it, outside of any syn-
chrony, even before and beyond any look on our part, according to an
absolute anteriority" (7).

Similarly, Derrida's cat is staged within the scene of an "*animalséance,*" a charged locking of gazes in which the human, in this case
Derrida himself, is "caught naked, in silence, by the gaze of an animal,
for example the eyes of a cat...the gaze of a seer, visionary, or extra-
lucid blind person."[120] His cat is introduced, that is, within the same
logic as the specter. As with the ghost of Hamlet's father, the scene
turns on a visor effect, on the startling anteriority of a spectral gaze
that, as Derrida puts it in this instance, spawns the abyssal situation of
"seeing oneself seen naked under a gaze that is vacant to the extent of

being bottomless" (381). The spectral animal visually channels the disquieting half-presence of a "life" never cosubstantial with terrestrial
Time, History, and Being.[121] By framing his encounter with his cat
in the same terms he uses to frame the ghostly visitation of Hamlet's
father, Derrida risks collapsing the material difference between the
body of an actual animal and the prosthetic armor of a fictional specter,
conflating the body of his cat with the "paradoxical corporeality" of the
prosthetic dress that the spirit of Hamlet's father dons in order to
make an appearance on the historical stage.[122]

Meeting the "bottomless gaze" of a spectral animal is, for Derrida,
a deeply ethical encounter capable of dislocating the composure and
presumed priority of the human subject.[123] "As with every bottomless
gaze, as with the eyes of the other, the gaze called animal offers to my
sight the abyssal limit of the human," he writes (381). Yet this ethical
encounter with animal alterity is, as Rey Chow says of critical theory's
fascination with human alterity, deeply idealistic.[124] The "real cat" that
Derrida takes pains to distinguish from a simply tropological function
is transubstantiated, despite his protestations, into one figure in a line
of suspenseful figures emptied of historical substance and summoned
to deconstruct ontotheological "sign[s] of presence."[125] Is a materialist
critique of life in biopolitical times—a politics of what Derrida himself raises as "the industrial, mechanical, chemical, hormonal, and genetic violence to which man has been submitting life for the past two
centuries"[126]—possible when animals are summoned as specters with
at best "an appearance of flesh" on their "bodiless body," when they are
assigned to a limbo economy of life and death and thus positioned as
never fully subject to histories of violence and exploitation?[127] Does
not thinking of the animal as specter risk depoliticizing the argument
that Derrida simultaneously makes in "The Animal That Therefore I
Am" for animals as mortal creatures vulnerable to the capitalizing machinery of the past two centuries? If on the one hand Derrida initiates
a politics of animal sacrifice specific to "carno-phallogocentric" cultures
of the West,[128] on the other hand he remains transfixed with animals
as first metaphors for *différance* as an uncanny force undermining ontological discourses in the West, including Marxist ontology. Derrida's

cat—herself partly an engineered product of material institutions of pet ownership that Derrida occludes by declaiming her "absolute alterity"[129]—is ultimately suspended as a historical subject and rendered an arch-figure of deconstruction.

I do not take issue with Derrida's efforts, alongside those of theorists such as Paul de Man and Hayden White, to undermine metaphysical truth claims by insisting that they are ineradicably haunted with traces of the tropological. What is at stake, rather, is how the tropological trace, supplement, or specter may itself be surreptitiously reified through its articulation to talismanic signs of animality. For the metaphors of the "pigheaded" animal and the "prophetic dog" that lace Derrida's deconstruction of the Marxian discourse of fetishism, and that animate the notion of hauntology he offers in its stead, are far from transparent. That the animal specter may itself covertly function as a fetish within deconstruction (a site where the transcendent foundations that deconstruction challenges are reconstituted in the immanent form of animal-gods) is matter for concern, given that articulations of animality and spectrality can, on the one hand, lend figures of deconstruction a character of compulsive inevitability and, on the other, drain animals of their historical specificity and substance.

Allow me to pinpoint, before moving on, how Derrida's conflation of spectrality and animality indeed puts him at risk, as Žižek says in relation to Deleuze, of being an "ideologist of late capitalism." The Animorph toys cited by Žižek to back his claim that Deleuzian "becomings" ideologically resonate with actual capitalism could also be cited in relation to Derrida's concept of "animot" and his meditations on spectral bodies. According to the logic within which Derrida invokes animal life, specters simply *are* (or rather *appear*, given that the ontologically self-evident is precisely what an apparition perturbs). To suggest that specters perturb hegemonic structures of power assumes that they appear out of some ghostly volition from within immanent fissures in architectures of presence. The rubric of rendering suggests, by contrast, that capitalism is biopolitically invested in *producing* animal life as a spectral body. Whether it be as semiotic or as biological stock, whether on reserve as mediatized sign or as mere material, animals and other signs of nature are kept in a state of suspension that Derrida himself characterizes as a state of "interminable survival."[130] It is difficult to dissociate the logic of the specter from a biopolitical logic of capitalization bent on producing, administering, and circulating life as an undying currency. Capital, in other words, is arguably less invested in the metaphysics of presence that Derrida confronts than in the spectral logic of a "paradoxical corporeality" that infernally survives.[131] Derrida himself draws attention to a biopolitical violence constituted by the power to keep animal life in a limbo economy of interminable survival, one equal to if not greater than the violence of liquidating animal life and extinguishing species. Nor is he unconcerned with the rising hegemony of "techno-tele-discursivity" and spectralizing media.[132] Whenever Derrida historically engages with the field of capitalism, that is, he acknowledges that a spectral materiality is often the very currency of exchange rather than a source of disturbance.

Taking recourse once again to the argument that Hardt and Negri leverage in *Empire,* the logic of the specter offers little resistance to market cultures geared toward biopolitical production. Globalizing market cultures advance biopolitically, argue Hardt and Negri, by exploiting and producing the aporias, ambiguities, and in-between states that postmodernist and hybridity theorists have deemed resistant. "The affirmation of hybridities and the free play of differences across boundaries," they write, "is liberatory only in a context where power poses hierarchy exclusively through essential identities, binary divisions, and stable oppositions."[133] The logic of the specter, likewise, is perturbing only within a field of power invested in binaries of life and death, presence and absence, specie and speculative value—binaries that capital, in its "necromancy," has arguably always exceeded.[134] It is therefore crucial to consider that Derrida's *animalséance* may ideologically reinforce rather than trouble "the spectral reign of globalized capitalism."[135] That said, resisting the spectralization of animal life does not mean reverting to an equally perilous empiricism that would fixate on animals as carnal proof of presence. As the double sense of *rendering* suggests, the logic of the specter and the logic of the specimen (conceived as the reduction of animals to the ostensibly transparent literality of their bodies) are flip sides of animal capital and signal the double bind with which capital achieves a biopolitical lock on "life." If draining the historical substance out of virtualized animals represents one valence of rendering, recycling animals as mere material represents the other.

I have attended at some length to Derrida's work, given that it constitutes one of the most sustained ethical engagements with "the question of the animal." However, the spectral animal invoked by Derrida makes a significant reappearance in Akira Mizuta Lippit's *Electric Animal: Toward a Rhetoric of Wildlife* (2000), a book that, as I have noted, serves as something of a recurring foil for this book's theorization of animal capital. Like Derrida, who is fascinated with an animal specter that looks at Man from a paranormal time and space in which it is neither dead nor alive, Lippit theorizes animals as undying spirits that survive their mass historical "vanishing" within modernity to be reincarnated in the technological media.[136] Building on a Derridean notion of supplementarity, Lippit seeks to locate "traces of animality" in language and in the technological media, where a carnophallogocentric symbolic order is infiltrated by animal affect (26). Metaphor, suggests Lippit, is one such site. Like Berger and Derrida, Lippit encourages the sense that there is a primal link between "the animal and the metaphor." He fuses them in the notion of "animetaphor": "One finds a fantastic transversality at work between the animal and the metaphor—the animal is already a metaphor, the metaphor an animal. Together they transport to language, breathe into language, the vitality of another life, another expression: animal and metaphor, a metaphor made flesh, a living metaphor that is by definition not a metaphor, antimetaphor—'animetaphor'" (165). As animals "vanish" from historical modernity, continues Lippit, a spirit or trace of animality—ultimately an indestructible code—is salvaged by the technological media. He contends that cinema, even more consummately than linguistic metaphor, "mourns" vanishing animal life, that is, preserves or encrypts animality in its affective structure of communication (196). Cinema bypasses linguistic registers, Lippit argues, to communicate via rapid surges of nonverbal affect long associated in Western culture with an animal's electrifying gaze and sympathetic powers of communicability

(196). Cinema communicates, in other words, by means of affective transference in the form of the spell-binding gaze between animal and human that Derrida describes as an *animalséance*.

In proposing that an essence or structure of animal communication survives the historical disappearance of animals to transmigrate into the cinematic apparatus, Lippit takes to its logical conclusion the margin allowed in Derrida's text for reducing the body of the animal to a kind of stage armor or "technical prosthesis."[137] Only by idealistically speculating in the animal as a rhetorical currency transcending its material body can Lippit propose such "a transfer of animals from nature to technology."[138] Thus while *Electric Animal* provides a brilliant recapitulation of discourses of the "undying" animal in Western philosophical, psychoanalytic, and technological discourses, Lippit ends up *buying* the idea of the undead animal that he surveys and rearticulating it to an aesthetic theory of cinema.[139]

Like Deleuze and Guattari, Lippit idealizes affect as a discharge of "pure energy."[140] To idealize affect as animal is, almost by definition, to naturalize it, deflecting recognition of affect as a *preideological* means and effect of power. As Jennifer Harding and E. Deidre Pribram argue, it is not only possible but imperative that "the critical component of power" be added to the theorization of affect.[141] Their comparative analysis of Raymond Williams's "structure of feeling" and Larry Grossberg's "economy of affect" offers two examples of cultural materialists who resist the idealization of affect as an "anarchic excess threatening to disrupt the structures of power" and instead bring affect into view "as a technology of power."[142] Like Deleuze and Guattari, Grossberg differentiates between emotion and affect. Emotion, for Grossberg, is "the product of the articulation of two planes: signification...and affect."[143] Affect, on the other hand, is dislodged "from the circuit of meaning relations" and occurs "prior to or outside of meaning."[144] Yet to say that affect operates outside of meaning structures is not to say that it escapes relations of power, as Deleuze and Guattari (and Lippit) intimate. On the contrary, Grossberg contends that power is not coterminous with ideology or systems of signification alone but encompasses the production and circulation of asignifying energies. Rather than idealizing the alterity of animal affect, as Deleuze, Derrida, and Lippit are variously prone to do, one of the questions this book poses is How does animal affect function as a technology of capital?

The Deleuzian and Derridean figures of animality I have traced unravel the presumption that *Homo sapiens* is an all-powerful presence and self-same subject. Yet in liberating animality from the metaphysical strictures of Western thought and reenvisioning animals as pure intensities and undying specters, these poststructuralist discourses may inadvertently resonate with market forces likewise intent on freeing animal life into a multiplicity of potential exchange values.

Automobility, Telemobility, Biomobility

Not only automotive corporations but telecommunication corporations as well appear to favor animal signs as affective technologies. In 2005, Bell Mobility (a division of Bell Canada, the nation's largest telecommunications company) revived the tired symbology and sedimented sentiment accumulated in Canada's national animal with an ad campaign featuring two digitally rendered beavers, Frank and Gordon. The Bell "spokesbeavers," in company with the popular "spokescritters" of Telus Mobility ad campaigns (see chapter 3) and the faithful canines featuring in Fido wireless phone ads, bring into view a burgeoning bestiary of animal signs in telecommunications culture. They also draw attention to a guiding contention of the following chapters, namely, that the (neo)liberal market discourses that have most successfully hegemonized the sign of animal life in the twentieth and twenty-first centuries are those seeking to naturalize mobility as cultural ideology and material artifact. The frequency and effect of rendering technological mobility under the sign of the *moving* animal (in both the physiological and the affective senses of the word) will thus be a consistent concern as I track animal signs through market cultures.

In the ad campaign, Frank and Gordon parody white, heteronormative Canadianness. Although the campaign constitutes a "wry" take on the codes of white normativity structuring the project of national identification and intimates that in their ironic animal wrappings they are rendered harmless, it effectively rearticulates them as natural and uni-

versal traits of the postnational citizen of capital.[145] Unlike the Nissan
Animals ad campaign, the discourse of mobility that Frank and Gordon
represent does not pivot on animals as tropes of physical prowess. The
digital beavers are notorious "couch potatoes" who instead trope mobility as a purely virtual exercise in teletechnological roving. Even the
average Joe, according to the animal appeal of Frank and Gordon, can
have the world at his feet when he connects through the wireless technologies and services of Bell.

One print ad in the campaign renders a particularly imperial discourse of telemobility (see Figure 2). Only a single beaver appears in
this ad (let us assume that it is Frank), and he is shown listening to
music on headphones plugged into a Bell mobile phone. Frank wears,
ironically, a luxuriant fur coat over his own simulated pelt as he lounges
on a massive wingback chair of red "imperial leather," to borrow from
Anne McClintock. Like the *Maclean's* spread, this ad turns upon the
double entendre of animal rendering, as the beaver historically trapped
for its pelt in colonial North America (nearly to the point of extinction)
is resurrected as a computer-rendered virtual animal, indeed one with
a mock penchant for the material trappings of empire his species once
yielded. It plays, that is, on the double value of the animal as specimen
and specter. Again, as in the *Maclean's* image, the ironic layering of
fake fur on fake fur in the Bell ad has an effect of displacing the reality
of material violence—and literal traffics in animal nature—onto a past
empire of capital, reducing nature's mastery to a harmless source of
simulacral enjoyment in an era of postindustrial capitalism.

Alongside the discourse of virtual mobility the ad poses, it insinuates
a discourse of *class* mobility. With his possession of a wireless mobile
phone, the lowly, working-class beaver shoots up the social ladder to
become a member of the ruling establishment. The ad suggests that the
material exploitation of labor, as well as of nature, is a thing of the past
and that a neoliberal marketplace equalizes low and high within a single
global leisure class. In the fantasy of wealth without work that marks
the current era of "millennial capitalism," as Jean and John Comaroff
analyze it, "capital strives to become autonomous of labor," not to mention nature.[146] The beaver that symbolically served to naturalize nation-
building and belonging now simultaneously serves to naturalize the

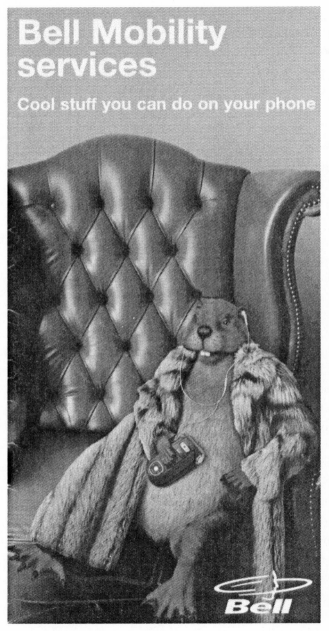

Figure 2. The new fur-clad class of subjects who enjoy virtual mobility. Bell Mobility, a division of Bell Canada, featured one of its famous duo of spokesbeavers on a 2005 flyer.

neoliberal image of capital as a terrain of consumption transcending production (7).

An eclectic array of cultural discourses and material practices come under analysis in the chapters that follow. Each chapter, with the exception of the first, renders a counterhegemonic genealogy of animal capital in relation to technologies and discourses of mobility under the headings of "automobility," "telemobility," and "biomobility." By contrast, chapter 1, "Rendering's Modern Logics," is devoted to laying some historical groundwork for the odd couple that uncomfortably shares the modern lexicon of *rendering:* the business of animal recycling and the faculty of mimesis. It leverages their lexical connection into an argument for cohistoricizing the business of animal recycling and the economy of mimesis within a "tautological time" and logic of capitalist biopower (in the terms of Negri).

Chapter 2, "Automobility: The Animal Capital of Cars, Films, and Abattoirs," resists a stock image of Fordism by reckoning with the historically repressed (and unfinished) business of animal rendering. *Automobility* names a network of ideological and material exchanges entangling three Fordist moving lines in the politics of animal capital: the animal disassembly line, the auto assembly line, and the cinematic reel. The consumption of animal disassembly as affective spectacle through tours of the vertical abattoir, the material rendering of animal gelatin for film stock, and the mimicry of seamless animal motion integral to cinema's and automobiles' symbolic economies are interimplicated in this chapter. To resist consigning automobility to a distinct historical period of Fordist capitalism that has been ostensibly closed with the arrival of post-Fordist economies, the latter half of the chapter engages two contemporary advertisements for the Saturn Vue sports utility vehicle and examines the ways that automobility is rearticulated in the present.

As becomes clear in chapter 3, "Telemobility: Telecommunication's Animal Currencies," wherever affect is mobilized as a technology of capital there stands, it seems, an animal sign. This is the case with the discourses I analyze under the heading of "telemobility," discourses mimicking the communicability and ostensible immediacy of animal affect. Rather than equating telemobility discourse solely with the present, this chapter begins with Luigi Galvani's early experiments in animal electricity in the 1780s. Animal electricity is not just the name Galvani gave to the lifelike spasms he induced in dead frog legs but a trope for the wireless long-distance communication with "animal spirits" he claimed to conduct through an invisible nervous fluid in animal bodies. From Galvani the chapter leaps to the pathological experiment posed by Thomas Edison's 1903 filmed electrocution of Topsy the elephant, a demonstration of electricity's ostensibly instantaneous communication of affect doubling as a public execution of a murderous animal. Chapter 3 takes up telemobility discourse as it is recalibrated in late capitalism, finally, by studying the advertising archive—stocked with signs of species biodiversity—of Telus Mobility Inc., Canada's second largest telecommunications corporation. Through the monkey metaphors that feature prominently in Telus's ads, the company's fetishistic discourse of telecommunication can be pressured to divulge the neocolonial relations of race, nature, and labor supporting it.

Chapter 4, "Biomobility: Calculating Kinship in an Era of Pandemic Speculation," engages with predictions by the World Health Organization and other agencies of a coming pandemic. A fixation in pandemic discourse on *zoonotic* diseases—diseases capable of leaping from animal to human bodies via microbial agents such as the H5N1 avian flu virus—is symptomatic of how formerly distinct barriers separating humans and other species are imaginatively, and physically, disintegrating under current conditions of globalization. This chapter examines how human-animal contact is constituted as a matter of global biosecurity in pandemic discourse as well as how zoonotic origin stories function to racially pathologize a specter of entangled ethnic-animal flesh. Yet if human-animal intimacy is pathologized in the cultural discourse of pandemic, it is contradictorily fetishized as an object of desire in concurrent cultural discourses. I examine the affective flip side of pandemic speculation in this chapter by looking at Gregory Colbert's popular photographic exhibit of human-animal intimacy, *Ashes and Snow*. Touring the globe in what Colbert calls his "nomadic museum," *Ashes and Snow* disseminates a vision of posthuman kinship composed of orientalizing images of entwined ethnic-animal flesh. The affects of fear and desire accruing to the permeability of the species line in the current era of globalization are tremendously productive of forms of animal capital, as this chapter attempts to show, in large part because they serve as visceral means and effects of power.

Finally, the book's postscript, "Animal Cannibalism in the Capitalist Globe-Mobile," glances at the carnal tautology of animal cannibalism (the feeding of rendered remains of ruminants back to livestock), a practice that erupted into crisis in North America in 2003 with the discovery of several Canadian cattle with bovine spongiform encephalopathy, or mad cow disease. The closing of the U.S. border to Canadian beef and livestock, and the resurrection of discourses of national purity as both countries strove to exonerate themselves of the pathological excesses of animal capital, provide a parting glimpse into the complex material and cultural politics of rendering. As disease incubators threatening to expose capitalism's harrowing protein recycles, animals return in excess of the anticipated returns of rendering. If mad cow disease constitutes something of a privileged material symptom of rendering's logic, the cannibalism of representational economies in late capitalism that Jean Baudrillard terms *simulacra* is arguably its double. This book works from within the double binds posed by the supplementary economies of rendering and their harrowing symptoms while at the same time taking stock of possible openings for protest.

Chapter 1

Rendering's Modern Logics

To render: "to reduce, convert, or melt down (fat) by
heating"; from Old French rendre, to give back. And
indeed rendering does give back. Animal byproducts
that would otherwise have been discarded have for
centuries been rendered into fat which is an essential
ingredient in the manufacture of soap, candles, glycerin,
industrial fatty acids. More recently, animal protein
meals have been produced as feed supplements for
companion and meat-producing animals, poultry, [and]
fish, and fat is used as a biofuel.
> —National Renderers Association Inc.,
> "North American Rendering: The Source of
> Essential, High-Quality Products"

Michael Taussig opens *Mimesis and Alterity: A Particular History of the Senses*
(1993) with the dizzying scene of "the ape aping humanity's aping"
from Franz Kafka's short story "A Report to an Academy."[1] The narrator in Kafka's story has been invited by the academy to give an account
of his former life as an ape captured by Europeans on the Gold Coast.
He recalls how, by mimicking his captors, he contrived to become-
human, thereby escaping his fate as a colonial specimen destined for
the Zoological Garden or the variety stage. The ape ends up, instead, a
self-improved gentleman recalling his rapid evolution before an audience
of similar gentlemen who are suddenly indistinguishable from the so-
called performing monkey.

Confronted in this scene of aping by the profound *mise-en-abyme*
of mimesis (not to mention by the confoundment of human and animal),
Taussig professes renewed wonder at the mimetic faculty. Mimesis, he
writes, is "the nature that culture uses to create second nature, the faculty to copy, imitate, make models."[2] To his credit, Taussig complicates

the dazzling "nature" of the mimetic faculty—"if it is a faculty," he writes, "it is also a history" (xiv). Engaging with colonial histories of mimesis tracing back to moments of "first contact," Taussig draws attention to the profound overencoding of the mimetic faculty by modern discourses of primitivism (73). Nevertheless, Taussig's opening appeal in his book to approach "the inner sanctum of mimetic mysteries" with something akin to reverence arguably proves as seductive as his assertion of the historical character of mimesis.³ Contrary to his efforts to historicize mimesis within colonial discourses and relationships of power (as well as their postcolonial reversals), Taussig encourages readers to replace constructivist critiques popular in the current academy with an attitude of appreciative "wonder" at the power of mimesis (xix). This is at a time when the faculty of copying and imitation has never been more immanent, arguably, to the means and ends of capitalism. Indeed, within the context of animal capital—which at once connotes a metafetishistic time and terrain of capitalism and denotes actual traffics in animal signs and substances (see the Introduction)—this strikes me as nearly equivalent to asking us to abandon critique of capitalism's conditions and effects. For the power of the mimetic faculty and the fetishistic grip of naturalized capitalism cannot, arguably, be separated. Certainly Taussig knows this; his own work has been seminal to furthering the analysis of colonial capitalism's reliance on forms of mimetic as well as economic power and of colonized subjects' resistant deployments of mimesis.⁴ I agree with Taussig that the theoretical outlook of "constructionism" tends to uphold "a dreadfully passive view of nature."⁵ But in his desire to give nature, in the form of the mimetic faculty, a more active role in culture than constructionism tends to allow, Taussig arguably swings too far the other way and idealizes mimesis as a force—even a marvel—of nature.

In the Introduction to this book I proposed the rubric of *rendering* as an alternative to Taussig's language of mimetic reenchantment. Rendering also connotes "the faculty to copy, imitate, make models," as in the practice of rendering an object's likeness in this or that medium. Yet rendering simultaneously denotes the industrial business of boiling down and recycling animal remains, with the aim of returning animal matter to another round in the marketplace. In the Introduction I termed this the "double entendre" of rendering, noting that while rendering has multiple senses, the accommodation of these two particularly divergent logics within the space of its one signifier is deeply suggestive of the complicity of representational and material economies in the reproduction of (animal) capital. In the supplementary workings of these two senses of rendering, mimesis comes into view as an immanent "faculty" of capitalism in the twentieth and early twenty-first centuries. In view of this contention, it becomes more difficult to grant the timeless innocence Taussig does to the mimetic faculty when he invokes "its honest labor [of] suturing nature to artifice."[6] The rubric of rendering compels us to consider, instead, how the "honest labor" of mimesis—indeed, how the very idea of copying as an unmotivated, innocent faculty— itself becomes a fetishistic resource of capitalism (see, for instance, the tropes of biological aping in the marketing discourse of Telus Mobility Inc., closely analyzed in chapter 3).

What follows is not an attempt to demystify mimesis, in Marxist fashion, according to the belief that under the mystique of the mimetic faculty lie the real workings of power. My aim is to show, on the contrary, that mimesis *constitutes* the real workings of power, at least partially. The material rendering of animals is not the empirical "truth" that gives the lie to its other, the representational economy of rendering; the two are the immanent shapes mimesis takes in biopolitical times. In this chapter, then, I seek to lay some groundwork for studying mimesis in the theoretical and historical context of biopower. I propose to do so by way of an eccentric pair of genealogies. In the first genealogy, I track back from Taussig to examine an earlier fascination with the animal nature of mimesis in twentieth-century cultural theory, returning to the writings of Walter Benjamin, Theodor Adorno and Max Horkheimer, and Roger Caillois (rather than to the ancient discourses of Plato and Aristotle, where many Western histories of mimesis begin).[7] The second genealogy traces the rise and rhetoric of industrial rendering as it emerged in Europe and North America around the turn of the twentieth century to capitalize on the surplus of animal waste.

What justifies this unlikely pairing of genealogies is not only the rubric of rendering, which the economy of mimesis and the business of animal recycling share, but also the perception that both constitute age-old and universal practices. Such a perception obscures recognition of the historically specific field of power organized by rendering's modern logics. In repeatedly gesturing toward their archaic origins, the cultural and industrial discourses of rendering that this chapter traces encourage the sense (whether inadvertently or deliberately) that they are timeless and universal practices rather than historically embedded within the relations of capital. Against the naturalization of rendering's modern logics, this chapter works toward coimplicating them in the "tautological time" of capitalist biopower theorized by Antonio Negri.[8] Building on Negri's suggestion that the history of capitalism undergoes a paradigmatic shift when the time devoted to capitalist production extends to cover the entire time of life itself, I propose that in the double sense of *rendering* a different but related history of biopower is inscribed.

Finally, as a methodological statement, the odd couple posed by this chapter's two genealogies of rendering bespeaks an effort to erode the disciplinary boundaries of the humanities and the sciences, boundaries that continue to bifurcate the study of culture and nature, culture and economy.

First Genealogy: Capitalist Mimesis

As suggested by the personability of the primate in the Kafka story relayed by Taussig, mimesis has been understood by most twentieth- and twenty-first-century cultural theorists as a "two-way street" irreducible to either culture or nature, history or biology.[9] Kafka's scene of aping brings mimesis into view as at once an animal faculty *and* a historical relationship of power, exceeding both essentialist and antiessentialist attempts to pin it down to one or the other.

However, an increasingly irreconcilable contradiction is arguably at play in the desire, evident in the work of theorists such as Taussig, Adorno, and Benjamin, to identify the oscillation or dialectic between history and biology that mimesis represents as a source of subversive alterity. This desire can be glimpsed in the fact that often when mimesis is invoked in twentieth- and twenty-first-century cultural discourse it is linked to a prehistoric figure of biological mimicry. Consider, for instance, how Michel de Certeau traces the origins of mimesis to the fathomless "depths of the ocean" in *The Practice of Everyday Life* (1984).[10] Although de Certeau is theorizing the resistant practice of bricolage ("making do") when he invokes the watery origins of life, bricolage turns on an idea of mimesis as a faculty continuous with "the immemorial intelligence displayed in the tricks and imitations of plants and fishes" (xx). De Certeau biologizes the tactical practice of making do by claiming that from "the depths of the ocean to the streets of modern megalopolises, there is a continuity and permanence in these tactics" (xx).[11] Intimating that the subversive potential of imitation is continuous with the deep nature of biological mimicry is a recurrent gesture within cultural discourses of mimesis in the twentieth century, one that contradicts their simultaneous efforts to historicize the contingency of mimesis and power.

The representation of mimesis as a dialectic between nature and culture was perhaps most persuasively articulated earlier in the twentieth century when an explosion of technological media (photography, film, radio, advertising) was arousing anxiety that the mimetic faculty might not in fact transcend its imbrications in capitalism's mass modes of reproduction.[12] The hopes of dialectical criticism were pinned to the mimetic faculty at the very moment, arguably, when the historical subsumption of its nature-culture dialectic into an immanent order of capitalism appeared all too possible. Taussig's engagement with mimesis in the "older" anthropological language of sympathetic magic has precedents in writings from this period (xiii). Walter Benjamin, cited heavily by Taussig, hinted in his 1930s writings that a sympathetic faculty for forging resemblances between unlike things can never be wholly denatured, not even through the instrumentalization of mimesis by the mass media of capitalism. In a famous passage in "The Work of Art in the Age of Mechanical Reproduction" (1936) in which he described the loss of aura—a loss that for Benjamin was symptomatic of capitalism's momentous historic reduction of mimesis to mere technological reproductions of likeness—he wrote that "to pry an object from its shell" is "to destroy its aura."[13] Benjamin's trope of a mollusk existence pried by technologies of mechanical reproduction from its biological environment implied that the mimetic faculty that capitalism threatens to denature archives the primordial origins of life itself. Yet although capitalism endangers the mimetic faculty by technologically harnessing it to mass reproduction (reducing the alterity of mimesis to the reifying order of the mimetological, to use a distinction later theorized by Derrida),[14] Benjamin invested hope in mimesis as an irrepressible biological inheritance destined to ultimately survive and subvert its instrumentality for anthropocentric capital.

On the one hand, Benjamin's work catches sight of mimesis as a political history flashing up in the moment of crisis provoked by capital's powers of mass reproduction. On the other hand, however, his work is prone to idealizing mimesis and to nostalgically evoking a "time immemorial" in which self and other, human and nonhuman, animate and inanimate, were linked by relations of mimetic resemblance rather than by relations of abstract equivalence.[15] Taussig himself is wary of Benjamin's tendency to exoticize mimesis "in the dance and magic of the primitive world."[16] In various short writings — "Doctrine of the Similar," "On the Mimetic Faculty," and "The Lamp," among others — Benjamin risks undermining the politicization of capitalist mimesis (of cinema, in particular) advanced in "The Work of Art in the Age of Mechanical Reproduction" by intimating that mimesis constitutes an innate biological compulsion, one threading back through an almost Lamarckian natural history. "The gift which we possess of seeing similarity," he writes, "is nothing but a weak rudiment of the formerly powerful compulsion to become similar and also to behave mimetically."[17]

It is important to note that linking mimesis to a prehistoric image of biological mimicry is well in keeping with Benjamin's contention that mimesis is the very means of dialectical movement across culture and nature (a movement policed and perverted by Enlightenment rationality and the reifying forces of capitalism). Benjamin saw mimesis as the spark that illuminates resemblances between culture and nature, in resistance to the Enlightenment reason that objectifies and polarizes them. In the same vein, mimesis is pivotal to the redemptive work of constellation, that practice of historical materialism that for Benjamin involved interrupting myths of historical progress by bringing past and present together within the dialectical instant of *Jetztzeit,* or "now-time."[18] Given that the mimetic faculty represents the means, for

Benjamin, of breaking down the chronological distance and cognitive distinction between cultural and natural history, present and past, his images of primordial mimesis were designed to have a counterhegemonic, defamiliarizing effect. However, what remains to be considered is how far mimesis—and the dialectical images it catalyzes—can be claimed to serve the counterdominant work of historical materialism versus the degree to which the dialectical production of startling nowtime may instead be indistinguishable from the fetishistic functions of the market. Capitalist mimesis (and the mimicry of animal capital, more particularly) appropriates the method, if not the political motives, of the historical materialist insofar as market discourses also dialectically associate capitalist mimesis with the "primitive" domain of biological mimicry.

Significantly, it is around an image of mimesis as an animal leap into the past that the question of now-time's subsumption was raised by Benjamin himself, who was cognizant of the potential difficulty of distinguishing between the dialectical flash that disrupts myths of progress and the fetishistic frisson of perpetual newness "immanent to the productivity of capital."[19] It was in relation to the fashion industry, which perhaps most typifies capital's cooptation of the shock of newness, that Benjamin wrote, "Fashion has a nose for the topical, no matter where it stirs in the thickets of long ago; it is a tiger's leap into the past."[20] Aware, perhaps, that his own evocation of mimesis as a primordial compulsion was deeply susceptible to fetishism, Benjamin attempted to draw a distinction within the mimetic spring of the tiger. "This jump," he said in relation to the fashion industry, "takes place in an arena where the ruling class gives the commands. The same leap in the open air of history is the dialectical one."[21]

Benjamin's writings on mimesis are closely associated with those of Adorno and Horkheimer, who were similarly fascinated with the "archaic character of mimesis," in the words of Gunter Gebauer and Christoph Wulf.[22] Adorno formulated mimesis as a "nonconceptual affinity" between self and other, an immediate, surrendering relation of culture and nature.[23] While profoundly aware of capitalism's ability to instrumentalize mimesis to a degree that cast serious doubt on its disruptive potential, Adorno, like Benjamin, nevertheless held out hope for its ultimate noninstrumentality for power, that is, hope for the alterity of mimesis. If not exactly the rudimentary compulsion that Benjamin explored, what typified the alterity of mimesis for Adorno was a "living experience" still glimpsed in its original, not yet disenchanted state in so-called primitive cultures, for which nature ostensibly continued to represent an otherness evading objectification and conceptual mastery.[24] Adorno believed that only aesthetic experience could restore the vitality of such a mimetic immediacy of culture and nature.

As Taussig notes, Adorno and Horkheimer were acutely aware that "civilization does more than repress mimesis" and that mimesis can be mobilized in the service of totalitarianism, anti-Semitism, and racism.[25] Both Benjamin and Adorno and Horkheimer affiliated mimesis with the primal sense of smell—the "most animal" of the senses (66). "Of all the senses," wrote Adorno and Horkheimer, "that of smell . . . bears clearest witness to the urge to lose oneself in and become the 'other.'"[26] In Benjaminian terms, smell can affectively trigger memories that have been buried or repressed, causing the past to flash up in the present. Yet if redemptive possibilities accrue to smell as a sensory means of identification and a mimetic porthole into the collective unconscious (or animal past) of humanity, smell can also be organized to serve the political ends of anti-Semitism and racism via the arousal of "primitive" passions of hate and fear. Just as fashion has a nose for the topical, exploiting the affective value of a dialectic between past and present, so fascism and racism have historically exploited associative articulations of Jews and other racialized groups with animality, or "biological prehistory," as Horkheimer and Adorno put it (67).[27] The effect is that racialized subjects are viscerally experienced as biological "danger signs which make the hair stand on end and the heart stop beating" (180).

While understanding mimesis as "a repressed presence not so much erased by Enlightenment science and practice as distorted and used as hidden force," the work of the Frankfurt School nevertheless betrayed its own entanglements in a primitivist fantasy of the "other" of technological modernity.[28] It was tinged, in other words, with the paternalistic aesthetics of a Europe sick unto death of its own technological sophistication and seeking a revitalization of experience through the contemplation and collection of the alterity of non-European cultures ostensibly living in a closer mimetic relationship with nature. Intellectuals such as Adorno and Horkheimer, seeking a way out of the claustrophobic advance of European fascism, on the one side, and the reifying powers of commodity culture on the other, looked to mimesis as a repository of prediscursive or "primordial reason."[29] Yet the persistent association of this primordial reason with other cultures exoticized in their closeness with nature betrays the historical immanence of their own formulations of mimesis and alterity to Eurocentric culture.

Roger Caillois's "Mimicry and Legendary Psychasthenia" (1938) was part of the efflorescence of mimetic theories spawned under the double specters of fascism and capitalism during this period.[30] One of the founders of the Collège de Sociologie (a Parisian avant-garde group including Georges Bataille and Michel Leiris), Caillois turned to the study of insects to carve out a pathological theory of biological mimicry (17). Insects mimicking the appearance of leaves, twigs, or stones revealed, for Caillois, a vertiginous "luxury" or mimetic excess by which animate and animal life appeared irrationally driven to approximate inanimate life, stasis, and even death. He christened this animal death wish *"le mimetisme"* (17). Caillois's elaboration of biological mimetism, like the "mimetic impulse" theorized by Adorno and the "compulsion to become similar" sketched by Benjamin, argues for "a deeply internalized tendency in all living things to deliver themselves up to their surroundings."[31] The playing dead of insects and animals signals not a survival mechanism protecting an organism against predation, Caillois contended, but a perverse death drive that he formulated as a "temptation by space."[32] *Le mimetisme* lures creatures into losing their distinct outlines and will to life by provoking them to seek an *"assimilation to the surroundings"* (27). "What mimicry achieves morphologically in certain animal species," elaborated Caillois, schizophrenia unleashes in human subjects—a loss of subjectivity and a *"depersonalization by assimilation to space"* (30).

Caillois's formulation of the relationship between mimesis and schizophrenia has been rearticulated, with a difference, in the poststructuralist philosophy of Deleuze and Guattari, who elaborate becoming-animal as an affective compulsion and involuntary "desubjectification."[33] For Deleuze and Guattari, "becomings" radically challenge the reduction of mimesis to relations of imitation, because *imitation* continues to connote a dialectic of nature and culture, original and copy, in which the two terms retain their binary distinction.[34] However, in first theorizing mimesis in terms of a pathological becoming exceeding imitation, Caillois in effect removed mimesis from a field of social power and returned it to the secret biological life of an organism subject to involuntary, inexorable drives.

Moreover, as Denis Hollier notes, "Caillois does not find it worthwhile to remind us that [an animal] can only play dead because it is alive. His entire analysis proceeds as if playing dead and being dead were one and the same."[35] If such an indifference to the "vital difference" is possible in the work of Caillois, how much more will market discourses elide the material difference, or exploit the aporia, between death as a mimetic feint and death as a fatal effect of capitalism's logics? The mimicry of the market fetishistically imbues commodities with a semblance of vital life while materially reducing life to the dead labor and nature of capital; market logics indeed render "the vital difference" indifferent by converting life into a mimetic *effect* transcending material distinctions between the living and the dead. Caillois's formulation of mimetism as a death instinct compelling animate life to revert to an inanimate state—his suggestion that a "return to an earlier state, seems here to be the goal of all life"[36]—itself can be read as a discursive displacement of the violence of capital's commodifying logics onto a theory of a pathological and regressive nature. Caillois's discourse of animal mimetism, that is, formulates as a biological compulsion what is in effect the market's reifying drive to convert all nature into capital.

Taussig ultimately recognizes the danger of "resting mimesis on a psychological or biological base-line such as a 'faculty' and buttressing it with notions of 'the primitive.'"[37] He asks, "can we not create a field of study of the mimetic which sees it as curiously baseless, so dependent on alterity that it lies neither with the primitive nor with the civilized, but in the windswept and all too close, all too distant, mysterious-sounding space of First Contact?" (72). Yet wary of idealizing the alterity of a mimetic faculty or power that perennially represents a surplus of "otherness" eluding capture, I propose that as capitalism has expanded in the twentieth and early twenty-first centuries to become an intensive and universal logic constitutive of life itself (that is, as capital has become animal), it is important to confront the harrowing possibility that mimesis may be wholly immanent to its biopolitical workings. It is this historical subsumption of mimesis into the cultural-economic machinery of capitalist biopower that "rendering" provisionally signposts. Negri's engagement with the Marxist problematic of real subsumption through the notion of "tautological time" will help me to elaborate the importance of resisting the appeal of mimesis as alterity in order to reckon with the material history of mimesis as rendering. En route to situating rendering in the time of real subsumption, however, let me first supplement this first genealogy with its industrial double.

Second Genealogy: Animal Recycling

Animal rendering shares, with prostitution, the euphemism of being the "oldest profession in the world." In an Errol Morris documentary film, *Gates of Heaven* (1978), a rendering executive describes the industry in the proverbial tense of the euphemism: "Rendering is one of the oldest industries . . . it dates back to the time of the Egyptians. It could be the oldest industry in the world, it could be, it's possible."[38] These words in Morris's filmic text defer rendering to the distant past and to the very delta of civilization, a gesture consonant with the official rhetoric of the industry. For instance, the first sentence of the rendering history offered in *The Original Recyclers,* a book published in 1996 by the National Renderers Association (NRA), similarly euphemizes a capitalist economy of rendering by tracing its origins back to the immemorial beginnings of Time itself.[39] According to the NRA, the story of rendering stretches back to even before the ancient Egyptians, back to the mythical moment when *Homo sapiens,* through the act of cooking animals over a fire, broke out of an enmired state of nature and inaugurated History: "Although rendering as an organized and cohesive industry has been around for only 150 years, the process of melting down animal fats to produce tallow and other fats and oils probably got its start when *Homo sapiens* began cooking meat over a campfire and saving the drippings" (2). Around this primal scene of rendering—in

the loaded moment when the raw becomes the cooked as an inaugural
mark of civilization—*Homo sapiens*, meat, fire, and cooking as the rudimentary technique of rendering are etched as timeless anthropological
signs. Rendering as a modern and "cohesive" capitalist industry flickers
in the mythic firelight of an originary human practice. The surplus captured by the modern industry is refracted through the half-light of the
animal "drippings" gleaned by early humans around the campfire, reflecting surplus value as nothing more than a natural remainder separated out through the primary technology of cooking. The scene suggests that *Homo sapiens* entered into the historical record the instant he
discovered himself, through the act of rendering, to be *Homo oeconomi-
cus*. Moreover, industrial rendering is cast as simply the evolved and
"cohesive" expression of an economizing impulse that first prompted a
glimmer of historical sense in prehistoric Man (the revolutionary idea
of saving drippings for the future) and launched humans on the path
of progress. Via this depiction of rendering, animal capital melts back
into a timeless tableau of use value, appearing to be anthropologically
continuous with an age-old practice of using every part of an animal.

As dangerous, then, as euphemisms that depict political cultures of
prostitution under capital as merely the modern expression of a timeless and inevitable practice are euphemisms that install rendering as a
sign of natural industriousness at work in the world since time out of
mind.[40] For all of the signs that have come to appear universal in the
euphemistic discourse of rendering—animal sacrifice, conservation,
waste, and surplus value ("cooking meat over a campfire and saving the
drippings")—are in fact historically, culturally, and politically contingent. Just as Gayle Rubin historicizes the "traffic in women" in relation
to "a systematic social apparatus which takes up females as raw material" and fashions them into objects of exchange, rendering notates
semiotic and material traffics in animal life specific to the social relations of capitalism.[41] The second genealogy presented here thus resists
the universality claimed by the rendering industry, emphasizing instead
rendering's specificity as a marginalized, malodorous, yet massively
productive industrial culture of capital. While the bulk of this book
engages with rendering as a biopolitical logic including, but invariably
exceeding, its economic referent, the following genealogy brings it into

view as an industry deploying particular material and rhetorical technologies at specific historical junctures to reproduce capitalism.

Genealogizing rendering as a capitalist industry itself immediately entails "splitting," however, because the animal recycling denoted by rendering has, over the past few decades, been usurped by the now-popular use of rendering to denote postindustrial cultures of digital animation. I have already suggested that in its modern usage rendering has long accommodated a balance of power between its at least double connotations; it has popularly referenced representational practices as well as the recycling of animal remains. At the turn of the twenty-first century, the balance seems to have tipped to the extent that rendering no longer popularly evokes the industry that breaks down animal hides, bones, blood, and offal but instead evokes the new culture industry that traffics in 3-D images of life assembled out of algorithmic bits of code. Digital capitalism appears to have successfully spirited away the bad affect associated with the boiling down of animal remains, reinventing rendering as an aesthetic notation for the field of computer-generated images. The reinvention of rendering by digital capitalism arguably depoliticizes both industries, associating ongoing traffics in animal material with technological virtuality, on the one hand, while identifying computer-generated graphics with biological stock, on the other. *Render farm,* the name given to facilities that cluster together processors in order to amass the "horsepower" needed for computer-generated imagery, provocatively articulates virtual with biological animal capital to coin a new mode of technological production. For instance, viewers of *Bee Movie* (2007) learn in one of the film's behind-the-scenes special features, that the movie required 23 million "render hours," in the new language of computer labor power. Caught in the midst of the reinvention of rendering by digital technologies, it is important to consider that computer-imaging technology supplements rather than displaces its industrial precursor, enabling advanced capitalism to pursue contradictory semiotic and biological traffics in animal life. For the present purposes, I confine myself to a genealogy of industrial rather than postindustrial rendering while nevertheless flagging the fact that what seem like two wildly disparate and noncontemporaneous practices—the one pursuing the carnal recycling of animal matter,

the other a representational recycling of lifelike effects whose prototypes are invariably animal—can be placed in political relation, via a
theory of rendering, as concurrent and complicit logics of capital.

A genealogy of modern rendering might begin by revisiting its relation to the industrialization of slaughter in Europe and North America
in the nineteenth century. In her study of French abattoirs, *Animal to
Edible,* Noëlie Vialles remarks that the word *abattoir* appeared in France
around 1806, "at the same time as Napoleon's major reorganization of
slaughtering and butchering."[42] Napoleon's project of modernization involved, crucially, the "exile" of the sensoriums of slaughtering and rendering to outlying precincts far from the eyes and noses of an urban polity
(22). In the nineteenth century public culture began to be sanitized and
sensitized through myriad practices, disciplines, and reforms best discerned, perhaps, by Foucault. According to Vialles, the institutionalization of enclosed, monitored facilities devoted solely to animal slaughter
in compliance with new regulations and sensibilities around "suffering,
violence, waste and disease, 'miasmas,' and finally animals themselves,"
helped to materially and ideologically prepare conditions for the massification of slaughter (19). "The quantities dealt with were henceforth
on an industrial scale and called for suitable organization," writes Vialles.
"It was a development that led ... to the remarkable 'vertical' abattoirs
of Chicago," where the mechanized moving-line production proto-
typical of Fordist capitalism would find one of its first applications (22).

The exile of slaughter to a "clandestine" space of public secrecy was
reinforced, notes Vialles, with attempts to euphemize the industrialization of animal sacrifice (22). The term *abattoir* was coined to name
"the 'no-place' where this massive and methodically repudiated slaughter" took place (23):

> The general meaning of *abattre* is "to cause to fall" or "to bring down
> that which is standing." It is primarily a term in forestry, where it refers
> to felling; subsequently, it came to be used in the mineral world, where it
> denoted the action of detaching material from the walls of a mine tunnel.
> It also belongs to the vocabulary of veterinary surgery, and particularly
> when applied to a horse it means to lay the animal down in order ... to
> give it medical attention. (23)

As euphemisms, *abattoir* and *abattre* sought to equate the "felling" of animals with the felling of trees or minerals (and even with the veterinary treatment of a sick animal), so that "the slaughterer becomes a wood-cutter, and blood is almost edulcorated into sap" (23). Yet, as Vialles adds, attempts to euphemistically deflect the violence of industrial-ized slaughter often failed, as *abattoir* itself came to assume the taint of all that it had been designed to disavow.

Symbiotic with animal slaughter, rendering was also being reformed into an industrial, mass, yet inoffensive culture of capital over the course of the nineteenth century in Europe and North America. From the nineteenth century to the present, the rendering industry has inno-vated many material technologies for scrubbing itself clean of the acrid, malodorous signs of its carnal commerce.[43] Retreating out of an urban field of vision was just one step in the reorganization of slaughter and rendering; doing everything possible to prevent the sensory revolt triggered by smell has arguably been even more critical to the affective management of animal capital. As slaughter and rendering were turned into mass operations in the nineteenth and twentieth centuries, suppressing the "olfactory obtrusiveness" haunting rendering's traffic in "perishable substances" became something of an industry obsession and *the* sensory index of its progress.[44] Modern renderers became acutely conscious of olfactory leakage from the industrial cooking of animal remains and of a populace whose senses risked being offended by reminders of a grisly business exiled to the margins of public con-sciousness. The containment of smell has been integral to the incon-spicuous "no-place" of public secrecy within which modern rendering has achieved invisibility.[45] Recalling the importance placed on smell by both Benjamin and Adorno and Horkheimer as a sensory trigger of mimetic identification, the control of smell is suggestive, moreover, of the containment and management of affect aroused by a potential identification with animal others subject to sacrifice. Smell's manage-ment enabled public culture in *"knowing what not to know"*[46] about the "anonymous flesh" on their dinner table.[47] The rendering industry has striven to spirit away all sensible traces of the historical—that is, dying—animal, preventing the smell of animal remains from reaching the nostrils of consumer culture by promptly converting perishable nature into perennial capital.

Alongside strategies of sensory and affective containment, the rendering industry also employs euphemism, as I began this section by noting, to divert recognition of its specific productivity under and for capitalism. When capital's clandestine traffic in animal bodies emerges, from time to time, out of the odorless and invisible "no-place" it has sought to inhabit in modernity, it takes rhetorical flight into the past by reciting, as the rendering executive in *Gates of Heaven* does, its fathomless ancestry. In his "case study of animal by-products recovery from the Neolithic period to the middle of the twentieth century" in an article in a 2000 issue of the *Journal of Industrial Ecology*, Pierre Desrochers adds academic argument to the popular euphemism of rendering as the "oldest industry in the world."[48] Desrochers offers sweeping, transhistorical evidence of rendering as an age-old practice, erasing its specific character under the political economy and cultural logics of industrial capitalism. "The oldest glue discovered so far," writes Desrochers, "was made by Neolithic cave dwellers living southwest of the Dead Sea some 8,000 years ago. It was made from collagen (the fibrous protein taken from animal skin, cartilage, and bone) and was used to waterproof rope baskets and containers" (32). Desrochers proceeds to classify glue derived from animal remains in Europe and America around the turn of the twentieth century as a product of the same "human creativity" that rendered the 8,000-year-old Neolithic specimen (35). In brief, Desrochers argues that while contemporary Western industrial culture claims to have improved on wasteful economic practices of the past by assuming itself the first to achieve "closed loop" production, an industrial ecology of waste recovery has been in practice at least from the mid-eighteenth century on.

For Desrochers, in fact, rendering dissolves into an ageless syntax for an economical and ecological reuse of waste in evidence from time out of mind, as he collapses waste recovery practices of "the Neolithic city of Çatal Hüyük" with those of "the Roman era" and further proceeds to suggest that "the same process was also going on in North America, where Plains Indians turned bones into, among other things, fleshing tools, pipes, knives, arrowheads, shovels, splints" (32). In a work that is a history rather than a genealogy, Desrochers reduces profoundly disparate cultures and eras to the common sense of rendering (and displaces recognition of a specifically modern, capitalist logic of recycling with evidence of rendering's universality). Not surprisingly, when his history "progresses" to industrial cultures of the nineteenth and twentieth centuries, Desrochers places them in sweeping continuum with the industriousness of Neolithic, Roman, and Plains Indian cultures. "Market incentives," according to Desrochers, are a natural extension of the proverbial economism according to which *Homo sapiens* is universally moved to "create wealth out of residuals" (38).

Within such an epic narrative of rendering, a capitalist industry is equated with indigenous practices of rendering, enabling dissimulation of its specific economic, political, and cultural motives. An animal sign mediates just such an identification with indigeneity in the collection of articles published by the NRA in *The Original Recyclers*.[49] A photo profile of a buffalo appears on the frontispiece of the book, accompanied by these words: "The buffalo exemplifies the rendering industry because the American Plains Indian appreciated the value of utilizing the whole animal." The collection of essays in the volume—tracking technological advancements and the creation of new markets capable of absorbing the ever finer surpluses being skimmed off of animal remains—are insidiously framed under a totemic (and dangerously static) figure of indigeneity and use value.[50]

In the first article in the same book—"The Rendering Industry— A Historical Perspective"—Frank Burnham further indigenizes the modern industry by placing it in lineage with native Northwest Coast cultures. In this case, the totemic figure is a "rendering-like process" practiced by the Tsimshian on the Nass River in British Columbia. Burnham relays a lengthy citation from the early ethnographic account of Robert F. Heizer, who tells how the Tsimshian rendered oil or "grease" from small fish called eulachon to use both as a foodstuff and in trade with the neighboring Tlingit. Heizer's account is saturated with paternalism for savages capable of favoring "one of the gamiest foods ever concocted" and for the "rank riches" of the eulachon trade, poking fun at its smelly "aura."[51] Given that the eradication of smell has been, as I have suggested, one of the rendering industry's most sensitive indexes of progress, Heizer's ethnocentric account describes "other" practices of rendering as crude predecessors to those used by the modern industry, relegating them to a primitive past and even to a pungent prehumanity.

The "potlatch grease" rendered by the Tsimshian—given away in ceremonies that were considered lavishly wasteful by colonial governments in Canada and first prohibited in an 1885 statute[52]—mediates social relations of exchange very different from those mediated by capital. West Coast potlatch ceremonies have long been overdetermined not only by the racist precepts of colonialism but by a Eurocentric ambivalence toward "waste," an ambivalence fixating on the potlatch as both a threatening and fascinating figure of excessive expenditure.[53] The history of the "fat-splitting" industry in *The Original Recyclers* calibrates a canny balance of identity and difference in relation to the ethnographic figure of "potlatch grease" Burnham recites, at once inviting a blurring of incommensurable cultural logics of rendering (and, by naively identifying "fat" as the natural surplus of both, effectively misrecognizing the difference of capitalist surplus value) *and* carefully distinguishing the industry's superiority over its crude precursors. The "rendering of wealth" in native West Coast cultures is both mimetically identified with and differentiated from the wealth rendered by a Euro-American "fat-splitting industry"—enabling the fantasy of rendering's timeless universality *and* the ethnocentric refusal of historical coevality with indigenous economies.[54]

If an evocation of its indigenous roots is one means through which the rendering industry naturalizes its logic, emptying "waste" of its historically contingent properties is another. Yet waste as a specifically modern preoccupation is both materially created through industrial economies of motion geared toward the massification of capital and discursively created through colonial hierarchies distinguishing the rationality of industrial capitalism from the irrationality of indigenous economies associated with the potlatch. It is in this Foucauldian sense that waste is *produced* as a modern subject.

"As the kill rate rose in the nation's slaughter houses from tens to hundreds, even thousands, of animals per week," writes Burnham in relation to the U.S. rendering industry around the turn of the twentieth century, "without the renderer the problem of disposing of these inedible byproducts of the beef industry would have become one of horrendous proportions."[55] The rendering industry—evoking its etymology in the old French *rendre*, "to give back," as the NRA does in the epigraph used to open this chapter—will formulate itself as the redeemer of the animal carnage of mass capitalism. "And indeed rendering does give back," declares the NRA, riding on a rhetoric of reciprocity that disguises the fact that rendering returns animal waste to another capitalizing round in the marketplace rather than releasing it into circuits of value outside of those circumscribed by the profit motive.[56]

Yet rendering convincingly poses as an ecological service that atones for carnivorous capital. It is through the idea that recycling offers an antidote to the unbridled greed of industrial culture (through the idea that recycling curtails capital's compulsion to unlimited consumption and production) that the even more total capitalization of nature promised by rendering evades notice. Rather than being simply *posterior* to mass production (recovering what is left over after economic exploitation), the rendering of animal by-products is arguably entwined in the material and discursive conditions of possibility of modern capitalism. It is important to counterintuitively consider the rendering of waste as a condition as well as an effect of the pace and scale of industrial capitalism. More than just mopping up after capital has made a killing, the rendering industry promises the possibility of an infinite resubjection ("return") of nature to capital. The "industrial ecology" metaphor of the closed loop valorizes the ecological soundness of waste recovery and recycling just as the rendering industry effectively opens up a renewable resource frontier for capitalism.

The rendering industry promises to redeem waste as an "unrealized abundance," a seemingly innocent project that in fact stores the political promise of capital's potentially endless renewability by securing the material grounds of capitalism beyond the limits of nonrenewable "raw" materials.[57] As Desrochers notes, it is predominantly around the rise of industrial rendering that the idea of the material "loop" or "recycle" is put into historical circulation, a new figure of material, cultural, and political sustainability that curls a teleological trajectory of historical progress into the even more totalizing round figure of capital as a

closed loop. Thus, while inconspicuously appearing to be an after-
thought of capitalist production, the rendering industry radicalizes the
nature of capitalist production and consumption. The secondariness encoded into waste recovery diverts recognition of the rendering industry's
pivotal role in opening up recycled material as a new resource frontier
for capitalism. In his book *By-Products in the Packing Industry* (1927), the
early American economist R. A. Clemen noticed that the "manufacture of by-products has turned waste into such a source of revenue that
in many cases the by-products have proved more profitable per pound
than the main product."[58] In *Nature's Metropolis: Chicago and the Great
West* (1993), William Cronon likewise notes that according to the books
of Philip Armour, one of the most powerful American meatpackers
around the turn of the twentieth century, it was only as by-products
that animals returned as capital: "Armour estimated that a 1,260-pound
steer purchased in Chicago for $40.95 would produce 710 pounds of
dressed beef. When sold in New York at an average price of 5 and ⅜
cents per pound, this beef would earn only $38.17—a clear loss without
deducting production and transport costs. Only by selling by-products
could the packers turn this losing transaction into a profitable one."[59]
Rather than salvaging an ecological ethic of use value for cultures of
capital, as it portrays itself as doing, the rendering industry scouts out an
internal frontier ensuring capitalism will be able to continue its restless
drive for economic expansion, training a new gaze inward on itself to
cannibalize its own second nature. Here "second nature" literally describes the cooked wastes that are captured and returned, through the
sphincters of the rendering industry, to the mass metabolisms of industrial capitalism from whence they came.

The emergence of a rendering industry thus signals a shift in both
the material and the symbolic conditions of capital, from a predominantly raw diet of so-called first nature to one increasingly contingent
on recycled nature. With the industrial consolidation of rendering,
capital begins ingressing on itself, prompted by a budding appreciation
of the returns to be made from the capture and reconstitution of its
own cooked residues. Contests over labor and nature at the imperial
and colonial frontiers of market cultures in the nineteenth and twentieth
centuries—the very narrative of the frontier as capitalism's expansion

outward to exploit the receding rawness of "first natures"—has arguably been supplemented by the probing of capital into the entrails of its own industrial cultures, with a new prospecting and staking out of waste not as spare change but as undiscovered inner space. The outward-looking gaze of capital toward the conquest of so-called raw colonial resources and markets is accompanied, around the turn of the twentieth century, with a studied appreciation for cooked natures already at least once chewed over and spit out by industrial capital, those second-, third-, and fourth-order materials deemed "waste."

It is possible, arguably, to track a distinction between formal and real subsumption not only in the material history of labor, as Marx does, but also in the material history of nature. The *"formal subsumption of labor under capital"* points, for Marx, to a stage in which forms of labor deriving from outside of capitalist social relations are incorporated into its processes.[60] As he writes, "Capital subsumes the labor process as it finds it, that is to say it takes over an existing labor process, developed by different and more archaic modes of production" (1021). By contrast, the real subsumption of labor signifies "the development of a *specifically capitalist mode of production . . .* [that] *revolutionizes* their actual mode of labor and the real nature of the labor process as a whole" (1021). The achieved passage to real subsumption is historically aligned by many, including Negri, with postmodernity and with forms of immaterial rather than material labor (that is, with the socialized labor of reproducing the social conditions of production). However, theoretical debates surround Marx's claim that the formal subsumption of "archaic" modes of production is a historical precondition of real subsumption, debates raised by postcolonial and feminist critiques of the Eurocentric teleology posed by Marx's contention that an advanced stage of (European) capitalism is the necessary precursor of communism.[61] Gayatri Chakravorty Spivak, for instance, argues that the material politics of the "socialization of the reproductive body" of the subaltern woman has been foreclosed by "the tradition of Marxism and continues to be excluded."[62] The genealogy of rendering I have been tracing suggests that it is not only the reproductive bodies and labors of (subaltern) women that have been excluded from a Marxian problematics of subsumption but the reproductive resources of animal nature as well. A genealogy of rendering shifts the critical discourse on real subsumption away from its historical focus on human (European) labor and social subjectivity and opens a repressed history of nature's subsumption. I will pursue this proposition in the final section of this chapter.

A critique of rendering's rhetoric of "return"—and my contention that the material renewability promised by the industrial ecology of "closed loops" serves an ideological vision of capital as biopolitical total-ity—suggests the need to be wary of a logic of recycling first formu-lated for cultures of capital over the remains of animals. Among the many cultural mythologies thrown into question by a study of rendering is one that valorizes recycling as a redemptive, subversive retort to capi-talism (a mythology with currency in many contemporary green social movements). Resource and animal conservation discourses need to be examined for how they may inadvertently advance rather than antago-nize the hegemony of capital. For a logic of recycling first developed around animal rendering arguably supplements the wasteful hyper-production and consumption of commodities with an ecological ethic of material efficiency and waste recovery that surreptitiously supports the sustainability of capitalism.

To more specifically locate the claims I have made regarding the internal resource frontier that renderers discover for capitalism in the entrails of its own industrial metabolisms, let me track back to a series of discourses that produced waste as a new subject of attention around the middle of the nineteenth century. The "pioneer industrial ecologist" Peter Lund Simmonds (1814–97) was one key agent of the emerging interest in waste as capital *in potentia*. A journalist who worked for the British Department of Science and Art, Simmonds created a large illus-trative collection on the reuse of waste products for London's Bethnal Green Museum and supervised numerous other exhibits on the produc-tive recapitalization of industrial by-products. In an introduction pre-pared for a guidebook to the animal products collection of the Bethnal Green Museum (1872), Simmonds declared: "It is one of the most impor-tant duties of the manufacturing industry to find useful applications for waste materials. Dirt has been happily defined as only 'matter in a wrong place.'"[63] Around the same time that Ernst Haeckel coined the

neologism "ecology" to describe "the nascent science of nature's house-
holds," Simmonds was formulating the sympathetic science of rendering as a sorting, distributing, and returning of waste materials to their
proper place, that is, the place where they regenerate as capital.[64] In
the discourse of industrial ecology pioneered by Simmonds, a capitalist
economy began to approach the totality of a natural ecosystem through
the material mimicry of Nature promised by industrial rendering. Anticipating contemporary discourses of biomimicry, Simmonds energeti-
cally promoted the idea that "modern industrial economies should mimic
the cycling of materials in ecosystems."[65] Simmonds wrote: "When
we perceive in nature how nothing is wasted, that every substance is
re-converted, and again made to do duty in a changed and beautified
form, we have at least an example to stimulate us in economically applying the waste materials we make, or that lie around us in abundance. . . .
There is no waste in Nature."[66] In suggesting that substances "again
made to do duty" in an ecosystem are equivalent to substances returned to the industrial loop to render another generation of capital,
Simmonds helped a political economy to mimetically pass as a natural
economy by subtracting profit motives from the equation. However, in
Animal Products: Their Preparation, Commercial Uses, and Value (1875),
Simmonds unmasked the motives behind the budding appreciation of
waste: "As competition becomes sharper, manufacturers have to look
more closely to those items which may make the slight difference between profit and loss, and convert useless products into those possessed of commercial value."[67]

In the context of turn-of-the-century North America, as Cecelia
Tichi discerns in *Shifting Gears: Technology, Literature, Culture in Modernist America* (1987), the "rubric 'waste'" emerges in different ways to
organize a multitude of powerful interests (66). From Thorstein Veblen's
indictment of wasteful consumption in *The Theory of the Leisure Class*
(1899) to conservationist calls to save wilderness and natural resources
by figures such as Gifford Pinchot and Theodore Roosevelt to Ford's
excision of any inefficient expenditure of labor or materials from auto
assembly lines, "the term 'waste' is crucial" (57). As Tichi writes,
"Ford's 'Learning from Waste' argued to the fraction of the inch and

the hundredth of a cent that Ford plants maximized natural resources and manpower in order to serve the American public" (65). Most important, notes Tichi, the "rubric 'waste'" made sense only within the context of a discursive episteme that viewed the world in component parts or pieces (66):

> Waste . . . presupposes a certain form of intellectual analysis of a condition or situation. The analysis must include a breaking-down, a dis-assembly of the way something works. To pronounce a situation or condition wasteful is to have first scrutinized the whole of it by breaking it down into its component parts. To call it wasteful is to have seen or devised a better, more efficient way of doing things. That can only be accomplished by an intellectual dis-assembly and re-assembly. (64)

Tichi traces the scrutinizing disassembly out of which "waste" would emerge as a peculiarly capitalist obsession to the time-motion studies of Eadweard Muybridge, Étienne-Jules Marey, and Thomas Eakins. A burgeoning interest in waste "owed much to the contemporary interest in the visualization of motion in space" promoted by the time-motion studies of all three, studies that helped model a trim, lithe "economy of motion" for industrial capitalism (77).

If Simmonds likened the industrial "loop" of rendering to Mother Nature's biotic recycles, Marey and Muybridge more specifically targeted the efficiency of the animal body as an organic prototype for the fluid "economy of motion" that industrial assembly line production hoped to model. Marey used a "chronophotographic" gun to capture visuals of birds in flight, sequential stills that could be assembled to recreate a semblance of continuous motion—a key organic effect chased by modern technologies of capital. Using a device he called a zoopraxiscope, Muybridge likewise reassembled his photographic stills of animal movement (most iconically, that of a galloping horse) into what amounted to a technological preview of the motion picture, turning the visual breakdown of animal physiology back into a model of apparently seamless mobility. The physiological studies of Muybridge and Marey are often cited as "protoanimations" paving the way for cinema.[68]

Time-motion studies seized not only on the body of the animal but also on the body of the laborer, another of industrial capitalism's primary objects of "intellectual scrutiny." It was through the scientific management principles promoted by Frederick Winslow Taylor that time-motion ideologies originating in the study of animal bodies developed ergonomic implications for an industrial culture of moving assembly lines requiring workers to perform repetitive motions with increased mechanical efficiency and speed. Emerging in the 1910s as a "patron saint of efficiency," Taylor used a stopwatch to conduct a different species of time-motion study.[69] He "separated seemingly simple [laborer's] tasks into their smallest components, analyzed each for excess or extraneous motion, then worked to reformulate them so precisely and economically that they required no excess mechanical motion of the worker's body or his tools."[70] Choosing as his subjects not birds in flight but miners shoveling coal, Taylor "shot" their manual motions and zoomed in to produce a series of temporal stills that made the inefficient motions buried in each micromotion perceptible. From there it was a matter of splicing out wasteful or extraneous movements and reschematizing a molecularly streamlined laboring force. "Essentially Taylor saw in industry the opportunities that sequential stop-motion photographs were providing the visual experimenters Thomas Eakins, Étienne Marey, and Eadweard Muybridge in the 1880s and 1890s," writes Tichi.[71] "His objective was to find the one best way to accomplish each work task, then to standardize that way" (78). Through an unprecedented subjection of bodies to microscopic performance measures, time-motion technologies and knowledges *produced* wasteful movement as a matter of reform and as a negative surplus that could be shaved off and converted into savings for the capitalist.

Taylor's principles of scientific management stimulated a biopolitical reorganization of far more than the movements of the "workingman." They informed the conservation science of Gifford Pinchot, who began to manage against the waste of natural resources to ensure the material future of generations of American capital to come. In his 1908 "The Slaughter of the Trees," Emerson Hough juxtaposed photographs of forests laid waste with images of the orderly results of the new methods of scientific forestry advocated by Pinchot as head of the U.S. Forest Service. As for the slaughter of the animals, Upton Sinclair's *The Jungle* (1905) records not only the infamous "speeding-up" of the moving lines that Taylorism inspired but also the pursuit of "porkmaking by applied mathematics," summed up in the popular quip "They use everything about the hog except the squeal."[72] In his description of "Durham's," a fictional rendering plant, Sinclair writes:

> No tiniest particle of organic matter was wasted in Durham's. Out of the horns of the cattle they made combs, buttons, hairpins, and imitation ivory; out of the shinbones and other big bones they cut knife and toothbrush handles, and mouth-pieces for pipes; out of the hoofs they cut hairpins and buttons, before they made the rest into glue. From such things as feet, knuckles, hide clippings, and sinews came such strange and unlikely products as gelatin, isinglass, and phosphorous, bone black, shoe blacking, and bone oil. . . . When there was nothing else to be done with a thing, they first put it into a tank and got out of it all the tallow and grease, and then they made it into fertilizer.[73]

The rise of the rendering industry can be placed in the broader context, then, of a complex of scrutinizing, disassembling, and sorting practices biopolitically registering nature and labor as ever more minute units of potential value, units no longer able go unnoticed or to evade being "again made to do duty" for capital, as Simmonds put it. That waste is a product of the time-motion technologies and rationalizing imperatives of Euro-American capital rather than a preexisting, eternal use value is borne out even by the rendering history sketched in *The Original Recyclers*. For there Burnham notes that in the California cattle economy of the 1850s, when the market for animal products was almost entirely in hides and tallow, meat was considered a waste product and was "abandoned on the range" for coyotes and other wild animals.[74] This anecdote turns upside down not only the idea that meat constitutes an animal's universal use value but doxologies holding that waste is a self-evident given rather than a fickle sign factored out by market forces.

The rendering industry has for too long enjoyed an understated role in the history of capitalist modernity. Animal stock strained from the boilers of rendering plants is converted into glue, glycerin, gelatin, bone meal, soap—seemingly amorphous substances that are in fact deeply implicated in mediating both the material and the symbolic hegemony of cultures of capitalism. The rendering of hides and tallow from California cattle in the 1850s was historically entangled, for instance, in soap's colonial career as a mass commodity and material signifier marketing a gospel of white supremacy to the so-called dark corners of the globe.[75] The discourse of speciesism that the modern rendering industry institutionalizes underpins the economic and cultural power of a white European humanity over "others of whatever sort."[76] A politics of rendering cannot be reduced, then, either to the material politics of producing and consuming animals as meat and material by-products or to the cultural politics of fetishizing the origins of mimesis in biological mimicry.[77] It involves continuously coimplicating both in the historical conditions and effects of power.

"Mere Jelly"

In "The Point Is to (Ex)Change It: Reading *Capital*, Rhetorically" (1993), Thomas Keenan draws attention to an enigmatic expression made by Marx in his analysis of labor time as the hidden quantity or measure of exchange value. Marx described the abstract element common to all commodities, the element that constitutes the measure of their equivalence and hence exchangeability, as the "mere jelly *[Gallert]* of undifferentiated human labor."[78] Marx's choice of words brings homogeneous labor time into view not only as an abstract measure of value but also as a visceral *substance,* opening up a materialist conception of labor time crucial to Antonio Negri's subsequent theorization of real subsumption and tautological time.

Yet if "mere jelly" is metaphorical, for Marx, of labor time as the homogeneous substance produced by and underpinning the system of exchange value, it is also uncannily evocative of the animal fats and gelatins being *literally* extruded during his lifetime, in unprecedented industrial quantities, from the rendering machines of capitalism.[79] I want to use Marx's words as a lever into Negri's theorization of tautological time, a time that finds one of its historical examples, it seems to me, in the industrial closed loops of animal rendering. The example of rendering does not fit comfortably, however, in the history of real subsumption developed by Negri. For one thing, it locates a logic of real subsumption in the material metabolisms of industrial capitalism rather than in the postindustrial terrain of immaterial social labor where Negri locates it. Moreover, reading Marx's expression literally (rather than only rhetorically) summons another material history into view besides that of human labor, which remains focal to Negri's materialist theory of time. Marx's enigmatic evocation of "mere jelly" suggests that human labor and (animal) nature are cosubstantial matters of real subsumption, or rather it emboldens me to extend Negri's theory of tautological time beyond the figure of human labor and life to which it is tethered. While "mere jelly" can be leveraged against the labor-centrism of Negri's work, it could by the same token be leveraged against Marx himself. After all, Marx was the first to inscribe a species distinction within the critique of capital by distinguishing human "species-being" from animal "species-life" and by claiming that the essence of the former, epitomized in forms of social labor, constitutes the historical subject of subsumption.[80]

Before continuing, let me briefly situate Negri's formulation of tautological time in relation to his longstanding political commitments and prodigious efforts to theorize time as substance. Negri wrote "The Constitution of Time" (2003), in which the notion of tautological time appears, while in prison, voluntarily serving out the remainder of a sentence for terrorist activities in Italy against the state (activities of which he was later cleared). In the revival of interest in this and other works subsequent to the success of his collaborative work with Michael Hardt on *Empire* (2000) and *Multitude* (2004), the Italian Autonomia and Operaismo (workerist) communist movements with which Negri has been associated achieved wider influence. The notion of tautological time elaborated in "The Constitution of Time" is particularly germane to Negri's later analyses of biopower and reveals the importance of a materialist conception of time as substance to the theorization and practice of communism. However, from his early workerist involvements to his reinvention, with Hardt, of "the proletariat" as global multitude, human labor has remained at the center of Negri's work.[81] Although Negri has affiliated his thinking with environmental social movements on multiple occasions, the history and politics of capitalist nature have by and large remained a subsidiary concern. I want to end this chapter by exploring how Negri's formulation of tautological time may have a specific bearing on the politics of rendering and animal capital while at the same time proposing that to extend his work in this direction requires confronting the species distinction latent in his key concept of *ontological production*.

"The Constitution of Time" opens with an excerpt from *Capital* in which Marx narrowed in on labor as the "value-forming substance" of a commodity and determined that this value is measured in units of time. The remainder of Negri's text is devoted to troubling Marx's understanding of time as the formal *measure* of value by elaborating on his simultaneous insights that time also emerges as the content or *substance* of production. Negri maps the end of time as measure and the emergence of time as substance onto the distinction between formal and real subsumption first conceptualized by Marx. In an era of achieved real subsumption (which for Negri is equivalent to the postmodern era), time can no longer be treated as an extrinsic measure, an externality linked to the existence of use values surviving outside the rule of exchange value. That is, time no longer constitutes a transcendent quantity out of which a certain number of daily hours are apportioned to specifically capitalist production or out of which the capitalist working day is carved. Time may have been transcendent under conditions of formal subsumption, in which use values and social relations of production originating outside of capitalism continued to provide a measure of comparative difference or contrast to the logic of exchange value produced in the social relations of capital. However, under conditions of real subsumption, claims Negri, there is no longer "possibility of recourse to an external element" off of which to measure capitalist production.[82] When capitalism overtakes everything once outside of it, to use a spatial metaphor for the temporal conquest Negri traces, time ceases to transcend the amount of time allocated to capital's reproduction and becomes, instead, immanent to or identical with it.

To approach the matter from an another angle, in an era of real subsumption the time devoted to reproducing capital is no longer contained within the discrete outlines of a working day but expands to cover the whole time of life, such that there is *no* time that is not devoted to producing for capital. Thus, as Negri writes, real subsumption consists in an *indifference* between the labor time of the work day and the rest of time, or in a seamless "*flow* between labor and time" (29). This can help us to understand his claim that "to say that time measures labor is here but a pure and simple tautology" given that they have effectively become one and the same thing (25). In the tautological time of real subsumption, continues Negri, we are therefore confronted with "the impossibility of distinguishing the totality of life (of the social relations of production and reproduction) from the totality of time from which this life is woven. When the entire time of life has become the time of production, who measures whom?" (28–29).

Within the tautological time of real subsumption, however, Negri also sights radical potentials. He claims that "this final tautology seems to us to be extraordinarily productive from the theoretical and revolutionary standpoint. For now we know that time cannot be presented as measure, but must rather be presented as the global phenomenological fabric, as base, substance and flow of production in its entirety" (29). When time is brought down to earth and realized as the immanent substance of production, though it may be productive or constitutive of capital its very recognition as *constitutive* opens up the possibility of changing time. "In destroying time-as-measure," Negri writes, "capital constructs time as collective substance. This collective substance is a multiplicity of antagonistic subjects" (41). For Negri, the time of communism is in the making whenever time is collectively seized as the social substance of life. I will return to this point shortly in order to suggest that the tautological time of produced nature ("mere jelly") likewise needs to be considered in its potentials and that an alternative to market life hinges not only on recognition of the constitutive time of subsumed labor but also on the constitutive time of subsumed nature.

The history of time traced through the concepts of *labor's* formal and real subsumption—a history marked, as Negri couches it, by a passage from extensive forms of (material) labor to intensive forms of (immaterial) intellectual and linguistic production—can be differently traced through the example of *nature's* subsumption that rendering gives. However, the question of nature's subsumption remains largely undeveloped in Negri's work by virtue, I want to suggest, of his species-specific conflation of ontological production—the immanent, creative activity focal to his theory of constitutive time—with human labor and life. In other words, a hidden tautology is arguably at play inside Negri's very formulation of tautological time, such that to speak of ontological production and to speak of human social labor becomes effectively one and the same thing. "Every productive activity, every human action," writes Negri, in a sentence that explicitly reveals their conflated status in his text, "is within this [time's] *Umwelt [environment]*" (35). The *genus* of immanent life, as it were, is rendered equivalent to the *species* of human constitutive activity by virtue of privileging the labor time (that is, the life time) of the latter in the concept of ontological production. A limit in Negri's thinking thus appears in the form of the closed loop within which production and human labor definitionally refer back to and reinforce one another.

While it could appear to be simply stating the obvious that production and human labor are one and the same thing, it is the assumption of their equivalence that marks a limit within Negri's theorization of real subsumption. To the extent that ontological production—the immanent constitution of life—is reduced not only to *human* labor but, more particularly, to the *immaterial* labor of language beings performing their species-specific work of social-symbolic production, Negri's work repeats rather than revolutionizes humanist ideology for our times, an ideology founded on the speciesist differentiation of human and animal on the grounds of language possession and labor.[83] There is little room in Negri's humanist philosophy of immanence to account for the material labors and lives of other species that have also become coextensive with the reproduction of capital.

Interestingly enough, in view of Marx's figure of "mere jelly," it is in the context of a short meditation on petroleum (oil) and energy in "The Constitution of Time" that Negri does briefly remark that "Nature is also a problem of subsumption."[84] Against the idea that oil provides a natural—that is, external—basis of value, Negri contends that "no *standard*, no *meaning* is given outside of collective time; no nature is given because *nature is realized subsumption*" (65). Nature, like time, is glimpsed as immanent to the time of capital's production and reproduction, reduced to the substance of exchange value rather than idealized as an ontology transcending the social relations of capital.

Reading Negri in dialogue with political ecology can be helpful in elaborating his brief comment that "Nature is also a problem of subsumption." James O'Connor suggests, not unlike Negri, that in our current era the reproduction of capital's conditions of production and the whole of "life itself" have become one and the same thing. Writes O'Connor: "Traditional socialism pertains to the production and reproduction of capital. Ecological socialism pertains to the production/reproduction of the conditions of production."[85] Ecological socialism struggles to "redefine conditions of *production* as conditions of *life*" (308). In O'Connor's view, "capitalist threats to the reproduction of production conditions are not only threats to profits and accumulation, but also to the viability of the social and natural environment as *means of life and life itself*" (12). What differentiates Negri's and O'Connor's approaches, however, is that whereas Negri privileges the social labor of a human multitude in the politics of "life," O'Connor suggests that nonhuman producers, in the ecological sense of the word, are also subsumed into the ontological conditions of capitalist production. Feminists have long criticized Marx for having overlooked the unpaid domestic, sexual, and affective labors of women in the reproduction of the conditions of production, a critique that it is now clear also concerns other species—and they are legion—whose lives have become coextensive with the ecological conditions of capital.

Negri's brief comment regarding nature's subsumption can be further elaborated by means of an essay written by Martin O'Connor, who is not to be confused with James O'Connor (although the two are in fact closely affiliated through the journal cofounded by the latter, *Capitalism, Nature, Socialism*). There are striking similarities between Negri's theorization of an era of real subsumption and O'Connor's theorization, in "On the Misadventures of Capitalist Nature" (1994), of a "mutation in the system of capitalism" resulting in what he calls "capitalism ecologized."[86] "In what we might call the *ecological phase of capital*," writes O'Connor, "the relevant image is no longer of man acting on nature to 'produce' value, henceforth appropriated by [a] capitalist class. Rather it is of nature (and human nature) codified as *capital incarnate*" (131). His words describe a historic shift from the externality to the immanence of nature in terms almost identical to those with which Negri describes the passage from the formal to the real subsumption of labor time. "What formerly was treated as an external and exploitable domain is now redefined as itself a stock of capital," states O'Connor.

"Correspondingly, the primary dynamic of capitalism changes form, from accumulation and growth feeding on an external domain, to ostensible self-management and conservation of the *system of capitalized nature* closed back on itself" (126). The industrial closed loop of animal rendering—and the rhetoric of industrial ecology accompanying it—is remarkably suggestive of such a tautological system of capitalized nature "closed back on itself."

Yet again, whereas Negri implies that ontological production and politics are coextensive with human social labor and life, Martin O'Connor embeds human life and labor within the larger problem of nature's subsumption. The "flow" between the time of life and the time of production that Negri theorizes can be placed within the broader purview of ecologized capitalism, a time of subsumption within which "capital is nature and nature is capital" (132). The production of *this* tautology is contingent, among other things, on a *"semiotic expansion of capital"* into nature and on the discursive production of nature as *participatory* subject (126). O'Connor recalls a parallel that Jean Baudrillard draws between the socialization of labor and of nature in the mid-twentieth century via his claim that "the doctrine of participation and of public relations [is now] extended to all of nature."[87] Writes Baudrillard, "Nature (which seems to become hostile, wishing by pollution to avenge its exploitation) must be made to participate."[88] Even if, as O'Connor argues, the command of a socialized, participant nature "operates primarily at the ideological, or *social imaginary,* level"—even if the image of a participatory nature is "a vicious fraud" and the ability to totally subsume nature an impossibility—a tautology of capital and nature is nonetheless at stake.[89]

Martin O'Connor maintains that, while "traditional Marxism followed liberal political economy in treating the 'natural' domains as external to capital and exogenously determined" (136), the challenge facing poststructuralist political ecology is to conceive of an immanent critique from within the time of nature's real subsumption. Indeed, ecological reckonings risk losing their antagonistic force in the immanent order of capitalized nature described by O'Connor. For the calculations, in capital's ecological phase, of its own damages—"all of these *extra costs to be priced,* and these reclamations of *values to be taken into account and conserved"*—themselves are redeemed as a form of "good currency" insofar as they reproduce capital as an abstract universal (135). Inasmuch as capital takes the measure of its own ecological depredations—or represents the universal "unit of measure by which such an assessment might be made," as O'Connor writes (145)—we end up in a tautological trap similar to the one that Negri theorizes in relation to time as at once measure and substance of labor. Any attempt to challenge the rendering of capitalist nature, then, has to be sprung from inside the jaws of this tautological trap, one posing a seemingly impossible conundrum: saving nature has become synonymous with saving capital.

In the carnal business and rhetoric of modern industrial rendering, it is already possible, I have suggested, to glimpse the seeds of a tautological time of capitalist nature, one in which nature is indeed redeemed, through a conservationist logic of waste recovery, as capital. For Martin O'Connor, the 1992 Earth Summit in Rio de Janeiro provides the postmodern example of an enfolding of ecological discourses of conservation and sustainability into the system of capital. "The proclaimed objective of Rio 1992," he notes, "was to save the planet—to save natural heritage, cultural heritage, genetic diversity, vernacular lifestyles, and so on" (132). Yet the rhetoric of sustainability that achieved global currency around the period of the Rio Summit "[has become] an unheralded boon in capital's own project of enlarged reproduction" (128). For when "capital is nature and nature is capital," writes O'Connor, "the terms become virtually interchangeable; one is in every respect concerned with *the reproduction of capital, which is synonymous with saving nature. The planet as a whole is our capital, which must be sustainably managed"* (132–33).

In struggling to construe a retort to capital from inside this tautological trap, it is important to recall that Negri perceives tautological time as being "extraordinarily productive from the theoretical and revolutionary standpoint."[90] Like Time, radical potentials accompany the death of transcendent Nature and its reduction to the historically produced nature, or "mere jelly," of exchange value. Nature, incessantly spatialized and essentialized in Western culture as a domain of ontology existing outside of history, comes into view as subject to time, as the immanent substance rather than the external measure or form of history. While "mere jelly" suggests that the substance of exchange value is inert, homogeneous, and passive, in the very fact of nature's becoming subject to history there arises the radical possibility that nature might be produced differently, as the "collective substance" of communism.[91] Yet contesting the passivity implied within this image of the time of *produced nature* requires, among other things, opening the theoretical closed loop in Negri's work to include nonhuman actors in the collective, constitutive work of ontological production.[92] This is not the same thing as symbolically soliciting and socially fantasizing nature's *participation,* in the sense relayed by Baudrillard. For while both participatory and constitutive nature are a reflection of nature's immanent as opposed to transcendent ontological status, the former represents an effort to ideologically pacify nature ("which seems to become hostile") to the unifying rule of capital, whereas the latter represents an effort to recognize that life, time, and nature are composed of "a multiplicity of antagonistic subjects."[93] Only when the multiplicity of nature is counted among these antagonistic subjects—only when the residual humanism of giving a human multitude all of the production credits for the immanent constitution of life worlds is contested within the praxis of communism itself—is it possible to truly do justice to the hope of realizing life as a collective substance.[94]

I want to end this chapter by returning to the example of oil that Negri raises in his brief nod to the problem of Nature's subsumption. I am struck by one significant difference between the example of oil chosen by Negri and the example of "mere jelly" posed by rendering. The difference is this: whereas fossil fuels are a *nonrenewable* resource, animal fats and oils are *renewable,* a distinction that arguably has some theoretical bearing on the analysis of tautological time. While Negri theorizes the passage from formal to real subsumption along the lines of a paradigmatic shift from a class politics of labor time to an ontological politics of human life time, it might further extend his analysis to rethink formal and real subsumption in their broader ecological entanglements with the nonrenewable and renewable resources of nature. Indeed, if the logic and history of industrial capitalism have been largely coextensive with investment in and exploitation of nonrenewable fossil fuels, a logic of biopower can perhaps be said to emerge when the economic and ideological investments of capital shift onto the renewable "life" resources of nature. The modern rendering industry was ahead of its time insofar as it introduced this shift into a field of industrial capitalism otherwise predominantly invested in the extraction of nonrenewable resources.

By the turn of the twenty-first century, an economic and ideological shift in investment to the renewable resources of nature has become pervasive. New technologies of biocapitalism seek to command the renewability of nature not so much through the mundane recycling of animal remains as through knowledge/power over the genetic codes of life. The (formal) subsumption of nonrenewable nature, linked to discourses of scarcity around the depletion of nature as an external and exhaustible resource, is now widely supplemented by the (real) subsumption of renewable nature, linked to economies of sustainability serving the potentially infinite reproduction of capital's conditions of production. While the rendering industry would now appear to be an outmoded industrial player within the postindustrial nexus of biotechnologies and bioinformatics, it has ironically achieved new purchase in a greening marketplace speculating in post–fossil fuel futures. Under the shadows of peak oil production and global climate change, growing interest in biofuels rendered from renewable animal and vegetable sources has once again positioned the carnal business of rendering, oddly enough, at the resource frontier of capital. The present-day international rendering industry is more than eager to promote itself as a producer of biofuels, not only because it can smell the market potential but also because public concern over the pathological effects of feeding rendered material back to livestock has put pressure on the industry to seek other markets for animal by-products. In the late twentieth and early twenty-first centuries, global outbreaks of bovine spongiform encephalopathy (BSE, or mad cow disease) in animals and humans, traced to the tautological practice of feeding protein meals rendered from animal remains back to livestock, have placed the so-called invisible industry under public scrutiny (see the discussion of the practice of animal cannibalism in this book's postscript). This has prompted the industry to explore other ways it can recycle animal remains back into the market.

At the dawn of the twenty-first century, "biosecurity" is the new catchword of the rendering industry.[95] The connotation is that traffics in biological capital must be secured against pathological agents that threaten it from without, when in fact the pathological agent that poses the greatest threat, BSE, is an immanent product of its own closed loops. Securing biological capital against the pathological is ultimately a contradiction in terms because, as I will have cause to remark elsewhere in this book, the pathological is but another name for nature as an immanent materiality that proves to be far from passive. Through the rhetoric of biosecurity, moreover, the business of animal recycling allies itself with the rhetoric of security perpetuated by the second Bush administration in its war against terrorism. While the late twentieth-century revolution in the life sciences and biotechnology has provoked a massive shift in capital investment to the renewable resources of nature, economic and ideological investment in nonrenewable reserves of oil persists for one reason: waging permanent war in the so-called defense of life depends on it. A comment relayed by Andrew Ross in his analysis of media images of the 1991 Gulf War clarifies the constitutive role of oil in a global economy of war: "Donella Meadows, co-author of the seminal 1974 *Limits to Growth*, pointed out in a Dartmouth College teach-in that there is only one activity in our society for which alternative energy could not provide a substitute for oil—war itself, especially war on the scale of rapid mobilization demanded by the Gulf War. The war, then, was fought, as Grace Paley commented, to ensure the future of war."[96] The future of war, the "zero time" of total death that Negri identifies elsewhere in "The Constitution of Time" with the "*nuclear State*,"[97] is deeply entangled in the carbon politics of capital's depletion of oil reserves and thus in the perverse destruction of its own ecological conditions of possibility. How can the environmental and social unsustainability of permanent war be reconciled with the biopolitical turn to renewable nature as capital's conditions of existence? Does not permanent war contradict Martin O'Connor's claim that, in an ecological phase of capitalism, the reproduction of capitalism becomes "*synonymous with saving nature*"?[98] Is it possible that the material unsustainability of permanent war can be account-balanced, at least in the social fantasy of sustainable capitalism, by biocapitalism's powers of redemption and creation?

The renewable "life" resource on which the rendering industry capitalizes is, in the end, animal deadstock. It is because the rendering industry's parasitism on life is so literal, among other reasons, that the industry provides an exemplary case study of capitalist biopower. The literality of its industrial closed loops likewise provides a material example of tautological time that tests the limits of Negri's ontological politics and contributes to historicizing the problem of nature's subsumption. As for the other logic of rendering with which this chapter opened—the faculty of copying associated in twentieth-century cultural discourse with the timeless antics of aping and biological mimicry—it too can be historicized, as I have suggested, as a problem of subsumption, that is, as an immanent function of capital.

The case studies developed in the following chapters track how animals are materially reduced to mere jelly even as they are contradictorily rendered lively signs of technological mobility. Yet while this book's working supposition is that the economic and cultural logics of rendering do not transcend their productivity for capital, it does not abandon hope of resistance. It proposes, instead, that any resistance to animal capital will need to derive from inside the closed loops of tautological time. While it has become a theoretical commonplace to invoke immanent resistance within the discursive field of capitalism, the following chapters challenge the normative limits of immanent critique by refusing the assumption that it is constitutively human. Negotiating the dangers both of anthropomorphizing and of pathologizing nature, it is possible to trace how animal capital breeds forms of antagonistic life, often in the form of unpredictable, unruly, or diseased natures erupting within the substance of exchange value. Revising material history to include what Martin O'Connor calls "nature's resistance" involves not finding, but politically *producing,* signs of antagonistic nature as part of the collective work of changing time.[99]

Chapter 2

Automobility: The Animal Capital of Cars, Films, and Abattoirs

The animal disappears in its suspension.
—NOËLIE VIALLES, *Animal to Edible*

The birth of Fordism is routinely sourced to the year 1913, when Henry Ford "set in motion the first example of assembly-line production in Dearborn, Michigan."[1] In citing Ford's Highland Park plant in Dearborn as North America's "first example of assembly-line production," the moving lines that the plant materially mimicked are quietly displaced from historical consciousness. For rarely recalled or interrogated is the fact that Ford modeled Highland Park's auto assembly line on moving lines that had been operating at least since the 1850s in the vertical abattoirs of Cincinnati and Chicago, with deadly efficiency and to deadly effect.[2] Ford, deeply impressed by a tour he took of a Chicago slaughterhouse, particularly with the speed of the moving overhead chains and hooks that kept animal "material" flowing continuously past laborers consigned to stationary and hyper-repetitive piecework, devised a similar system of moving lines for Dearborn but with a crucial mimetic twist: his automated lines sped the assembly of a machine body rather than the disassembly of an animal body. The auto assembly line, so often taken as paradigmatic of capitalist modernity, is thus mimetically premised on the ulterior logistics of animal disassembly that it technologically replicates and advantageously forgets in a telling moment of historical amnesia.

I retrieve Ford's visit to the slaughterhouse as a visceral point of connection between two seemingly unrelated moving lines, one that sparks this chapter's historical examination into the contingency of automobility on both the material and the semiotic logics of animal rendering. What changes when Fordism is revisited as a complex of mimetic relations, when Highland Park is viewed as a copy of a prior animal disassembly line rather than as the original template of mass production, and when capital is read within the more diffuse outlines of an abysmal logic of rendering that precedes and exceeds Fordism proper? How might the mass cultures and mass media associated with Fordism need to be revised in view of their unexamined premises in the recessive and excessive politics of animal capital? In this chapter I probe for signs of animal capital in half-sedimented histories of Fordism in an effort to defamiliarize the compacts of mass production and consumption, the methods of scientific management (with all of their Taylorizing prods and prompts), and the general economy of power that Fordism has come to popularly signify. The familiar view of Fordism changes in every aspect when confronted with a material politics of animal capital it has largely left unscrutinized, and even helped to repress.

Tracking how animal life is put into contradictory circulation as both a carnal and a symbolic currency implicates Fordism in a double logic of rendering overlooked by a long line of critiques that take the human, in the privileged figure of the laborer, as the focal historical subject of industrial capitalism. Even Antonio Gramsci's famous neologism "Fordism"—which brings into political focus not only the social production of "a new type of worker and of man" but shifting nexuses of social persuasion and force beyond those managing class[3]—leaves a metaphorical and material production of animals in place as the ulterior sense of Fordism. Gramsci interrogates industrialism's "victory over man's animality" in a passage in his prison notebooks titled "'Animality' and industrialism," yet "man" remains the primary subject whose nature is physically and symbolically at stake, while the fashioning of modern capitalism's animal subjects is paradoxically displaced from the sign and politics of "animality" (298). The animal sign in one of the key objects of Gramsci's critique—Frederick Winslow Taylor's depiction of the worker as an "intelligent gorilla"[4]—thus remains unchallenged. The

simian encoded in the Taylorist science of labor organizes systems of
scientific management around a figure of animal mimesis, that is, around
the figure of a gorilla predisposed to the labor of mass production as a
species of mechanical aping.[5] In his prison notebooks, Gramsci seizes
on Taylor's image of the trained gorilla for the reductive figure of manual labor it poses, however not for the figure of animal nature it presupposes.[6] The figure of the animal as a mimetic automaton capable of
copying the same simple physical task over and over again is inadvertently accepted in Gramsci's critique of an American industrialism that
strips its labor of skill and intellectual agency, reducing it to the brute
repetition of mechanical motions.[7] Entwined in the covert figure of
the animal automaton, moreover, is a figure of mimesis; the animal nature of mimesis and the mimetic nature of animals remain pivotal assumptions underpinning modern capitalism's social and economic
projects. If industrial capitalism's "new human type" is confronted in
critical terminologies of Fordism, its underlying animal prototypes remain largely unproblematized, even unconscious.[8]

Bill Brown suggests that "the task . . . of producing the history which
lingers within neglected images, institutions, and objects" is the task of
producing a "material unconscious."[9] He evokes Fredric Jameson's theory
of literature's political unconscious but contests Jameson's equation of
the literary with ideology, proposing instead a new referentiality or a
"new materialism" that approaches literature as a "repository" of submerged histories (18, 4).[10] To formulate history as the material unconscious of literature, Brown invokes Walter Benjamin's notion of the
mimetic "shock" that illuminates history not as a past chronology of
finished events but as unsettled fragments still up for revision, thawing
and heaving up different types of debris under the messianic heat of a
backward glance that views the past as a series of open rather than
reified accounts. As Brown writes, Benjamin holds that alternate, undeveloped histories hang as suspended subimprints of photography and
film, awaiting future "developers" who might make them materialize.[11]

In place of the "photographic metaphor" of the Benjaminian optical unconscious, Brown privileges the literary "plate" as a teeming site
of repressed, as-yet undeveloped material histories (14). For Brown,
the "referential excess" of ostensibly negligible remarks in literary texts

constitutes an unactivated link to "the material everyday," to a repository of "ephemera that have yet to attain historicity" (5). Flaubert's
seemingly superfluous mention of a barometer in his description of
Mme. Aubain's parlor in "Un coeur simple," for instance, constitutes
more than a move to generate a mimetic reality effect;[12] in Brown's
reading, the barometer is where history unintentionally leaves a sensible
trace in the text, where the text retains signs of a material contiguity
or brush with history beyond what it consciously sought to capture
through its mimetic designs (17). Brown argues, moreover, that the
material unconscious is a historical negative that requires "active development" to appear (14). Only when a literary "plate" is bathed in the
catalytic solution of an active reading—in a "certain kind of attention,
concentration, or inhabitation that is unwilling to understand the seemingly inadvert as genuinely unmotivated" (14)—can the ostensibly
incidental imprints made by history's material pressure on literary texts
be brought to consciousness.

I approach Fordism as a tangle of repressed and unresolved material relationships that can be "developed," in Brown's sense, to trouble
"the dominant cultural memory" of capitalist modernity (5). Looking
back on seemingly unrelated images and institutions heaving in the
historical mound of turn-of-the-century North America, this chapter
reopens the complex relations of Fordism, resists its reification as a fixed
historical image, and provokes a reckoning with its unsettled accounts.
Against the perception that Fordism represents a clearly delineable and
now defunct stage of modern capitalism, "automobility" names a complex of cultural and economic relationships that are by no means finished and that exceed historical containment in the past. The material-
semiotic network of automobility emerges, but does not end, with three
early time-motion economies: animal disassembly, automotive assembly,
and moving picture production. *Automobility* refers to the "moving" effects of cars and cinema, effects achieved by technologically as well as
semiotically mimicking the seamless physiology of animals in motion.
Yet it also refers to the unacknowledged material contingencies of car
and cinematic culture on animal disassembly, sites where they literally
depend on the remains of animal life and are implicated in the carnal
business of animal slaughter and rendering. At the same time, industrial

slaughter emerges not only as a space of production through a triangulated reading of automobility's moving lines but also as a space of
consumption and spectacle. The network of automobility culturally
institutes talismanic tropes of animal life *and* materially drives the displacement and death of historical animals according to the double logic
of rendering. The rendered material of automobility's moving lines
archives an "unconscious" death wish on animal life that is radically,
yet productively, at odds with the fetishistic signs of life articulated
through the animal tropes so predominant in time-motion discourses
of automobility (starting with the animal studies of Eadweard Muybridge and Étienne-Jules Marey).

Unlike Benjamin and Brown, however, I do not begin with the visual
or literary excess unwittingly captured on a photographic or literary
"plate" but rather seize on and amplify seemingly incidental linkages
connecting the material and symbolic economies of cars, films, and
abattoirs. I have already staked out Ford's visit to a Chicago meatpacking plant as one incident around which the relations of Fordism
can be reopened to and through an analysis of the animal capital of
automobiles and of slaughter. I will also delve into the materiality of
film stock production to trace the inconspicuous yet pivotal role that
photographic gelatin[13]—derived from the waste of industrial slaughter—has played in the development of moving pictures and mass
imagery. Gelatin is among those seemingly negligible but in fact significant points of entry into the material unconscious of culture. In my
reading, it marks a "vanishing point" where moving images are both
inconspicuously and *viscerally* contingent on mass animal disassembly,
in contradiction with cinema's framing semiotic of "animation."[14] To
take seriously such seemingly tenuous connections between cars, films,
and abattoirs as Ford's visit to a packinghouse or the visceral role of
animal gelatin in photographic and film culture demands that one indeed be "unwilling to understand the seemingly inadvertent as genuinely unmotivated."[15]

Because animals have been identified with the unconscious insofar
as it is has been conceived, in the Freudian tradition, as a subterrain of
primordial drives pacing in "an unaging and undiminishing state," it is
especially important to reiterate Brown's formulation of the unconscious

as *material history*.[16] As Brown puts it, one must "understand the unconscious as material history and history as the unconscious, as the necessarily repressed that can be rendered visible in sites of contradiction or incomplete elision."[17] Reformulating the unconscious as a terrain of recessive and excessive material history becomes paramount when it is a matter of developing counterhegemonic genealogies for animal subjects lavishly accorded mythological and rhetorical existence yet strictly denied historical being. Against an understanding of animals as "perpetual motion machines" that "live *unhistorically*," I develop the material unconscious of capitalist modernity as the denied, disavowed historicity of animals and of animal rendering.[18]

Touring the Vertical Abattoir: Slaughter's Cinematic Disposition

While this chapter will implicate cars' and films' mimicry of animal life in the industrial economy of slaughter, I begin here by implicating, conversely, the material space of animal disassembly in a logic of spectacle usually identified with cinematic culture. The lineaments of cinema can arguably be glimpsed in the animal disassembly lines of Chicago's stockyards, where animals were not only produced as meat but also consumed as spectacle. Under the rafters of the vertical abattoir there rolled a moving line that not only served as a technological prototype for automotive and other mass modes of production but also excited new modes of visual consumption.

Animals hoisted onto moving overhead tracks and sped down the disassembly line constituted one of North America's first "moving pictures." Such a contention requires that, like Jonathan Crary or Geoffrey Batchen, one excavate for the discursive rather than empirical conditions of visual culture, for the "assemblage" of percolating knowledges and desires that intersected with material practices and technological equipment to put images into motion.[19] *This* moving picture was being consumed on guided tours of Chicago's Packingtown at the same time that Eadweard Muybridge's zoopraxiscope, a device that put still photographs into motion under the zoosign of animal life, was beginning to capture attention as a novel mimetic machine bringing Americans closer to the attainment of mass motion picture technologies.

When Chicago hosted the World's Columbian Exposition in 1893, Muybridge's zoopraxiscope was among its many exhibits. It was displayed in the exposition's White City alongside other cutting-edge mimetic technologies such as Eastman's portable Kodak camera, flexible film, and Edison's Kinetoscope motion picture camera, all promising spontaneous visual capture of life in motion.[20] Visitors were apt to stray from the attractions of the White City, however, and venture into the bloody outer attraction of the neighboring "bovine city," where an unprecedented technology of animal sacrifice—the moving disassembly line—was also on display.[21] As Louise Carroll Wade notes, over one million people paid a visit to the bovine city, or the Chicago stockyards, in 1893, the year of the exposition.[22] "Guided tours of the yards and packinghouses were 'as popular as a ride in the Ferris wheel and far more interesting'" in the opinion of many visitors.[23] Across the river from Chicago's White City, in dark Packingtown, lay the spectacle of animal disassembly, the material "negative" of the mimetic reproduction of life promised by the new technological media on the other side. The mimetic media were, for a brief historical instant, dangerously contiguous with their material unconscious.[24]

In the time-motion efficiencies on display in the vertical abattoirs of Packingtown, cattle were forced to walk up chutes to an elevated landing so that the gravitational pull of their own bodies would propel them down the disassembly line. Hogs, by contrast, were simply seized by their hind legs and hurtled along by means of an overhead rail. In the description of Durham and Company's disassembly line in Upton Sinclair's *The Jungle* (1905), provisions made in the architecture of mass slaughter for its recreational viewing make a significant appearance. The slaughter of cattle could be viewed "in one great room, like a circus amphitheater, with a gallery for all visitors running over the center."[25] As for "the hog's progress" (37), it could be viewed in

a long, narrow room, with a gallery along it for visitors. At the head there was a great iron wheel, about twenty feet in circumference, with rings here and there along its edge. Upon both sides of this wheel there was a narrow space, into which came the hogs at the end of their journey; in the midst of them stood a great burly Negro, bare-armed and bare-chested. He was resting for a moment, for the wheel had stopped

while men were cleaning up. In a minute or two, however, it began slowly
to revolve, and then the men upon each side of it sprang to work. They
had chains which they fastened about the leg of the nearest hog, and the
other end of the chain they hooked into one of the rings upon the wheel.
So, as the wheel turned, a hog was suddenly jerked off his feet and borne
aloft. At the same instant the ear was assailed by a most terrifying
shriek. . . . The shriek was followed by another, louder and yet more ago-
nizing—for once started upon that journey, the hog never came back; at
the top of the wheel he was shunted off upon a trolley, and went sailing
down the room. (34–35)

Evidently, Chicago's "great packing machine" capitalized not only on a
rapid mass processing of animal material but on a booming interest in
viewing the life and death passions of animals and laborers, intertwined
ethnographic subjects of industrious capital.[26]

In his analysis of American amusement culture around the turn of
the century, Brown suggests that in thrill rides such as the Ferris wheel
or roller coaster (modeled on industrial bucket wheels and coal carts),
"the pleasure industry merely replicates, while controlling, the physiological trials of modernity."[27] Tours of slaughterhouses, already a popular
sideline of Chicago's Packingtown as early as the 1860s, were designed
to showcase the tremendous efficiency with which American culture
managed its material nature. Slaughterhouse tourism also promised
to fascinate and disturb tour-goers with the somatic sights, smells,
and sounds—the "physiological trials"—of doomed animals and gore-
covered laborers. Brown's understanding of the supplementary economies of work and play in turn-of-the-century North American culture
is borne out by the analogy Sinclair uses to convey an effect of the
speed with which Packingtown's labor strove to keep pace with the continuous flow of animal bodies: "They worked with furious intensity,
literally upon the run—at a pace with which there is nothing to be com-
pared except a football game."[28] Through the riveting view from "the
stands," as it were, the disassembly line doubled as spectacle, or sport.

Chicago's stockyards, then, revolved not only around the rationalized reduction of animals to meat and the myriad commodities rendered from animal remains but around a supplementary economy of
aesthetic consumption built into the line, with the kill floor doubling

as a "circus amphitheater" where the raw footage of the "slaughtering machine" rushed at a staggering pace past visitors.[29] Moreover, tours of slaughterhouses involved much more than *visual* consumption of the commotion of slaughter. The stockyards were also an overwhelming olfactory and auditory theater, filled with the "sickening stench" of blood and the death cries of animals.[30] "The uproar was appalling, perilous to the eardrums," writes Sinclair. "There were high squeals and low squeals, grunts, and wails of agony. . . . It was too much for some of the visitors—the men would look at each other, laughing nervously, and the women would stand with hands clenched, and the blood rushing to their faces, and the tears starting in their eyes" (35). A visceral, affective response to the raw footage of the moving disassembly line was part of the gripping experience offered by meatpackers. Rather than an undesirable effect, emotion and tears produced through exposure to the sensorium of slaughter were arguably integral to the spectacle of slaughter. If, according to its own material calculations, the machinery of mass slaughter had managed to capture "everything but the squeal," thanks to the supplementary business of slaughterhouse touring even the squeal returned as capital.[31] For the affect (nervousness, tears, fascination) produced through exposure to the surplus sights, sounds, and smells of animal death was captured and converted into capital through the business of slaughterhouse tours (tours that Sinclair in turn textually rendered to sensational effect).

That the business of slaughterhouse touring promised significant returns for meatpackers is evinced by the fact that in 1903 Swift and Company published a *Visitor's Reference Book* that it distributed to tour-goers "as a Souvenir of a visit to the plant of Swift & Company at Chicago, Ill., U.S.A., and as a reminder of the modern methods and activities of the American Meat Packing Industry."[32] The booklet also reveals, however, that touring slaughter was at the same time a risky business, one that meatpackers needed to mimetically manage in order for the affective surplus of animal disassembly to be converted into capital rather than into political agitation of the sort inspired by Sinclair's novel. At its most basic level, the *Visitor's Reference Book* functioned as an advertising pamphlet designed to remind people of Swift and Company's "Arrow S" trademark when they next went to purchase meat. Among the biopolitical aims pursued through early tours of the stockyards, after all, was that of persuading a nation to desire meat as a regular part of its diet. The affective sights, sounds, and smells generated through what was then, according to its booklet, Swift and Company's slaughter of "twenty-five hundred cattle, seven thousand hogs and seven thousand sheep per day" thus needed to be carefully managed to prevent moments of human-animal identification from triggering metabolic revolt in tour-goers (causing them to sicken rather than salivate at the prospect of meat) or political exception to the rationalized slaughter of animals.

For Swift and Company's illustrated souvenir booklet to perform its deeper function of mimetically managing against the potential for affect to revert into counterproductive forms of metabolic and political revolt, its designers intuitively chose to recapitulate the tour through the eyes of a little white girl no older than six or seven years of age. The booklet, through text and drawings, depicts the path of a white family through the organized "stations" of animal disassembly, moving from Station 1, "Live Hog Pens," to Station 14, "Beef Dressing," capped with a visit to Swift's "Oleomargarine Factory" and canning facility. The little girl is a cursor pointing to and eagerly pulling her family through each station. She inhabits the space of slaughter as if it is second nature to her, as if by virtue of being human the animals are as much her own property as they are Swift and Company's.

At Station 2, "Beginning Hog Dressing," the little girl is shown sitting genially on a railing that separates her from a hoisting area where hogs are "shackled to the moving wheel," as happy in the presence of what is underway on the other side of the rail as she would be in a park feeding ducks (see Figure 3). In the "Beef Cooler," she gestures expansively at a row of dangling beef carcasses beside which she stands in intimate quarters (see Figure 4). A model citizen who visits sites of national pride and feels utterly secure inside the nation's economic space, she also relays what Lauren Berlant terms "the infantile citizen's faith in the nation."[33] She shows by example—through her utter lack of alarm and her casual, cheery demeanor—that the scene of slaughter is perfectly natural and nonthreatening. As the subject deemed most likely to embody a sensitive (potentially hysterical) response to her

Station 2

Beginning Hog Dressing

A FTER a rest and a shower
bath the hogs are driven, a
dozen or more at a time, into a
pen at the base of the automatic hoisting wheel.
Each one is then shackled to the moving wheel
which raises the hog steadily until the shackle
hook is dropped to a sliding rail. On this rail
the animals pass the skilled dispatcher who starts
eight hundred an hour on the journey through
the dressing and cleaning rooms to the vast coolers.

Figure 3. "Beginning Hog Dressing," in Swift and Company Visitor's
Reference Book *(1903). From the Advertising Ephemera Collection of the
Rare Book, Manuscript, and Special Collections Library of Duke University.
Database A0340–05, Emergence of Advertising On-line Project, John W.
Hartman Center for Sales, Advertising, and Marketing History.
http://scriptorium.lib.duke.edu/eaa/. Reprinted with permission.*

environment, the little girl thus functions as an affect meter at each
station. Displaying nothing but confidence and curiosity, she communicates that animal disassembly is the furthest thing from traumatic,
both for the animals undergoing it and for the humans watching it. In
short, she models the proper response to slaughter, one that Swift and
Company may at some level have cannily understood becomes more
difficult to recognize as pathological or sadistic when embodied by a
little girl.

Yet as she is illustrated perched on the railing, with two hogs shackled upside down behind her, the little girl marks, even as she polices,
the most precarious site of slippage between the spaces and powers
partitioning humans and animals in the slaughterhouse. Though she is
almost identical in shape and body mass to the animals strung up behind her, Swift and Company seem to be making the wager that even
the subject who, due to her age and gender, is most powerless within a
social hierarchy of humans is absolutely powerful in relation to the
animals behind her by virtue of her species difference. The certitude of
her absolute humanity is truly ensured, however, only by her sparkling

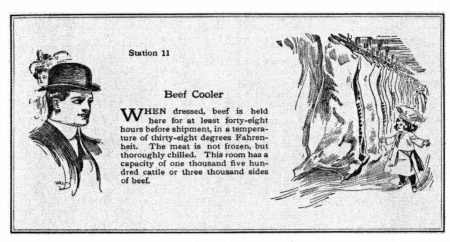

Figure 4. "Beef Cooler," in Swift and Company Visitor's Reference Book
*(1903). From the Advertising Ephemera Collection of the Rare Book, Manuscript,
and Special Collections Library of Duke University. Database A0340–11,
Emergence of Advertising On-line Project, John W. Hartman Center for Sales,
Advertising, and Marketing History. http://scriptorium.lib.duke.edu/eaa/.
Reprinted with permission.*

whiteness. It is doubtful that Swift and Company would have risked such a wager—would have dared manage against the dangerous slippage between human and animal in the space of slaughter via the subject whose social powerlessness strongly invites the substitution—with a little colored girl, whose racialization has historically involved mistaking her for an animal. The mutual coding of whiteness and humanness is pivotal to the success of the mimetic management operated by the figure of the little girl.

Swift and Company thus communicate their supreme confidence in the absolute difference of human and animal by giving the little girl license, in their illustrations, to play on the physical barrier dividing human and animal. Her starched white dress—matched with a white hat of the sort worn by head chefs (demarcating the power of the one who eats from that of the one who is eaten)—further amplifies her humanness as an impenetrable barrier that secures against human-animal slippage in the slaughterhouse. The dress code of the rest of her family likewise bespeaks the affluence and security of an imperturbable white humanity. Her mother wears an elaborate black feather hat; her father is a tastefully muted figure who usually appears in the background on those pages on which he does appear. An older, bearded figure who could be the little girl's grandfather wears, in his intermittent appearances in the booklet, a top hat. That male figures are backgrounded throughout the booklet, seemingly there only to indulge the curiosity of a girl-child, further displaces recognition of the white masculinity and power consolidated in packinghouse capital.[34]

As well as an index of the tastefulness of the race and class who tour slaughterhouses (not to be mistaken with the races and class who work in them), dress, like whiteness, is a crucial code of humanness working to draw an unbreachable species line between humans and animals in the Swift and Company booklet. Not only does the little girl stand upright next to animals who have been turned on their heads; she is clothed, while they are flayed. She is dressed, while they are "dressed." At Station 13, "Sheep Dressing," her full suit of starched white clothing communicates her power over the sheep bodies toward which she casually points, bodies flayed of their "pelt, or skin" (as the booklet states) in an almost indecent graphic exposure. Whenever a hint of sadism lurks in the scene of a clothed figure of miniaturized power gazing on a shackled and "dressed" animal—whenever the suspended carcass looks almost human—the little girl is shown gazing not at the animal but back at her mother or father, deferring the look to them. Against the hallucinatory resemblance between the flayed body of a large steer and that of a human, the booklet averts her eyes and, by example, those of the public.

The message that tours of slaughter are not disturbing, that there is no reason to be haunted by the sights seen, is reinforced at the end of the souvenir booklet. There Swift and Company state that they are providing it as a "reminder of the sights of the Stock Yards," one enabling visitors "to see those sights again in memory." As its parting words suggest, the booklet was designed to be administered at the end of the tour, *after* the meatpacker had cashed in on an interest in animal death but *before* the affect excited by the spectacle of slaughter could cause upset in its twin economy, which depended on a literal consumption of meat products. Recursively training tour-goers in how they should be affected by and recollect slaughter, Swift and Company managed against the potential for affect either to provoke renunciation of meat-eating or to form into the prolonged shape of political activism.

In *Parallel Tracks: The Railroad and Silent Cinema*, Lynne Kirby argues that railroads trained audiences for filmic viewing: "As an ideological paradigm, the railroad created a subject invested in the consumption of images and motion—that is, physical displacement—for entertainment."[35] Slaughterhouse tours in a different way also created a subject invested in "physical displacement—for entertainment," a subject readied for cinematic experience through the viewing of the moving picture of animal disassembly. In tours, however, physical displacement was itself displaced onto animals and the progress of their breakdown, while human tour-goers were positioned as stationary bodies whose integrity was threatened only vicariously, by virtue of a potential affective identification with the animals. Both in the visual consumption of the rapid sequential logic of the moving line that they encouraged and in their stimulation of affect, slaughterhouse tours arguably also helped to lay the perceptual tracks for cinema. If, as Batchen suggests, it is "the unfolding of space through time that is cinema," the disassembly line as time-motion technology (and the slaughterhouse tour that paralleled its linear unfolding) realized a cinematic disposition prior to cinema proper.[36] The moving disassembly line mobilized the idea of "time itself as a continuous linear sequence of discrete moments," while the tour positioned the visitor's eye as a "tracking camera" (12, 117). The discrete, numbered "stations" strung together into a moving sequence by the pace of slaughter and the eyes of the tour-goer were analogous to the "frames" reeled at high speed past a cinematic audience to produce an ocular semblance of seamless motion. The technological mimicry of both moving lines thus suggests a complicity in their economies, although their material outcomes were radically divergent. The first propelled the dissolution of animal bodies into minute particles and substances; the second moved toward the resolution of image life. Tours of slaughterhouses can thus be read as protocinematic technologies, with this crucial twist.

In her study of modern French abattoirs, Noëlie Vialles suggests that the aesthetic logic shaping tours of disassembly lines is indeed strangely analogous to that framing the consumption of film. As Vialles

writes, tours of slaughterhouses regularly disturb visitors who notice
that the tour route "parallels the one-way path of the animals," the
path of no return.[37] This, arguably, is the threatening mimetic identification of human and animal that causes tour-goers in *The Jungle* to
laugh nervously. As Sinclair wrote, "Perhaps some glimpse of all this
was in the thoughts of our humble-minded Jurgis, as he turned to go
on with the rest of the party, and muttered: *'Dieve*—but I'm glad I'm
not a hog!'"[38] Yet, as Vialles adds, the parallel path of tour-goers and
animals is dictated by the time-motion logic of the moving line—"seeing round an abattoir in the opposite direction would be like watching
a film backwards; it would mean reconstituting the animal from the
starting point of the carcass, and that would be at least equally disturbing."[39] Tours of slaughterhouses, hints Vialles, follow the same insistent
sequential sense as the cinematic reel, a logic that frames the impassive
stages of deanimating animal life as an inexorable progression.[40] The
submission that packinghouse tours demand to the irreversible direction
of the moving line is also the submission on which cinema depends to
achieve its mimetic effects. The animated effects accumulating from
the time-motion momentum of cinema are ideologically complicit,
following Vialles's suggestion, with the production of an animal carcass. It is in this sense that the disassembled animal can be said to
constitute the material negative of cinema's mimetic effects. Here, in
particular, the double entendre of *rendering* describes the contradictory
vectors of time-motion ideologies insofar as they simultaneously propel the material breakdown *and* the semiotic reconstitution of animal
life across the modern spaces of slaughter and cinema.

   Their time-motion organization is not the only point of complicity
between the symbolic economies of slaughter and cinema, however.
Both moving lines are "moving" in a deeply affective as well as a technological sense. The excitement and communication of affect is where
the consumption of the moving picture of animal disassembly exceeds
merely visual consumption of image frames and offers a conditioning
in the "total" aesthetic experience which, shortly, would also be promised by cinema. The physiological response—the nervousness, laugh-
ter, or tears provoked by tours of animal disassembly lines—would
also be a feature of cinema-going. Recall, for instance, the legendary

physiological impact of the Lumière Brothers' *L'Arrivée d'un train en gare de la Ciotat* (1895), which caused audiences to instinctively spring out of the way of the train mimetically barreling toward them on the screen.[41] While animal death was generating an aesthetic surplus in the Chicago stockyards and being captured through the business of touring, mimetic technologies such as those represented by the zoopraxiscope and the Kinetoscope were pursuing a semblance of affective, immediate communication under the charismatic sign of animal life. While animals on the disassembly line were being consumed as visceral moving images, cinema was being fetishistically imbued with raw presence through the writings of modern film directors such as Dziga Vertov and Sergei Eisenstein. According to Lippit, Vertov and Eisenstein envisioned a "biology of the cinema" accruing not to cinema's ability to achieve naturalistic effects (which Eisenstein abhorred), but rather to an affective immediacy achieved by the filmic ability to cut and paste parts into a montage whose startling juxtapositions would strike directly upon the viewer's senses.[42] As Bill Brown notes, film theorists such as Tom Gunning, who take up Eisenstein's work to theorize early cinema as a "cinema of attractions," emphasize cinema's powers of "'direct stimulation' rather than [its] narrative logic."[43] The interest in cinema's powers to bypass discursive mediation in pursuit of a direct, affective immediacy was renewed later in the twentieth century by Michel Chion, who theorized the rendering of sound in cinema as no "mere imitation" or "replication" but as a visceral impact or sensory impression: "In fist- or sword-fight scenes, the sound does not attempt to reproduce the real noises of the situation, but to render the physical impact of the blow."[44] Cinema's "moving" effects, in this view, are associated with its ostensible ability to short-circuit linguistic, narrative, or discursive mediations and to communicate through "the rapid movement of affect from one entity to another."[45] The intensity of animal death on the disassembly line—the animal sights, smells, and sounds given "immediately" to the visitor's senses—is in this sense also the moving prototype of film as an affective technology. In both cases, however, what is rendered imperceptible are the discursive techniques and the capital investments mediating the animal attractions of slaughter and cinema.

Among other things, the visual-affective consumption of the moving picture of slaughter suggests that the "cinematic mode of production" theorized by Jonathan Beller, rather than historically distinguishing a postindustrial from an industrial era of capitalism (as Beller suggests), already limns Fordist modes of production.[46] Theorizing the cinematic mode of production in relation to a postindustrial "attention economy," Beller contends that a subject's "kino-eye," or film-eye, comes to constitute a "site of production itself."[47] "Paying attention" to and consuming images functions as a form of social-affective labor within the political economy of the visual formulated by Beller.[48] The productivity of the kino-eye, he argues, consists in suturing together cinematic images, a postindustrial extension of the industrial labor of assembling material units that is necessary to realize images as capital.

For Beller, the cinematic mode of production emerges in the passage from modernity to postmodernity, a passage that many cultural Marxists describe in terms of a progression from formal to real subsumption and from material to immaterial labor.[49] Thinking of a passage or progression from one to the other arguably fails to account, however, for the coexistence of the two in the vertical abattoir and in its double rendering of animal capital. The labor of workers physically toiling on the disassembly line (not to mention the travails of the animals) was already shadowed by that of touring subjects whose interest in recreationally exposing themselves to and curiously consuming the sensorium of slaughter was crucial to its production as spectacle. While the labor of slaughter and the labor of *consuming* slaughter were (and still are) clearly divided along class, racial, and ethnic lines, a kino-eye can nevertheless already be glimpsed working alongside animal disassembly and reconstituting it as a moving image.

If slaughter and cinema were linked by the shared time-motion logics organizing their visual unfolding and by their power to stimulate and capitalize on affect, the rise of cinematic culture was also literally—materially—contingent on mass slaughter. I turn now to develop the repressed material relationship between the rise of the cinematic image and what Akira Mizuta Lippit vaguely terms the *"vanishing"* of animals from modern life.[50] By implicating slaughter in the symbolic economy of cinema and cinema in the ulterior violence of animal disassembly,

I resist Lippit's valorization of cinema as a salvaging apparatus that shelters or encrypts vanishing "animal traits" (196). For if motion pictures repress their resemblance to the protocinematic "moving picture" of animal disassembly, they even more actively render unconscious their material contingency on slaughter.

The Rendered Material of Film Stock

For modern moving pictures to do more than trope animal mobility—that is, for cinema's animated effects to *literally* develop—they required the tangible supports of photographic and film stocks. It is here, in the material convolutions of film stock, that a transfer of life from animal body to technological media passes virtually without notice. To confront the animation effects of modern cinema with their carnal conditions and effects, one needs to tease out the animal ingredients of film stock via a material history of photographic gelatin. In 1873, a gelatin emulsion coating of "animal origin" was first widely adapted to photographic uses.[51] Gelatin—aka "animal glue"—is a protein extracted from the skin, bones, and connective tissues of cattle, sheep, and pigs. As Samuel E. Sheppard wrote in *Gelatin in Photography* (1923): "As is commonly known, gelatin and its humbler relative, glue, are products of animal origin, the result of the action of hot water or steam upon certain tissues and structures of the body.... The actual material consists of the leavings of tanneries and slaughter-houses—i.e., trimmings, so-called skips, ears, cheek-pieces, pates, fleshings, etc."[52] The suturing tissue of animal bodies is exchanged for what Sheppard calls the "physiological and biochemical unity" of image life in the duplicit, material-symbolic rendering of animals that helped to leverage cinema into historical existence (25). In the material convolutions of photographic and film stocks, in the viscosity of their "negative gelatin emulsions," resides an opaque politics of rendering (17). If we recall Marx's use of the visceral metaphor of "mere jelly" to describe the abstract measure of exchange value (see chapter 1), gelatin can be excavated as one site where the production of capitalist culture can be seen to always also involve the rendering of nature.[53]

The coating of choice for photographic and film stocks today as it was at the turn of the century, gelatin binds light-sensitive agents to a base so that images can materialize.[54] In 1884, when the word *film* was put into commercial circulation by George Eastman of the Eastman Dry Plate Company (soon to become the Eastman Kodak Company), the word "referred only to the gelatin coating upon the paper."[55] Turn-of-the-century dialogues between Eastman and Thomas Edison led to the incessant finessing of film stocks capable of yielding specific visual effects (sharpness, high definition, transparency) to corroborate the immediacy and vitality of moving pictures. Even today, the Kodak corporation acknowledges that it is gelatin that is the veritable "Image Recorder."[56]

Yet the manufacture of gelatin emulsions is shrouded in secrecy, historically involving a retreat into the darkroom to develop the writing with light that photography and film appear to magically execute. In an enigmatic bit of information proffered under the heading "Emulsion, the Image Recorder" on Kodak's Web page, the photochemical necessity of preparing sensitive gelatin emulsions in "total darkness" helps to obscure the already mystifying material conditions of image culture: "At this point, the remaining manufacturing steps must be performed in total darkness. Gelatin is dissolved in pure distilled water, and then solutions of potassium iodide and potassium bromide are carefully mixed with it. Silver nitrate solution is added to this heated mixture, and the desired light-sensitive silver halide...salts are precipitated as fine crystals."[57] The incidental reliance on animal remains that Kodak fails to acknowledge in the cloaked science of gelatin manufacture is a fly in the ointment of the company's emulsion mystique, a repressed debt that can, nevertheless, through the active "attention" Brown theorizes, be disinterred to reopen a material politics of modern cinema.[58] For modern cinema's mobilization and massification of image life is not only conditioned on time-motion sciences that take animals as organic metaphors of technological mobility; it is also materially contingent on what Sheppard referred to as "the leavings of tanneries and slaughter-houses."[59]

A study of photographic and film stocks shows that prior to the invention of gelatin emulsions in the 1870s, the development of image life already relied heavily on albumen coatings derived from egg whites and animal blood. With the industrialization and popularization of image production pronounced by Eastman's emulsion-coating machines, his affordable portable cameras, and his film development services, however, the relation of film's mimetic effects to a material politics of animal protein changed both quantitatively and qualitatively. As Sheppard writes, "In 1884 the first machine for coating gelatino-bromide emulsion paper was built by Walker and Eastman, and the production of these papers was begun on a large scale" (18). In 1888, when the Kodak camera was introduced to the public, Eastman machines were busy coating "about six thousand feet of negative film a day" with photographic gelatin.[60] It was film that Eastman Kodak also promised to develop for its customers—"You press the button, we do the rest"[61]— encouraging miraculous rather than material knowledge around the popular production of images. By 1911, "in addition to its regular snapshot film, Kodak was manufacturing over eighty million feet of motion-picture stock annually."[62] By the latter half of the twentieth century, the great "emulsion empires"—those of Kodak and Fuji Film—would measure their raw stock less in footages or mileages than in global lengths: "During a single five-day work week... workers at a Kodak film plant are able to coat enough 35 mm film to circle the globe."[63] Yet the material means of cinema were simultaneously being rendered invisible beneath the moving image's fetishistic effect of immediacy.

It was not just film manufacturers who began ingeniously capitalizing on the remains of animal life flowing from industrialized slaughter around the turn of the century; North American entrepreneurs were widely experimenting with ways to incorporate the surplus of slaughter into material compounds capable of passing as genuine animal articles. An innovative mimetic material known as hemacite—a mix of animal blood and sawdust compressed under high pressure to form a virtually indestructible substance—imitated ebony and other precious substances without the prohibitive cost, rendered as it was from industrial waste products.[64] Celluloid, though not composed of the "leavings" of slaughter, was among the efflorescence of synthetic materials being engineered to embody "a versatility and uniformity unknown to natural material," allowing them to be "molded into any desired form"

through mass modes of production.[65] Originally marketed by the Celluloid Manufacturing Company in the 1870s as a material capable of imi-
tating ivory, tortoiseshell, coral, and amber, celluloid substituted for the
look and feel of elephant tusks and other exotic parts of organic wildlife in luxury items such as hair combs, hand mirrors, and brooches.[66]
What Jeffrey Miekle calls celluloid's "power of mimicry" enabled it, as
the Celluloid Manufacturing Company stated in an early advertising
pamphlet, to assume "a thousand forms" and to pass as authentic so
peerlessly as to "defy detection."[67]

Beyond touting celluloid's mimetic power to pass as counterfeit for
ivory or tortoiseshell, its manufacturers also argued a case for substi-
tuting celluloid for natural materials on affective grounds of wildlife
conservation. The Celluloid Manufacturing Company declared that
just "as petroleum came to the relief of the whale . . . [so] has celluloid
given the elephant, the tortoise, and the coral insect a respite in their
native haunts; and it will be no longer necessary to ransack the earth
in pursuit of substances which are constantly growing scarcer."[68] As
Miekle notes, ivory was "the material [that celluloid] most imitated."[69]
In a Du Pont salesmen's handbook from 1919, the extinction of "great
herds of elephants" was thus invoked in the marketing cause of celluloid (17). A logic of imitation persuasively articulated with a logic of
wildlife conservation around the mimetic management of celluloid's
artificiality. As Miekle remarks, "Comments such as those of Du Pont
served primarily to associate celluloid with ideas of luxury and rarity,
to suggest that the American housewife enjoyed comforts formerly
available only in a sultan's harem. No evidence suggested a scarcity of
ivory during the early twentieth century" (17).

In his search for a flexible film base that could replace cumbersome
glass plates and liberate photography as a mass amateur pursuit, George
Eastman saw more than just this mimetic potential in celluloid. In
1889, Eastman replaced glass plate and paper supports with thin, roll-
able strips of transparent nitrocellulose plastic, or celluloid film, supplying one of the missing material conditions of mass motion picture
technology. Thomas Edison collaborated closely with Eastman in de-
signing the Kinetoscope motion picture camera around the new roll-
able film, radically advancing the technological mimicry of continuous

movement sought by early cinematographers. If a discourse of wildlife conservation buttressed celluloid's material bid to existence prior to its filmic adaptation, it would be articulated even more prominently to and through cultural discourses of photography and film, which pronounced a conservationist ideology in their call to shoot animals with a camera rather than with a gun (to go "Big Game Hunting with a Kodak").[70] Étienne-Jules Marey's "chronophotographic gun," whose sequential filmic cartridges allowed him to shoot animal and bird studies in a manner that replaced the taking of life with its mimetic capture, explicitly heralded the substitution of the camera for the gun.[71] Immuring wildlife on film was widely framed as a conservationist act; over a century later, the valorization of celluloid's conservationist logic still informs the cinematic theory of Lippit, who rearticulates film as a "virtual shelter for displaced animals."[72]

Yet when Lippit proclaims that cinema preserves "the traces of an incorporated animality" (187), he celebrates film's sympathetic features at the cost of overlooking its pathological relationship to animal life. For onto a base of celluloid first pitched as a conservationist alternative to endangered animal tusks, horns, and shells, Eastman applied a second substance, a gelatin emulsion encrypting cinema's contradictory contingency on animal disassembly, one pivotal to its mimetic power to develop lifelike images. In the translucent physiology of modern film stock—in its celluloid base and its see-through gelatin coating—it is possible to discern the "two-layered" mimesis through which modern cinema simultaneously encrypts a sympathetic and a pathological relationship to animal life.[73] Film thus marks a site where a contradictory logic of rendering is daringly, yet inconspicuously, flush.

With one notable exception, the materiality of film stock rarely erupted into historical consciousness to disturb the images it supported in increasingly global quantities. In "the great emulsion debacle of 1882" (when the Eastman Dry Plate Company was still selling emulsion-coated glass plates rather than flexible film), Eastman was almost ruined by a series of fogging, overexposing plates.[74] The failure of Eastman plates to properly develop images was traced back to the batch of gelatin from which their emulsion coating had been rendered. Through this early fiasco, Eastman discovered "that impurities in the gelatin itself can either promote increased sensitization or even complete desensitization" of image life, which compelled him to pursue "an absolutely uniform manufacturing standard" and to monitor for the undappled consistency of animal matter used in the production of photographic gelatin.[75] Emulsion formulas became closely guarded corporate secrets with the growing realization that advances in light-sensitive emulsions could significantly increase film speed and hence an image's fetishistic effect of mimetic immediacy.

In 1925, Dr. Samuel Sheppard, at the time an emulsion scientist working for Kodak, traced organic impurities in photographic gelatin back to the particularities of a cow's diet. Sheppard discovered that cattle who had eaten mustard seed yielded better film speeds, because a sulfuric substance in mustard oil accentuated the light sensitivity of silver halide crystals suspended in an emulsion. Sheppard's findings suggested that the failure of Eastman's plates in 1882 had been due not to the *presence* of an impurity in the gelatin but rather to the *absence* of an impurity: mustard seed had been missing in the diets of the animals from which the gelatin was rendered. The head of Kodak's research laboratory, Dr. C. E. Kenneth Mees, later recounted Sheppard's emulsion breakthrough to a lecture audience: "Twenty years ago we found out that if cows didn't like mustard there wouldn't be any movies at all."[76]

In New York's University of Rochester Library, holder of the George Eastman Archives, only one slim folder of documents makes reference to gelatin production.[77] In one document in the file entitled "Gelatin Is Simple Stuff" (an article from all appearances commissioned by Kodak for a broader audience), an anonymous writer states: "It was generally believed that gelatin's role in the photographic process was wholly passive. It merely sat there, quietly clutching billions of bits of silver halide."[78] In the flurry of research prompted by the 1882 "debacle," however, and following from Sheppard's discovery of the photochemical agency of allyl mustard oil, "gelatin graduated from a passive to an active part in the creation of photographic emulsions."[79] The same document reports that "in its pure state this allyl mustard oil was not of any value as a sensitizer; it was only as an impurity, an accidental, that it achieved its value."[80] In other words, sulfur sensitizers in mustard

were of use to Eastman only if they had been metabolized by an animal and were lodged as accidental trace elements in its physiological
tissue; in animal biology lay the irrational key to the technological
success of filmic mimesis. In the photochemical parable of the mustard
seed it is briefly acknowledged that the development of mass images
turns on a "sensible trace" of animal life, a contingency haunting Eastman's emulsion empire and therefore becoming subject to intense biopolitical controls.[81] "The problem," continued the anonymous writer,
"was solved by setting up to manufacture gelatin; if Kodak controlled
its making, its quality could be controlled, too."[82]

Eastman would indeed put Sheppard's discovery to work to gain
Kodak an emulsion edge by extending the corporation's control over
the life and death of animal stock. In 1930 Eastman purchased the
American Glue Company, a rendering plant that had been in operation
in Peabody, Massachusetts (the "tannery city"), since 1808. He renamed
it the Eastman Gelatine Corporation and began materially managing
livestock and its rendered remains exclusively for Kodak quality.
Tightened micropolitical control over the raw diet as well as the cooked
hides and bones of animals allowed Eastman to manage organic impurities in photographic gelatin, signaling the almost maniacal mastery over animal physiology that made the mimetics of photography
and film possible.[83] By 1939, between his two facilities at Kodak Park
in Rochester, New York, and Peabody, Massachusetts, Eastman was able
to manufacture nearly all of the gelatin Kodak needed. "And it was
gelatin made to specification; for by this time the key to gelatin's character had been found. Gelatin could be made so that the essential
'impurities' were present in precisely the right amount."[84] In its new
appreciation of gelatin's critical role in image development, the Eastman Gelatine Corporation skimmed only the most refined "stuff" off
the rendering vat for its manufacture of sensitive photographic emulsions, allotting B-grade gelatin to food and pharmaceutical markets and
no longer even bothering with animal glue. North America's appetite
for filmic images had spurred a reprioritization of rendered material,
one concretely reflected in Eastman's purchase of the Peabody plant,
his regearing of the facility toward the manufacture of photographic

gelatin, and his sale of the glue-making side of the business. By simultaneously fetishizing animals as naturally photogenic figures in motion (as in the protocinematic studies of Marey and Muybridge) *and* as the emulsion industry's most photosensitive substance (nature had seemingly designed animal physiology "with the photographic process in mind"),[85] modernity accommodates a wildly disjunctive discourse on animal life. The kind of animal sign rendered through this disjuncture is at least double: disembodied signifier of seamless motion *and* mere material processed in staggering quantities at accelerating speeds through the abattoirs and reduction plants of the West.

The degree of biopolitical control requisite for managing the animal "accidental" of mass image culture is brought into even greater relief when Kodak's material unconscious — that is, the image industry's repressed contingency on animal rendering — is seen to have encompassed a traffic in animal remains from all over the world. In the gelatin documents that sit inconspicuously in the Eastman archives, another article gives surprising insight into Eastman Kodak's heterogeneous global sources of animal bones, horns, and hides, revealing a transnational traffic dating back to the 1880s and flourishing up until the Second World War. In "Commentary on Dry Gelatine Raw Stocks in Storage" (1969), a report that from all appearances was intended solely for an internal corporate audience, we can glimpse the global heterogeneity of animal material that Eastman Kodak collected to render into gelatin. The report shows that the corporation organized its imported "dry stock" into taxonomical types in an effort to distinguish gelatin rendered from Chinese water buffalo from "Type IV (X) material" (sacred cattle dying a natural death on the Indian subcontinent) and "Type III material" (South American livestock).[86] Rendering a global heterogeneity of animal matter into homogeneous types capable of feeding the precision manufacture of photosensitive gelatin required navigating geopolitical difference as well as controlling physiological variabilities of animal matter. Rendering a global traffic in animal remains immaterial to image culture ("You press the button, we do the rest") entailed not only reducing animals from all over the world to the abstract substance of the sign of photographic and cinematic exchange (to "mere jelly") but also rendering the volatile geopolitics of a transnational traffic in animal remains historically "unconscious" to the popular culture of film.

As "Commentary on Dry Gelatine Raw Stocks in Storage" inadvertently exposes, gelatin indexes complex geopolitical histories in which the mimetic power of mass images is imbricated in volatile global flows of raw material. Although demand for Eastman Kodak photography and film stock spiked during the Second World War (driven by new military interests in aerial photography and propaganda film), information relayed by the "Commentary on Dry Gelatine Raw Stocks" in the Eastman archives shows that the war also seriously disrupted the global supplies of raw stock feeding Kodak's emulsion empire:

> The Japanese invasion of Southeast Asia completely disrupted the collection of Water Buffalo hides.... (The lack of shipping and also the submarine activity effectively prevented any substantial quantities of cattle bones picked up in India from reaching Europe—and even if such shipments had been possible, they would have been to no avail, since Germany occupied the areas in Belgium and France where the acidulating plants are located.) Likewise, very little Type III material got through to us from South America (2).

As the document reports, supply of "Type III material" further dried up when the "Peron military dictatorship took over the Argentine government in 1944, and an embargo on raw bone exports was put into effect" (3). Indeed, in the seemingly mundane historical inventory of dry gelatin stock is inscribed a loaded catalog of "political upheavals," giving us a glimpse into the material histories within which modern mass imagery was imbricated:

> "Hoof-and-mouth" disease, temporary embargoes, the closing of the Suez Canal in 1967 after the 6-Day Arab-Israeli war, squeezing of the Grist Osseine supply temporarily by the Calcutta "ring" or the Brussels "club," long-shoreman and shipping strikes, the India-China war, the India-Pakistan war, political upheavals in South America—all these and other factors influenced the supply picture from time to time, but we always were able to work around any particular problem with the help of our inventories (5).

Both the first and second world wars confronted Eastman Kodak with its vulnerable reliance upon foreign sources of gelatin, motivating Eastman to secure domestic supply and production of rendered material. The Eastman Gelatine Corporation became pivotal to Kodak's ability to continue and even accelerate its manufacture of film amidst global crisis.

One last item among the meager file of documents referring to gelatin in the Eastman archives—*A Handbook for the Men and Women of Eastman Gelatine Corporation* (1945)—allows the biopolitics of gelatin production to be developed from another angle. In this instance, automobility involved Taylorizing the worker into an "intelligent gorilla" of mass production, into a subject as scrutinized and standardized as the animal "accidental" of image culture that he or she helped to manufacture. In its handbook, "the Corporation" laid out the system of wages, benefit and insurance plans, and codes of conduct for its more than 350 employees.[87] This information is spelled out under the kindly gaze of "the Kodak family" father, Eastman, whose photo-portrait appears on the handbook's first page. Eastman's benevolence is reinforced with the information that the corporation supplemented employees' regular pay with annual wage dividends based on the value of its common stock, "paid in recognition of the contribution which loyal, steady, and efficient workers make to the success of the Corporation" (9). Like Ford with his wage of five dollars a day, Eastman generously afforded his laborers the ability to participate to some degree in the conspicuous consumption of the mass commodities they helped to produce, possibly even the purchase of pocket Kodaks that would allow them to better enjoy the week's worth of vacation time allotted employees of Eastman Gelatine each year.

The enticements of belonging to Eastman's family of trained gorillas were tempered, however, by "A Few Helpful Rules." The handbook emphasizes that the company had little tolerance for "Tardiness" and that it expected "Neatness." Under the heading "Personal Conduct," the training of its labor force took on a less persuasionary and more forceful aspect: "Everyone is expected to refrain from improper language and to avoid horseplay of any kind. To interfere with or disturb another in his or her work without reason is cause for discipline" (35). Again, an undertone of severity and surveillance laced the benevolent discourse of the corporation when it came to "Registering Your Time": "By registering your times of entering and leaving work on your time-clock card, you help to make sure that your pay will be correctly made out" (34). Yet as Marx first clearly discerned, there is an "extra" time of labor concealed in the wage relationship that is critical to the creation of surplus value. If one kind of surplus was being rendered at Eastman Gelatine by skimming extra value off of animal remains, the more classical surplus rendered from capital's workforce was skimmed off in the form of extra labor time. The employee time-clock card that is of such a piece with Fordism is a condensed figure of this concealed surplus mechanism of capital, an instrument of seemingly objective time accounting that renders invisible the differential between necessary and extra labor time so crucial to corporate profit margins. Industrial capitalisms' economies of motion and scale chase an increasing reduction of necessary labor time (through the "speed-ups" of moving lines that Sinclair described so acutely in *The Jungle*), bringing the time of labor under even more minute measure. Hence the warning extended by the *Eastman Gelatine* Corporation in its *Employee Handbook:* "Failure to punch your clock card cannot be excused except for some very good reason" (34).

It was not just the time of labor that was carefully clocked as an ostensibly objective value; monitoring the behavior and cleanliness of the corporation's workers was integral to the "purity" of the gelatin manufactured at Peabody. As the handbook explained to employees, "Gelatine is one of the most important raw materials used in the manufacture of photographic films, papers, and plates. . . . The gelatine used for this purpose must be of exceptionally high quality since the slightest impurity may affect the sensitivity of the emulsion" (6). At the Eastman Gelatine facility, the handbook stated, "good housekeeping is expected of everyone" to prevent material specks and motes from marring filmic emulsions and the mimetic magic of images (34). The handbook closes with a prohibition that calls to be read as an ironic summation of the invisibility demanded of the material nature and labor of mass visual culture: "No one is permitted to take pictures on Eastman Gelatine property without permission" (35).

Automobiles: Recreating Animals

Having theorized the protocinematic spectacle of animal disassembly and the "material unconscious" of film, I now turn to trace how the animal capital of cars is triangulated with that of slaughter and cinema. If Ford modeled his Highland Park plant in Dearborn, Michigan, on the moving lines of Chicago's vertical abattoirs, filmic and automotive productions in turn closely referenced each other's technological advances across the twentieth century. As Kristin Ross notes in the context of her study of modern French cinema, "the two technologies reinforced each other. Their shared qualities—movement, image, mechanization, standardization—made movies and cars the key commodity-vehicles of a complete transformation in European consumption patterns and cultural habits."[88] It is seldom recalled, moreover, that early Ford factories were themselves sites of cinematic as well as automotive production. In 1914, "Henry Ford established a Motion Picture Department in his Dearborn, Michigan automobile plant," writes Andrew Loewen, producing short films on a wide range of subjects including developments in industrial technology, history, warfare, and of course "the workings of Ford factories themselves."[89] In contrast to Beller's suggestion that the mode of cinematic production emerged *after* Fordism, Loewen splices automotive and cinematic modes of production in his theorization of the simultaneity of "auto-cinematic production," one that seeks to account for "the historical and operative inextricability of industrial automotive and cinematic social production" posed by Ford's Motion Picture Department (4). "In a departure from Beller's periodization and in marked contrast to theorists of immaterial labor more generally," writes Loewen, "cinema's birth inside the factory testifies to the emergence of intensive (subjective) labor within the extensive outlines of the Fordist paradigm" (5).

The biopolitical times of animal capital theorized in this book also cut across and complicate clear period distinctions within the history of capitalism, inasmuch as carnal and symbolic economies of rendering can be seen to operate concurrently in Fordist as well as post-Fordist eras. Just as it is important to discern forms of "intensive (subjective) labor" already at work in Fordist culture, however, it is also crucial to confront a dematerialized image of post-Fordist culture with capital's continuing contingency on the material bodies of labor and nature. In this section I suggest that the ubiquitous practice of metaphorizing cars as animal can be counted among the more powerful dematerializing forces of (neo)liberal culture and interrogated for the disavowal it enables of the escalating social and ecological costs of mobility. Through an analysis of a 2002 Saturn Vue campaign I suggest, moreover, that the rendering of animals marks a productive site of discursive continuity rather than discontinuity across Fordist and post-Fordist eras. For while the time-motion logics organizing assembly line production have been revised if not wholly dislodged by post Fordist systems of flexible production, what has stayed in place and indeed intensified is the mimetic productivity of animal signs deployed to manage capital's volatile material relations.

While automobiles were certainly fetishized as animal in early Fordist culture, animal metaphors proliferated in market discourses of the second half of the twentieth century as capital was increasingly diverted into the symbolic as well as the material production of cars. Massive investment of capital in the semiotics of advertising and branding is considered one of the key markers of post-Fordism and a sign of the paradigmatic shift in emphasis from material to symbolic economies within the history of capitalism. To give one concrete example of this shift in capital investment, according to *AdAge* the General Motors (GM) corporation spent $609 million in measured media in the first quarter of 2002 alone.[90] In the same year, one of GM's subsidiaries, the Saturn corporation, launched a $35 million ad campaign introducing its new sports utility vehicle (SUV), the Vue. In what follows, I track the animal capital of cars across the twentieth century to GM's Saturn "experiment" in the 1980s and to the post-Fordist culture of production that Saturn introduced within North America.[91] GM spawned Saturn in an attempt to compete with Japanese imports and to create an American answer to a "just-in-time" model of production (Toyotism) that sheds the material stockpiles, serial logic, and standardized mass units of Fordism in favor of maximum weightlessness, flexibility, and niche production. The popular sense promoted by Saturn that just-in-time production is *less material* in its conditions and effects than Fordist production is epitomized by its 2002 Vue campaign, one presenting a series of ecological dioramas in which the SUV emerges as a species of wildlife. As I have noted, rendering automobiles animal is a ubiquitous gesture in car culture, but its potent ecological articulation in the Saturn campaign can be read as symptomatic of intensifying contradictions in the current era between a dematerialized image of neoliberal culture that automobiles help to ideologically drive and all too material signs of their ecological and social depredations. As the Saturn campaign illustrates, animal signs have become key to managing the material contradictions of neoliberal culture at the level of mimesis.

A 2002 television ad for the Volvo Cross Country gives an initial glimpse into the mimetic value or capital of animals in car advertising. The ad, opening with a shot of the Cross Country as it speeds north, at dusk, toward an exotic arctic house, focuses on a female driver with a man asleep in the passenger seat beside her. The woman-car hybrid is the only body moving on the road. Suddenly, a herd of caribou erupt out of the dusk and stream across the highway, a latitude transecting the longitude of the car's movement directly within the cross-hairs of the driver's field of vision. The car comes to a stop: time and motion are for an instant suspended in a magical pause as the scene transacts a mimetic identification between the migratory animal collective and the Cross Country. The car and the caribou commune, it appears, by means of their common emotional sensors and innate powers of "affective computing."[92] The female driver, moreover, is essential to the consolidation of the mimetic moment: woman's biological wiring ostensibly attunes her to the mysterious unianimality of car, caribou, and driver. The male passenger, representing the rational consciousness of culture, remains oblivious to the magnetic call of the wild roused in the Cross Country and in his wife. After a second of still sensing, the caribou disappear into the night, the Cross Country resumes full speed heading north, and a sparse, parting text flashes on the screen: "Volvo for life."

The aesthetic interest generated by crossing animal and automobile (not to mention woman) at this biopolitical intersection is profoundly at odds with cars' ecological exploits and impacts. It is not just the repressed historical contingency of automotive assembly on animal disassembly that materially contradicts the fetishistic crossing of automobile and animal in the Volvo ad but the violent displacements of wildlife and their habitats that has occurred as cars, roads, and fossil fuel extraction have carved ever more deeply into animal territories over the course of the twentieth century.

Michael Taussig's analysis of the famous RCA Victor logo "His Master's Voice," in which a dog is shown listening quizzically to a sound reproduction emanating from the "ear trumpet" of an early phonograph, helps to illuminate the pivotal role of the animal in bending mimesis to market ends.[93] Taussig contends that in testing the mimetic power of the phonograph against the natural faculties of an animal, the RCA Victor logo cleverly plays on the dual connotations of "fidelity." "Everything," writes Taussig, "turns on the double meaning of fidelity (being *accurate* and being *loyal*), and on what is considered to be a mimetically astute being" (213).[94] As opposed to the car and the caribou in the Volvo ad, at stake in the RCA Victor logo is the testing of a canine's discerning sensors against the sound fidelity of the phonographic reproduction, a reproduction so convincing that the dog is led to believe that his master must be present inside the machine. As Taussig discerns, moreover, "Where politics most directly enters is in the image's attempt to combine fidelity of mimetic reproduction with fidelity to His Master's Voice," according to the twin connotations of fidelity as the machinic measure of a quality reproduction and as affective obedience, or faithfulness (223). In this drama of fidelity, a technological reproduction so true to life that it passes for original is tested on an animal's sensory and soulful faculties, with both complimentary and comic results: the dumb animal is bewildered, tricked by the perfect projection of his master's voice. The animal is simultaneously granted a natural talent for sniffing out the difference between the presence of an original and the imposture of a copy *and* discriminately put back in its place when its senses are outwitted by a masterful machine. The covenant between dog and master becomes an obedience lesson not only in recognizing the superior mimetic powers of machines but also in responding with affective loyalty to the market that calls to us through the powerful mimetic tool of the RCA Victor logo itself.

While the mimetically capacious machine invariably emerges from this biological test as superior, automobile discourses will obsessively repeat their challenge to an animal figure that is indispensable to the

mimesis of the market. As Taussig puts it, "The technology of reproduction triumphs over the dog but needs the dog's validation" (213).
The drama of fidelity reappears at the intersection of Cross Country
and caribou in the Volvo ad, where the car passes the biological test
posed by the caribou crossing its path. It is also rearticulated, with a
difference, in the Saturn Vue campaign. Before turning to the Saturn
campaign, however, let me first trace what amounts to a highly cursory
beeline through a complex century of automotive culture in order to
provide something of a connecting thread between Ford's visit to the
slaughterhouse, with which this chapter opened, and Saturn's deployment of animal signs in the current era.

According to James Flink, Ford "longed to rid the world of unsanitary and inefficient horses and cows" and thus set to work to replace
the horse, long the organic standard of physical transport.[95] Impressed
by the moving disassembly lines of Packingtown and the time-motion
studies of Muybridge and Taylor, Ford devised a mode of mass production that would indeed usher in a "horseless age."[96] Jonathan Crary
explicitly links the time-motion studies of Eadweard Muybridge to the
physical displacement of animal traction by new locomotive powers:
"The horse, which had been for thousands of years the primary mode
of vehicular movement in human societies, is symbolically dismantled
into quantified and lifeless units of time and movement."[97] In 1908, the
Ford Motor Company presented to the public its first mass-assembled
vehicle, the Model T. Ford models effectively displaced their "unsanitary" originals even as they retained, in the metaphor of horsepower,
"the traces of an incorporated animality."[98] As Lippit puts it, the horsepower engine is an "equine crypt."[99] By mid-century, the cars manufactured by the Ford corporation would begin to be explicitly marketed as substitute animals. With the release of the Ford Mustang and
the pony class of vehicles in the 1960s, the mimetics of the Ford corporation began to challenge wild rather than domestic animals as ultimate
models of seamless mobility and effortless speed. Indeed, in the 1970s
and 1980s, Ford launched a wild animal series with the Ford Mercury
Bobcat (1978), Lynx (1980), and Cougar (1983).

Although Ford's modeling of the automotive assembly line on the
disassembly of animals in the abattoir gave him a logistical head start

on mass production, in 1927 GM gained an aesthetic advantage over Ford under the presidency of Alfred Sloan. Sloan established the first Art and Color Department in the automotive industry, hired Harley Earl as its head, and turned styling into an economic priority (rather than a superficial flourish) of automobile manufacture. In GM's Art and Color Department, as in Ford's Motion Picture Department, it is again possible to see the immaterial or symbolic labor usually identified with post-Fordism already inseparably entwined with assembly line production. Earl's previous work on Hollywood film sets allowed him to bring "celluloid lessons" to bear on automotive sheet metal.[100] Under Earl, an aesthetic of organicism carried the mimetic capabilities of the automobile head and shoulders over the assembled look of Ford's Model T. Earl was known for producing full-size model cars out of clay to achieve effects of streamlining and organic curvature that could conceal the component make-up of mass-assembled vehicles.

The mimetic trajectory that led the Ford Motor Company to its Bobcat, Lynx, and Cougar series of the 1980s (and later to its current breed of wild off-road SUV) was one that the GM corporation also followed, often with an edge on ostentatious styling. GM pushed its streamlining aesthetics to the aerospace- and fish-inspired "finned" vehicles of the 1950s. The OPEC (Organization of Oil-Exporting Countries) embargo and the energy crisis of the 1970s forced GM to review its overblown aesthetic agenda, however, and to consider the manufacture of subcompact and energy-efficient cars. This historical bee line cannot begin to do justice to the complexity of the OPEC embargo and other events in the 1970s, a decade viewed by many as the historical turning point from modernity to postmodernity. For the purposes of this chapter, however, it can be seen to have led to GM's decision, in 1985, to spawn the Saturn Corporation with the aim, among other things, of surviving within a highly competitive global economy.

The Saturn Corporation is popularly viewed as a rogue division of General Motors determined to disassociate itself from its lumbering parent company by pioneering a flexible, post-Fordist culture of auto-mobility that the rest of GM would be wise to model. Saturn has been touted as a model of the "networked organization" that is "set up to achieve heterogeneous objectives of multiple stakeholders rather than to simply conform to the single goal of the American firm that seeks to maximize shareholder value."[101] Among the motives inspiring the Saturn project were the rapid loss, over the course of the 1970s and 1980s, of GM's domestic market to quality Japanese imports, its growing realization that among those choosing imports over cars of dubious quality "made in America" was an increasingly affluent constituency repelled by the masculinist brand cultures of companies like GM (namely, professional women), and its even more compelling insight that to continue making exponential profits the auto industry needed to avert losses of time and money caused by nagging labor disputes. GM's Saturn "experiment" refers, above all, to a model of labor-management relations incubated at the Saturn "learning laboratory" in Spring Hill, Tennessee, one whose inscription as a pedagogical rather than an economic project is indicative of automobility's increasingly mimetic means.[102]

Alongside its new participatory relationship to labor, the culture of Saturn also promotes the sense that its post-Fordist production of automobiles is no longer contingent on the material exploitation of nature. Massive stockpiles feeding the "volume production of standardized commodities" in Fordist culture are dispersed through a network of suppliers so that, rather than being stored in monolithic warehouses and tying the manufacturer down with weighty inventories, resources and parts can instead be ordered for the just-in-time production of customized vehicles.[103] These parts then pass through a cluster of self-directed work teams (heavily aided by electronics technologies) capable of assembling a range of computer-rendered models that are, finally, shipped out to customers through a web of retailers. Here, materials are summoned, sutured, and dispersed with the speed and seeming ease of technological communication. Yet this deterritorialized production scenario arguably entails an even greater command over material resources than that demanded by the Fordist assembly line. The fetishistic effect of immediacy and immateriality excited by a rhetoric of postindustrial production—so that a car's computer-rendered image appears to constitute its moment of production—displaces recognition of the intensifying material demands automobility places on people, resources, and environments globally.

The postindustrial image of a custom-designed automobile that appears to have a manifest rather than manufactured existence is epitomized by the Saturn Vue campaign I have been approaching. The Vue—"at home in almost any environment"—is just one SUV among many that serve to powerfully naturalize the cultural ideology and material technologies of neoliberalism that they represent. The tagline of Toyota SUVs is "You Belong Outside"; Ford SUVs, such as the Explorer, celebrate "No Boundaries." Before it changed its tagline to "Shift" in September of 2002 (fusing automotive gears and digitized cursors into a single function key of mobility), Nissan's Xterra was animalistically rather than fossil fuel "Driven." Yet an even more unabashed mimicry of automobile and animal emerged with the Vue ads. Two decades after GM created Saturn with the aim of manufacturing energy-efficient vehicles, the vision of the subcompact fell to the wayside as Saturn trumpeted the arrival of its SUV.[104]

The particular print ad from the Saturn campaign analyzed here, "Inhabitants of the Polar Region," is a two-page spread that enacts, even in its sprawling occupation of media space, the Vue's imperial promise of an unlimited traversal of terrestrial space (see Figure 5).[105] Organized as an interactive educational exercise, "Inhabitants of the Polar Region" invites readers to cross-reference three visual components: an illustrated animal panorama, a black and white numbered cut-out in the upper left-hand corner, and the taxonomic key of animal names in the lower left-hand corner. By cross-referencing all three, consumers are engaged in a learning game that involves the identification of wildlife species, including the Vue, which is the first species listed on the taxonomic key. Corporate pedagogy teaches natural history to consumers of the twenty-first century. The aura of early childhood evoked by its pedagogical address underscores the strategy used by the ad to manage automobility's economy of power: *mimetic* management of the relation of nature and culture. After all, children, like animals and "primitives," have been constructed as natural mimics who learn by copying.[106]

The taxonomic system of classification mimicked by the ad presents a synchronic cross-section of a state of nature, of naturally occurring biodiversity. As a synchronic slice, the ad presents a timeless "still," a

Figure 5. The advertisement "Inhabitants of the Polar Regions" (2002) appeared in a $35 million marketing campaign for the Saturn Vue SUV promoted by the Saturn Corporation, a division of General Motors.

representative range of animal life outside of contingent historical forces such as human management and exploitation. The Vue is not depicted in motion, as a moving picture, but as a still life object. If the ad puts time under suspension by inviting viewers to relive childhood as a period of primal, timeless schooling in mimetic identification, it also suspends motion. It is tempting to read Saturn's still life as a naturalist rendition of just-in-time production in which the time-motion economies of Fordist moving lines have been replaced by a post-Fordist instantaneity of conception and execution that oddly resembles a static state. The ad, in this reading, holds up nature as a mirror image of post-Fordist production space, with its rhizomatic network of independent contractors, self-directed teams, and participatory involvement of labor and nature. The ad could be read as posing bioregion and biodiversity as the ecological equivalents of the "networked organization," with different animal species representing its "multiple stakeholders." However, while "Inhabitants of the Polar Region" can be critiqued for its suggestion that a postindustrial economy has its natural counterpart in ecology, there is more going on in the ad. At stake in the Vue text is not only the naturalization of an economic reality conceived as external to the space of representation but the management of mimesis as itself a site of post-Fordist production.

In positioning the Vue within a painterly diorama in which time and motion seem suspended, the vehicle appears to be intent only on the mimetic movement of becoming like the animals around it. Yet what at first glance looks like a flat painterly plane upon which animals and automobile are rendered equivalent can be seen, on closer inspection, to be a differentiated topography containing at least two grades of mimetic fidelity. A close look at the lower left-hand corner of the Saturn ad (discernible only as a faint smudge above the legend in this reproduction of the image) reveals that the animal illustration has been signed by the hand of "K. Pendletton." The mimetic technology adequate to the representation of animal life, in other words, is the relatively rude naturalism of hand-drawn art. The Vue, on the other hand, asserts its difference through the enhanced mimetic technology it introduces into the visual ecology: the Vue is a computer-rendered image whose supernatural mimetic fidelity makes the hand-drawn images of the animals appear naïve in comparison. The taxonomic discourse of species identity that equalizes the Vue and polar species is simultaneously disavowed by the ad's use of an "advanced" representational technology for the car body in comparison with the one used to render the animals. A discourse of technological progress encoded in the digital sharpness of the Vue subtly distinguishes it from the surrounding wildlife with whom it at first seems to coexist. The wildlife is, in effect, demoted in the ecological hierarchy by the heightened representational fidelity of the SUV.

As in the RCA Victor logo analyzed by Taussig, the Vue ad's differentiation of levels of mimetic fidelity also naturalizes a relationship of mastery between culture and nature. The animals are demoted not just through the appearance of a body with superior fidelity but also by virtue of a narrative of time implied in the "evolution" of mimesis. The ad's ecological diorama positions wildlife as a predecessor of the Vue, consigning all but the Saturn "animal" to a frozen past, even to extinction (that several of the animals listed on the taxonomic key are endangered predicts their imminent "pastness"). Despite the valorization of the animal as an organic metaphor of automobility, or rather because of it, animals are consigned to being originals necessarily predating, and never matching up to, the second nature of capital. The anachronistic effect and nostalgic affect produced by the ad's imitation of a primary school textbook serves to reinforce the solo currency of the SUV body, whose cutting-edge verisimilitude projects it alone as a presence in the present. An evolutionary narrative of survival of the fittest is thus retooled along a trajectory of mimetic prowess. There is what Johannes Fabian calls a "denial of coevalness" insinuated within what at first looks like a synchronic tableau of coexisting wildlife.[107]

Moreover, the SUV performs its perfect autonomy. There are no tread marks showing the path from factory to wilderness, nor is there any need, it would seem, of a human operator. Yet the darkly tinted windshield at the same time makes it impossible to determine whether there is in fact a human subject inside the vehicle. As in the case of Foucault's reading of Bentham's Panopticon, the inability to confirm either the presence or the absence of a human operator introduces into the scene an aspect of surveillance that also contradicts the animal immanence claimed by the Vue. If the Vue is included in the list of animals composing the taxonomic key, its tinted windshields contradictorily hint at an invisible human presence—an imperial eye—overseeing the animal panorama. An ecotouristic gaze hides behind the windshield (and less subtly in the name *Vue*) to locate the sovereign act of consumption within the capitalist ecology.

Different color codings operate like molting coats in the Saturn campaign, allowing the Vue to coordinate with any environment. In a companion ad, a red Vue mimetically blends in with "creatures of the evergreen forest." This is niche marketing at its most literal. And, as in "Inhabitants of the Polar Region," in other ads in the campaign animal and automobile are again mimetically identified *and* distinguished along the lines of the different rendering technologies used to depict them (pictorial naturalism versus digital supernaturalism) and the hierarchy encoded in that difference.

Yet the controlled mimesis that intimately juxtaposes animal and automobile to calibrate their sameness and difference also holds the potential of igniting recognition of automobility's material contradictions. While roadkill is perhaps most emblematic of the violence at material intersections of animal and automobile, car culture materially displaces animals in far more systematic ways as well, through the infrastructure of roads and highways that transect animal habitat and through the incalculable costs of fossil fuel extraction. Moreover, if automobiles emerge, in part, out of a desire to replace the animal traction of the horse, across the twentieth and early twenty-first centuries they have also worked to outmimic animal life and to symbolically occupy the place of animal life. However, while the Vue campaign generates enormous affective energy by posing species and SUV in ecological intimacy, it cannot guarantee its ability to mimetically master the political volatility of their proximity.

Speculation and Specie

American stock market offices opened up and gathered momentum amid the noise, stench, and animal traffic of Chicago's stockyards. For nearly a century, speculative and specie value—virtual and carnal capital—shared the common designation of "stock."[108] By the 1970s, however, the period in which Fredric Jameson relates the rise of postmodernist culture to increasingly spectral flows of global capital, the animal trade at the Chicago stockyards was closed down.[109] Animals had become the too-literal, and faintly embarrassing, biological substance of the increasingly virtual sign of "stock." More and more remote from their animal correlates in material history, stock markets at the turn of the twenty-first century now appear to conduct sheerly ethereal global trades in fictitious capital.

In "Recollecting the Slaughterhouse," Dorothee Brantz traces the rise and demise of centralized public abattoirs in the West, both those founded in Chicago in 1865 and those built in Paris in the 1860s at the bidding of Baron Georges-Eugène Haussmann. In Brantz's diagnosis, the "post-industrial age witnessed the demise of the modern mass-slaughterhouse because it did not fit into the image of the so-called postmodern city."[110] Since the evacuation of slaughter from urban space in the early 1970s, "meat-market districts in New York and Chicago have been transformed into trendy hangout areas and loft neighborhoods, reinventing the slaughterhouse as an aestheticized space for consumption and entertainment" (122). Continues Brantz, "Just last year [2000], Les Abattoirs, a museum for contemporary art, opened in Toulouse, France, on the premises of a 19th-century slaughterhouse" (122).

Among the more notable postmodern rehabilitations of slaughter space traced by Brantz is that of Paris's La Villette abattoir, recently transformed into "a 'polyvalent cultural complex' that houses a science museum, festival space, and la Cité de la Musique" (123). Upon viewing an outdoor screening of a movie at the old abattoir, Brantz was struck by the superimposition of moving images on premises formerly devoted to animal disassembly. "Watching the film projected onto the former cattle market . . . was an eerie experience," she writes (123). Trying to capture a sense of the radical cultural shift La Villette undergoes as its former traffic in animal life and death is replaced with a spectral traffic in images and entertainment, Brantz declares that "the park of La Villette is not just architecture turned against itself. It is life turned on its head" (123). These are, resonantly enough, the terms in which Marx described the fetishism of the commodity, which "stands on its head, and evolves out of its wooden brain grotesque ideas, far more wonderful than if it were to begin dancing of its own free will."[111]

Yet in her recollection of the historical premises of postindustrial culture, Brantz inadvertently reinforces the hegemonic sense that postindustrial traffics in images and entertainment are no longer a material matter of life and death as opposed to the "deadly spectacle" and "carnivore feast" they historically replace (118). Through a cross-examination of the protocinematic consumption of slaughter, the carnal composition of filmstock, and the mimetic powers of automobiles, this chapter has sought to complicate the equation of industrial capitalism with materiality and postindustrial capitalism with immateriality, as well as to challenge the idea that the former is now "history." Given the heightened immateriality effects surrounding the production and consumption of neoliberal culture in an era of globalization, the carnal conditions and effects of capital more than ever need to be historically "developed," in Bill Brown's sense. Such an effect of immateriality was excited, among other things, by Kodak's announcement in 2004 that it was extricating itself from the material business of making film due to the digitization of image production. It is also an effect, as I suggested in my reading of the Saturn Vue campaign, of a discourse of post-Fordism that encourages the idea that automobiles spontaneously manifest in the space of just-in-time production.

At the beginning of this chapter I remarked that critiques that have taken humans (and in the Marxian tradition, workers) as the focal subjects of material history leave a whole biopolitical terrain of animal signs and substances—massively productive for cultures of capital—unexamined. Yet any biopolitical organization of human populations in the service of reproducing capital arguably presupposes a related organization of animal populations. As James O'Connor puts it, in reverse terms, the "history of nature . . . is in some small or large part the history of labor."[112] In the Fordist histories reopened by this chapter, the politics of labor and of nature are indeed inseparable. Fordizing and Taylorizing discourses intent on reducing workers to "the body part" best able to efficiently perform a piecemeal motion over and over again on the assembly or disassembly line presuppose the possibility of producing nature as a homogeneous and uninterrupted flow of material.[113] Yet, especially when this material is animal, such homogeneity is never absolute or guaranteed. As Vialles notes in the context of the abattoir:

> Job fragmentation is fully effective only in connection with material that is perfectly regular and always the same. Here, though, the regularity is only ever approximate; the suspended body retains traces of the unique life that once animated it: illnesses it may have had, accidents it may have suffered, various anomalies that may characterize it. The contingency and individuality of the biological sphere resist the formal rigour of technical organization.[114]

Automotive and meatpacking plants mark two sites where nature and labor have been most rigorously produced as parallel subjects of modern capitalism's time-motion economies but also where "the contingency and individuality" of laboring bodies has continuously erupted in protest. In the 1930s, sit-down strikes protesting speed-ups in assembly lines were devised in specific response to the time-motion logics structuring the work (and play) of mass culture. The violence used to break sit-down strikes in order to keep the Fordist lines running gives us a glimpse into the associated force required to feed a continuous stream of animal or other material onto the moving tracks of capital. In the second half of the twentieth century, wildcat strikes have emerged to protest a post-Fordist organization of labor through "disorganized" or spontaneous walk-outs of workers, simultaneously disrupting the workplace and subverting the legal framework that contains striking within union-management protocols. The identification of workers with the wildcat in impromptu walk-outs not only disrupts production and subverts a logic of union representation that many feel is compromised by unions' close ties with management in the post-Fordist era; it also breaks a mimetic monopoly on animal signs by hegemonic discourses of advertising and branding. Labor's identification with the wildcat in an unauthorized strike is dramatically different from the controlled mimesis at work, for instance, in the Cougar, Lynx, and Bobcat series marketed by Ford in the late 1970s and early 1980s.

However, while the histories of capitalist labor and nature are invariably entangled, when it comes to developing material histories of protest, human labor and animal nature are also incommensurable. Their incommensurability lies in the difference between human subjects of history, whose protests are inscribed within the horizonal possibility of representational politics (even when, as in wildcat strikes, labor chooses to preempt representational politics and engage in micropolitics), and animal subjects, whose protest is either mediated through a system of anthropocentric representations or remains utterly unintelligible. Even more than the most unintelligible figures of human life and precarity—subaltern women[115]—animals suffer the double binds of representation: they are either excluded from the symbolic order on the grounds of species difference, or anthropomorphically rendered within it.

Gayatri Spivak suggests that the "physiological inscription" posed by Bhubaneswari Bhaduri (a young Indian woman who hanged herself in 1926) becomes a "subaltern rewriting of the social text" only in its "distanced decipherment by another."[116] So, too, do animal signs of protest require "decipherment" if they are to politically disturb "the dominant cultural memory" of capitalist modernity and postmodernity.[117] This winds me back, finally, to Bill Brown's theory of the "material unconscious." Brown contends, if you'll recall, that literary texts retain marks of a material everyday, seemingly negligible or excessive marks that constitute traces or tips of undeveloped histories. While such marks signal entry points into material histories suppressed by hegemonic accounts, they are at the mercy of future acts of decipherment that alone can "develop" them and bring them to historicity.

Signs of animal protest awaiting counterhegemonic production are strewn all over the social texts of modernity, as yet unactivated links to repressed histories of animal capital. For instance, in his study of a Banff taxidermist by the name of Norman Luxton, Mark Simpson retrieves a letter in whose irritation is inadvertently etched the historical materiality of animal life that the taxidermist aims to put under suspension. In this case, the "physiological inscription" of animals' own rotting bodies protests the goal of producing animals as undying currencies:

> In a letter dated 4 June 1910, John Ambrose, a taxidermic colleague of Luxton's working in Winnipeg, writes to express his outrage about the condition of a shipment that has recently arrived: "I received the Sheep heads last Monday in a very bad condition, putrid, rotten and the majority full of maggots. It was a disgusting job to clean them and I think, they should not have been shipped in such a condition."[118]

More than the taxidermist bargained for, such a somatic assault is, as Simpson suggests, "one way in which flayed animals come to undo their butchers" (98).

Animal signs capable of protesting and competing with those metaphorically and materially rendered in service to cultures of capital are not found, then, but produced, as in Simpson's analytic production of a carnal disturbance in the business of taxidermy. While this chapter has developed particular histories of animal capital in relation to the triangulated economies of slaughter, cinema, and the automobile, I can only point to the importance of also developing histories of animal agency. For the rendering of animal capital is surely first contested by animals themselves, who neither "live *unhistorically*" nor live with the historical passivity regularly attributed to them.[119]

Chapter 3

Telemobility: Telecommunication's Animal Currencies

Electric Animals

Over the course of the 1780s in Bologna, Italy, an anatomist and obstetrician by the name of Luigi Galvani standardized the practice of inducing electrical reflexes out of severed frog legs to demonstrate his theorem of animal electricity.[1] In *Commentary on the Effect of Electricity on Muscular Motion* (1791), Galvani claimed that frog muscle was "the most sensitive electrometer yet discovered" (80), albeit one carved out of the flesh of a "headless frog" (27). The doctor's method of reliably arranging the raw material of his "animal conductors" (31) in a fashion that guaranteed repeatable results to any who modeled it quickly gained renown as "the Galvani preparation," a standardized production of animal specimens that he visually reproduced in drawings of his electrical laboratory. Galvani's etched and written records of his method remain an inadvertent concession to animal sacrifice as a founding condition of electrical communication: "We placed some frogs horizontally on a parapet, prepared in the usual manner by piercing and suspending their spinal cords with iron hooks. The hooks touched an iron plate; behold! A variety of not infrequent spontaneous movements in the frog" (xi–xii).

From the animal capital of cars, films, and abattoirs, I now turn to
a genealogy of telecommunication culture in the West, beginning with
Galvani's frog legs, exposed nerves and tendons twitching with the
sign of electrical life. "Telemobility" is this chapter's framing trope for
cultural discourses that metaphorically (and materially) render technologies of long-distance communication "animal." Galvani's belief
that animal flesh is a natural conductor of electricity—his notion that
the physical animal supplies a singularly sympathetic medium for chan-
neling the metaphysical current of "animal spirits" (68)—has been
rearticulated in subsequent cultural discourses of telecommunication
in the West, to considerable fetishistic effect. The genealogy developed in this chapter begins with Galvani's early experiments, moves to
the analysis of a twentieth-century animal electrocution, and ends with
a study of the early twenty-first-century advertising campaign of a
Canadian company that uses living species to represent the spirit of
wireless communication. In this respect, it follows the unorthodox
method of historical materialism proposed by Walter Benjamin, con-
stellating radically disparate images to produce a shock of illumination.[2]
As I myself have argued, however, the critical jolt produced by constel-
lating images can be difficult to distinguish from the mimetic means
and ends of capital itself, particularly when these means are tropes of
animal electricity that themselves excite shocking, long-distance connections.[3] My intent, however, is to develop three decidedly material
moments that will, first, break up or distort the fantasy of charismatic,
"animal" connection that excites capital and, second, complicate the
popular association of that fantasy with the present era of globalization by illuminating telecommunication's animal tropes and technologies at work in earlier cultures of capitalism.

Telemobility draws attention to cultural discourses that fetishistically articulate technological mobility not to and through the seamless
physiology of animals in motion (as do discourses of automobility) but
to and through animals' ostensibly innate capacity for a sympathetic,
even telepathic, communication of affect. At stake in telemobility's animal tropes is an ideology of immaterial and immediate exchange between bodies on the same virtual wavelength. I am particularly intent
on critiquing how the metaphorization of virtual mobility as animal in

telecommunication discourses of the twentieth and early twenty-first centuries has promoted what Régis Debray describes as a fantasy of "painless transmission," in disavowal of communication's violent political economies and material conditions of possibility.[4] While the spiritualistic effects of telemobility discourse have truly become a force to be contended with in current neoliberal culture, with "techno-tele-media apparatuses" exciting belief in a metaphysics of communication (and of capital) on an unprecedented scale, as I have suggested, they can also be glimpsed in earlier eras of capitalism.[5]

The tropes of sympathetic, affective communication that telemobility notates regularly turn on some rendition of Galvani's figure of animal electricity or, as Akira Mizuta Lippit has more recently theorized it, of the "electric animal." "In its most basic manifestation," writes Lippit in *Electric Animal: Toward a Rhetoric of Wildlife* (2000), "electricity determines the currency of technological communication."[6] Not unlike Galvani, Lippit is compelled by the vitalistic notion that the electric, or affective, act of technological communication is paradigmatically animal. Lippit identifies the rhetorical structure of the modern technological media, particularly photography and cinema, with animals' "transferential" mode of communication (191). "Transference is the means by which nonverbal energy circulates within the world," writes Lippit (191). It consists in "the rapid movement of affect from one entity to another," a direct, intangible exchange of "pure energy" between bodies (186, 196). This pathic mobility signals a power of communication that is simultaneously virtual and animal; indeed, in the figure of the electric animal, virtuality and animality no longer represent contradictory or dialectical poles (of spirit and matter) but become synonyms for a communicability that is spontaneous rather than mediated.

The figure of the electric animal encompasses Lippit's claim, first, that affect constitutes a prediscursive mode of communication that is quintessentially animal and, second, his suggestion that those technological media that communicate affectively are therefore animal in their rhetorical structure. One of the aims of this chapter is to show that the conflation of virtuality and animality in the figure of the electric animal has been deployed to spectacular effect by cultural discourses with a vested interest in occulting political economies of telecommunication.

When technological communication in the West is fetishistically identified with the "semiotic capacity" of animals—that is, with what Lippit describes as "a 'communicability or transitivity' that is affective rather
than discursive"—it no longer appears to be contingent on material relations of production and power (30, 49).

Yet even as Lippit himself risks reinforcing a fetishism of communication, he also initiates the important work of tracing a discursive
genealogy of the idea of the electric animal. Although animals have
been systematically denied logos in discourses of Western modernity,
Lippit surveys a host of thinkers who have been more than willing to
attribute to animals a quasi-magical power to communicate with other
bodies over long distances through the enigmatic transmission of affect. From Franz Anton Mesmer's experiments in animal magnetism
to Sigmund Freud's formulation of the unconscious as a terrain of animal drives and Joseph Breuer's configuration of hypnoid states, Lippit
traces a series of iterations of the figure of the electric animal that reveal
that, far from universal, it constitutes a decidedly modern, European
object of fascination. Within the discourses surveyed by Lippit, moreover, animals' lack of logos and purported surplus of electric affect have
been formulated as an inability to anticipate or have knowledge of
death, indeed, to die. He recapitulates the figure of the undying animal
as it accumulates across discourses of Western philosophy, science, and
psychoanalysis: "Because animals are unable to achieve the finitude of
death, they are also destined to remain 'live,' like electrical wires, along
the transferential tracks. Unable to die, they move constantly from one
body to another, one system to another" (192). A canonical figure of the
undead animal takes shape across heterogeneous texts that in different
ways consign animals to a spectral existence outside of the possibility of
language, time, and history—in short, outside of the horizon of death.
Like unconscious wishes, writes Lippit, animals "are indestructible,
undying, they are recycled constantly throughout the world" (191).

A metaphysical rather than material figure of animal life emerges
out of the general philosophical consensus, in the discourses surveyed
by Lippit, that "the animal never dies: it merely vanishes" (53). As with
the indifference to the sacrifice of amphibians in Galvani's laboratory,
the biological death of an animal is rendered epiphenomenal by this

logic. Rather than implicating the figure of the undying animal in the metaphorical and material means of capital, Lippit himself ultimately subscribes to the idea that "the animal" constitutes an indestructible current transcending biological life and death: "Undying, animals simply expire, transpire, shift their animus to other animal bodies" (187).

Foucault, by contrast, helps to bring the figure of the undying animal back into political focus as a means and effect of knowledge/power, recalling that it is in the coemergent discourses of biology and economy in the nineteenth century that "the animal maintains its existence on the frontiers of life and death."[7] It is arguably no coincidence that the animal "discovers fantastic new powers in the nineteenth century," as Foucault puts it.[8] In its new indifference to the material line between life and death, the figure of the animal shares the logic of another spectral ontology: capital. It was the spectrality of capital that Marx arguably sought to capture in his description of the "necromancy" of the market.[9] In likening commodity production to the dark, magical art of raising the dead, Marx sought to return a measure of horror to an abstract system of exchange value indifferent to "natural" systems of use value and to the embodied species value of things. In another startling use of metaphor in his early writings, Marx described money as "the galvano-chemical power of society," an equalizer that "makes impossibilities fraternize."[10] Whereas Marx metaphorically deployed Galvani's discourse of electrical communication to critique the mystique of money, this chapter sets out to investigate how tropes of animal electricity have also been deployed to hegemonic effect, exciting a fetishism of technological communication and, more broadly, a metaphysics of capital.

The Fetishism of Communication

In his seminal book *Primitive Culture* (1871), the so-called father of anthropology, Edward B. Tylor, wrote: "I will venture to assert that the scientific conceptions current in my own schoolboy days, of heat and electricity as invisible fluids passing in and out of solid bodies, are ideas which reproduce with extreme closeness the special doctrine of Fetishism."[11] Tylor considered the idea of animal electricity a residual

trace of "primitive" culture within the otherwise enlightened culture of
Europe, a culture distinguished by its scientific rationality from "lower
races" that Tylor saw as stalled in an ostensibly childlike stage of animistic belief.[12] I am acutely aware that this chapter risks repeating the
claim, represented by Tylor (and, indeed, by Marx), that fetishistic belief is a primitive practice that can be exorcized from social life, a goal
that, as Tylor's work shows, has been historically complicit in Western
ideologies of progress and a racist hierarchy of cultures.

The goal of exorcizing fetishism, of seeking to demystify social relations between people and things, has been most recently problema-
tized within the humanities by scholars associated with the emergent
field of "thing theory." In the company of other thing theorists such as
Bill Brown and Michael Taussig, W. J. T. Mitchell challenges the traditional anthropological presumption that only "primitives, children,
the masses, the illiterate, the uncritical, the illogical, the 'Other'" fall
prey to the animistic belief that pictures and signs are living.[13] He
contends that the belief that pictures and signs "are something like
life-forms, driven by desire and appetites" (6), a belief routinely identified with so-called savage cultures, in fact pervades cultures of capitalist modernity and postmodernity. Moreover, Mitchell cautions against
"the ineluctable tendency of criticism itself to pose as an iconoclastic
practice, a labor of demystification and pedagogical exposure of false
images" (8).

While I would very much like to avoid reenacting the iconoclastic
claim of being able to pull back a veil of false animal images from
telecommunications culture to reveal an underlying reality, I also want
to suggest that the current moment demands a rethinking, rather than
relinquishment, of the labor of demystification. In the introduction to
this book I offered "distortion" as a figure for a dialectical practice that
reflects the insights of immanent critique, refusing to privilege either
materialism or idealism as an oppositional vantage point from which
to expose the "lie" of the other. Yet while distortion acknowledges that
an immanent field of power does not admit of an outside from which
to launch a critical exposé, it nevertheless names a practice that remains committed to code switching back and forth between symbolic
and material economies of rendering (that is, modes of production of

animal capital) as a strategic means of antagonizing capitalism from within. The practice of distortion particularly chimes with the aims of this chapter insofar as telemobility represents the promise of a pure act of communication freed of that mundane domain of material transmission and reception in which distortion can be said to occur. Whether a deliberate manipulation or an unexpected glitch in the normally smooth machinery of transmission, distortion draws attention to the materiality of communication that is disavowed in telemobility discourse. However, it does so with the consciousness that the materiality it serves to recall is itself always a metaphorically mediated, and therefore "distorted," reality.

While the influence of immanent critique in contesting and complicating the "labor of demystification" cannot be underestimated, Mitchell's own picture theory arguably reveals the alternate pitfalls of recent engagements with fetishism that minimize questions of political economy in favor of making room for the irreducible mystery and alterity of things. After cautioning against forms of iconoclastic criticism that fail to recognize that they themselves are a "symptom of the life of images" and proposing, instead, "a mode of criticism that [does] not dream of getting beyond images," Mitchell arguably goes too far in entertaining a new spirit of acceptance of fetishism (8, 9). Imputing "desire" to things themselves in an example of fetishistic good faith, he distances forms of analysis that, while acknowledging the impossibility of ever "getting beyond images," would nevertheless insist that fetishism continue to be interrogated as an effect of power. If Mitchell swings too far toward the alternative he offers to demystifying critique, it is not so much because he invites cultural critics to stop censoring the "magical belief" (7) that animated things are living subjects, but because he encourages readers to personify pictures as *subaltern* subjects who embody a profound lack of power. Invoking Gayatri Spivak's work on subaltern women, Mitchell proposes that we "shift the question from what pictures *do* to what they *want*, from power to desire, from the model of the dominant power to be opposed, to the model of the subaltern to be interrogated or (better) to be invited to speak" (33).

The trope of the living image-subject who lacks or "wants" power is, Mitchell avers, "'only' a metaphor, an analogy that must have some limits" (10). Yet the analogy becomes increasingly naturalistic as he pursues its elaboration. Although Mitchell initially poses the subaltern woman as a model for pictures or things as "wanting" subjects (in itself a proposition deserving far more than the passing glance I am giving it here), it emerges that *animals* ultimately model "the subaltern status of images" for Mitchell (36). He invites readers to consider the "species identity" of images, asking us, "Suppose, for instance, that the desires of pictures were modeled on the desires of animals?" (36).

In identifying the fetishistic appeal of picture-things in the current era of global capitalism with the desires of animals, Mitchell associates that appeal with the utmost alterity and innocence of power. That "things" can actually be produced as life forms within current biotechnological modes of production—that the fetishism of commodities takes on a startlingly literal dimension as the reproduction of capital becomes identical with the reproduction of animal life itself (Mitchell himself foregrounds the cloned sheep Dolly as an example of this historical moment)—would seem to bespeak the urgency of developing new kinds of demystificatory critique adequate to the interrogation of the relationship between fetishism and biopower in the present. Yet it is in full view of Dolly that Mitchell chooses to shift the analysis of fetishism away from a critical vocabulary of power and toward a vocabulary of desire, ultimately the alterity of animal desire.[14] In metaphorizing pictures as animals who gaze at us across a "gulf unbridged by language" (a phrase that he borrows from John Berger), Mitchell replaces iconoclastic criticism with a form of cultural critique that risks serving as an accomplice to the tautological production of animal capital.[15]

In between the dual pitfalls of presuming to exorcize fetishistic belief and of infusing commodity-things with the alterity of animal desire, this chapter negotiates a critique of telemobility. To confront the fantasy of bodiless, virtual communication that telemobility notates, I will implicate it in animal rendering, in the double sense of the word that I have been exploring throughout this book. The fetishism of communication that telemobility notates can be shown to turn on the metaphorical figure of the electric animal *and* on the carnal medium of animal flesh, as Galvani's experiments suggest. The promise of virtual communication reaches a mimetic pitch—most persuasive, and at the same time, most contradictory—when the animal body is presented as its transparent, or natural, sign. In what follows, I seek to distort telemobility's promise of "painless transmission" by routing it through three historical scenarios that recall the material relations of power on which virtual mobilities are contingent.[16]

"Monstration"

While telemobility's promise of instantaneous, affective communication across bodies separated in space or time is arguably epitomized by neoliberal discourses of global telecommunication in the present, as I have suggested, it can already be glimpsed in Galvani's early experiments in animal electricity. The fetishism of communication played out on the flesh of Galvani's "animal conductors" subsequently cathects onto the promise of virtual mobility sparked by a series of technological media of communication: early telegraphs and telephones, the cinematic apparatus, mobile phones, and wireless Internet devices. Without wanting to claim that they are historically continuous in their material-semiotic means and effects, the scenarios that I develop in this chapter can nevertheless be constellated within a genealogy inasmuch as in all three a fantasy of painless communication reveals its contingency on the metaphorical and material rendering of animals.

I have already pointed to the first scene, laid out in Galvani's laboratory. The muscular spasms that Galvani incited in the flesh of animals was evidence, he believed, of an electrifying communication with invisible "animal spirits" (68). Nearly a century after Galvani's theory of animal electricity was discredited as mere pseudoscience, Thomas Edison fused the technological media to a different "animal conductor" in a public performance designed to demonstrate the instantaneous, and deadly, effects of electrical current. In January of 1903, Edison helped choreograph the public electrocution of Topsy, a six-ton Indian elephant on exhibit at Coney Island's Luna Park. Topsy was felled with 6,600 volts of alternating current to propagandize the mortal dangers of George Westinghouse's competing system of electricity. The electrocution of Topsy amplified the effect of the earlier execution of

William Kemler in North America's first electric chair, instituted in New York in 1890 according to Edison's design and with his assurances that a bolt of alternating current equaled instant (that is, painless) death.[17]

The showdown with Topsy not only promoted the idea that corporal punishment had found its apogee in the electrical switch; it also came to constitute ten seconds of some of the earliest live footage captured by emergent moving picture cameras. Topsy's execution served simultaneously as a public demonstration of the effects of alternating current and as a promotion piece for the cinematic branch of Edison's technological empire. While Topsy was the animal with the most cultural and physical capital to be sacrificed to technological advancement in the Edison era, numerous cats, dogs, calves, and sheep (as well as at least one horse) were similarly "westinghoused" at Edison's West Orange laboratory in New Jersey.[18]

A century after Edison's filmed electrocution of Topsy, the figure of the electric animal has been rearticulated in yet another demonstration of virtual communication, this time on behalf of a telecommunications corporation in the present. At the turn of the twenty-first century, Canada's second-largest private telecommunications company, Telus Mobility Inc., launched a concerted advertising campaign zoometaphorizing the powers of its mobile phones, high-speed Internet services, and telecommunications products as animal.[19] The live species continuously streaming through the Telus campaign function as visual metaphors of a charismatic power of communication flowing though all living things, including the commodity-things (mobile phones) that are vitalistically likened to them.[20] In its rendition of the idea of the electric animal, Telus excites belief in a wireless world in which global communication constitutes an innate animal capability rather than a political economy embroiled in global relations of material-semiotic production. Later in this chapter, I implicate the virtual mobility promised by the Telus corporation in the neocolonial resource and war economies of the eastern Congo in an effort to recall telecommunication's violent conditions and effects.

Borrowing from the film theory of André Gadreault, I will refer to these three scenes as "monstrations." Gaudreault distinguishes between two narrative layers of film. The first layer of narrativity, which he considers technologically built in or "innate," he terms "monstration."[21] This innate and "spontaneous" narrativity accrues simply to the physical "articulation of photographs which constitutes the shot" (72). On this level, prior even to any discursive content, "every shot tells a story merely by means of iconic analogy" (71). Narrativity at the level of monstration, which as Gaudreault claims is "bound solely and indissolubly to *mimesis*," consists in technological articulation as a physical act of *showing* prior to the signifying act of *telling*, which constitutes the second layer of narrativity (72).[22]

It is admittedly risky to detach Gaudrealt's theory of monstration from its specific object (the early cinema of attractions) and apply it to the disparate spectacles staged by Galvani, Edison, and Telus. I do so, however, because the notion of monstration helps to further illuminate the logic that links three animal spectacles, which are historically and culturally incommensurable on so many other levels. It is Gaudreault's formulation of monstration as a mode of mimesis that operates via "showing" rather than "telling" that emboldens me to critically adapt it to the scenes traced in this chapter. What is at stake here, however, is not exposing a logic of mimesis operative in the physical suturing of images into a narrative series but the logic by which the animal body is rendered a transparent or demonstrative sign of technological communication. The animal can be called monstrative insofar as it, too, has been identified with a prediscursive mode of mimesis. As Lippit suggests, while animals have been barred from logos and the domain of the symbolic in discourses of Western modernity (from "telling"), they have nevertheless been conceived as eloquent in their mute acts of physical signing and their sympathetic powers of affect (in "showing"). The scenarios I have introduced around Galvani, Edison, and Telus might be termed monstrations in the sense that they present the prediscursive mimesis of the animal body as an iconic analogy of the affective immediacy of technological communication; they metaphorically and materially present technological communication as an "animal utterance."[23]

The idea that a technological power of virtual communication becomes visible through the material analogy of animal life presupposes that animal life is itself transparent and that animals cannot but utter or "show" the biological truth of their own bodies. The notion that animals are capable only of a physical "system of signaling" and a "prewired response" saturates not only the Cartesian worldview inherited by Galvani but persists, as Derrida argues, in contemporary philosophical, psychoanalytical, and scientific discourses.[24] It is at work, suggests Derrida, in Jacques Lacan's claim that animals cannot lie because lying requires that one be a "subject of the signifier."[25] As this chapter will argue, moreover, Galvani, Edison, and Telus have coerced the displays of involuntary animal affect that they then present as transparent evidence of the spontaneity of technological communication. Calling the scenes examined in this chapter monstrations draws attention to their motivated *productions* of animal affect and reveals that affect is, at least in these instances, very much an effect of power.

In its partial rhyme with *monstrous, monstration* also brings the pathological into view. The pathological has come to popularly connote the affective sickness of being unable to feel the pain of others, and as such hints at violent contradictions in telemobility's promise of "painless transmission." However, the pathological carries other senses as well. Cary Wolfe notes that the association of the pathological with the realm of "the animal, the bodily, the contingent" is one of the legacies of a Kantian project of Enlightenment: "The Enlightenment (as completed by Kant) consists in the desubstantialization of the subject, its 'purification' from its substantial origin in nature, the animal, the bodily, the contingent, in what Kant calls, in *The Critique of Practical Reason,* the 'pathological.'"[26] The contradiction between the sympathetic mode of purely virtual communication that Galvani claimed to "monstrate" and its actual, pathological means appears to have been blatant in his laboratory, where animals were rendered under the logic of the specter ("animal spirits") *and* the logic of the specimen (frog legs). In Edison's staged electrocution of Topsy, the animal was sacrificed to a monstration of the instantaneous effects of electricity in a similarly undisguised exercise of pathological power. However, in the early twenty-first-century advertising campaign of Telus Mobility Inc., the pathological conditions and effects of virtual communication are nowhere to be seen. Following the mediological premise of Régis Debray—*"No more than there is any innocent medium can there be pain-*

less transmission"[27]—my critique of the Telus campaign will ask where the displaced substance of the sign of telemobility is to be located.[28] Where is the historical flesh, still visible in Galvani and Edison's operating theaters, that carries the terrestrial burden of clairvoyant exchange?

Luigi Galvani

If at first glance Galvani's laboratory etchings and scientific notations seem consistent with late Renaissance traditions, closer examination suggests that Galvani in fact prefigured the modern biopolitics of a Dr. Frankenstein. What Mary Shelley would fictionalize in *Franken-stein* had already been attempted by Galvani: a necromancy with dead nature's carnal parts and an obsession with achieving knowledge and control of life via knowledge and control of electricity. Etchings of Galvani's lab show bodies in pieces—frog and animal parts dangling from hooks, pinned to dissection plates, or suspended in jars of fluid—but also the detached human hand of science rhetorically executing and pointing (see Figure 6). Parts stand in for wholes in the metonymic discourse of science recorded by Galvani. Frog legs, which Galvani's etchings show stretched and flattened on a series of zinc plates littering the surface of the operation table, are presented as two-dimensional figures. Tables and plates are, by turn, viewed through the mimetic plane of the medical etching itself in a reiteration of demonstrative surfaces. In fixing a piece of nature on a plate to render a transparent impression of life, the aesthetic ideology of Galvani predicted that of the daguerrotype, the photograph, and the cinematic frame, each of which has required briefer periods of "contact" with the life mimetically impressed on the representational plane. In Galvani's discourse, the dead, deductive parts of specimens are presented as mere physical proxies standing in for the invisible animal being summoned in his scientific séance: electricity. The piecemeal animals on Galvani's lab table are therefore not the ultimate object of the scientific gaze, which is invited to pierce through the flesh of "brute beasts" to the phantom force of animal electricity inspiring their muscular movements.[29]

Physiology was beginning to gain legitimacy as a scientific discipline around the period of Galvani's early experiments in the 1780s.

Figure 6. Luigi Galvani's own etching of his laboratory, from Commentary on the Effect of Electricity on Muscular Motion *(1791).*

Just as the study of animal physiology conditioned the emergence of photographic and cinematic culture a century later (through the time-motion studies of Eadweard Muybridge and Étienne-Jules Marey), so did it support the emergence of a discourse of telecommunication that can be traced back to Galvani. Containing the "germ of modern wireless telegraphy" and constituting an early instance of telecommunications discourse, the case of Galvani thus gives a first glimpse into technological communication's contradictory contingency on metaphorical and material renderings of animal nature.[30]

Galvani was by no means alone in the occult pursuit of electricity as an invisible elixir of life. However, he was the most insistent in isolating animal bodies as the favored medium and repository of electricity.[31] In scientific debate with Alessandro Volta regarding his opposing theory of contact electricity (from which the voltaic pile would be derived), Galvani declared that Volta "attributes everything to metals, nothing to the animal; I, everything to the latter, nothing to the former."[32] Unlike Volta, Galvani located the source of electricity in metaphysical rather than physical nature, and more particularly in "the obscure nature of animal spirits, long sought in vain" (68). What disappeared from Galvani's discourse was the historical force—the profoundly physical techniques—that conditioned the wondrous electrical events he was able to host over animal bodies. When Galvani touched exposed nerves with a metal scalpel, inducing "excited motions" in the monstrous half-bodies of his headless frogs, he framed the contractions as a sympathetic call and response of animal spirits rather than as a confession incited from the flesh with the help of hooks and metal armatures (27). Despite what must have been Galvani's intimacy with the visceral substance of animal life—through the logistics of procuring and disposing of a seemingly endless stream of animal subjects, quelling the smell, texture, and resistance of bodies operated on half-alive or freshly dead, excluding pain from the hermeneutics of the animal reflex and nausea from his own reactions to his test subjects' rapid "decay and rot" (35)— the manhandling that mediated his metaphysics of animal electricity recedes from view. Galvani's belief that electricity is sympathetically channeled through "animal conductors" blinded both him and his viewers, it would seem, to the seemingly obvious role that pathological force played in provoking a "show" of virtual communication.

In what is considered the core of his commentary, "The Effects of Atmospheric Electricity on Muscular Motion," Galvani claims that fits of motion sprung in frog legs during an electrical storm were evidence of a sympathetic correspondence between electrical spirits resident in an invisible animal fluid and "like" agencies in nature. In an anterior realization of possibly *the* canonical trope of technological modernity, the electrical animation of the "spectre" assembled by Dr. Frankenstein out of parts collected from the "dissecting room and the slaughterhouse,"[33] Galvani erected a lightning rod on his parapet "when a storm arose in the sky" (36). To the rod Galvani "attached by their nerves either prepared frogs, or prepared legs of warm animals" (36). He notes that "as often as the lightning broke out, at the same moment of time all of the muscles fell into violent and multiple contractions" (36). Galvani took the results as evidence that an "inherent animal electricity" invisibly permeated the universe (41).

The ability of electricity to provoke "excited motions" in convincing mimicry of autonomous life soon became known as "galvanism," a popularization of Galvani's science attributed to his nephew, Giovanni

Aldini. Aldini is known for conducting electrical monstrations for the "admiration and pleasure" of more than select medical practitioners and audiences.[34] As Bernard Cohen notes, Aldini

> shifted the sober discussion of the new science from the laboratory, the academy, and the pages of scientific journals to the arena of public entertainment, performing bizarre spectacles as a professional showman. That is, Aldini became a mountebank, demonstrating the effects of his uncle's discovery by electrically animating the head of a calf severed from its body, causing the eyes, tongue, and mouth to move or twitch.[35]

In riveting performances orchestrated by Aldini, monstrations of animal electricity normally limited to the extortion of lifelike effects from dead animals graduated to the extortion of similar effects from human corpses. Galvani electrified spectators when he made a criminal "recently dead from a public hanging" sit bolt upright on the scientific stage.[36] Through the performance of "animal electricity," the mutilated or dead body was dissociated from the life it could continue to "sign" through muscular motions; the body was merely a conductor of a life force that existed independent of pathological substance. Though it never fulfilled its practitioners' hopes of reanimating the dead, the spectacle of galvanism nevertheless played an important role in producing life as a mimetic effect indifferent to the biological distinction between living and dead matter.

It is no surprise that electrical monstrations eventually crossed the speciesist divide in Aldini's entertainments; all along Galvani was intent on medically applying his theory of animal electricity to human health. His discourse of animal electricity simultaneously allowed for absolute distinctions between animal and human (the only ideological stance capable of justifying experiments on animals that would be unthinkable on a European humanity, with the exception, among other things, of criminal corpses) *and* the collapse of physiological differences between bodies as different as humans and amphibians (what was tested on frog legs could be therapeutically used on humans). This species ambiguity infects Galvani's lab drawings; the aesthetic tradition of cross-hatched etching carried over from Renaissance renderings of anatomy inevitably anthropomorphized the vertical, dangling frog

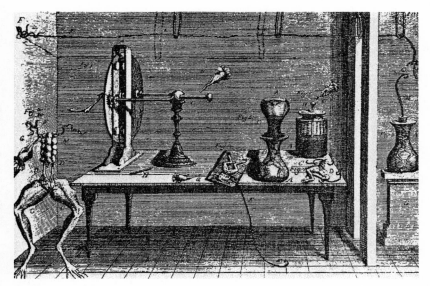

Figure 7. The ambiguous amphibian. Etching from Luigi Galvani's Commentary on the Effect of Electricity on Muscular Motion *(1791).*

legs. The frog's classically rendered thighs and calves are, uncomfortably, virtually indistinguishable from a human's, emerging as recognizably amphibian only at the feet (see Figure 7).

Thus Galvani soon began applying electrical stimulations rigorously tested on frogs to patients with nervous—that is, electrical—stagnations. Electricity, claimed Galvani, was "an aid for dislodging, dissolving and expelling from the nerves principles stagnant and impacted in them."[37] Significantly, Galvani saw electricity as a cure especially for patients suffering from stiffness of movement (rheumatism) and paralysis. It is tempting to read Galvani's therapeutic answer to physical stiffness and nervous stagnation (and his nephew's spectacular inducement of signs of life in the criminal corpse) as sites where medical culture reinforced a rising market liberalism seeking unobstructed flows of capital through the larger social body. Aldini's demonstration that the dead could be raised, or at least be made to continue "signing" life, historically coincided, that is, with the intensifying subsumption of life itself to capital's abstract law of motion.

Up to this point, I have argued that Galvani's construction of communication as a spirit session hinged on the metaphysical correspondence he monstrated between animals and electricity. Yet the "sympathetic magic" of virtual, long-distance communication was also contingent on a material exercise of "contact magic," a close-range manipulation of a piece of the body to establish a pathological connection.[38] For Galvani, who believed that electricity was an imperceptible nervous fluid most concentrated in animal tissue, the biological fluids of a frog became the chosen substance of electrical communication. That is, frog fluid was included as a fetishistic, material link in Galvani's metaphorical discourse of animal electricity. It is arguable that the flesh that Galvani dangled as bait to call forth "animal spirits" was inescapably fetishistic, *especially* when the hand of science seemed to indifferently point past it. For even in piercing through his specimens to the imperceptible "nervous powers" behind them, Galvani fixated on animals as electricity's most charged depositories.[39] His fixation narrowed in on the body of the frog, and again, on the specific substance that Galvani believed channeled invisible animal spirits: their bodily fluids. In his design of the battery as a technology for conducting and storing electricity, Galvani therefore placed frog fluids between two metals according to his belief that they were the source of its electrical charge.

The history of the technological media is packed with similarly talismanic incorporations of animal parts. Jonathan Crary recalls Descartes's instructions to use a "bovine eye" for the lens when constructing a camera obscura.[40] Martin Jay notes a similar substitution of a cow eyeball for a human one in the "famous scene of the slit eyeball in the Surrealist masterpiece *Un chien Andalou* by Dali and Buñuel in 1928."[41] Avita Ronell recalls the telephone's debt to animal "organ transplant[s]," from the "tympanum of pig bladder" in early Chinese telephones to the fur of the stuffed family cat used by Thomas Watson (partner of Alexander Graham Bell) "as an exciter for a frictional electric machine."[42] The history of the battery brings into sight more of a transfusion than a transplant but one that all the same marked the site of a physiological transfer of powers from animal to technological media.

Alessandro Volta later proved that it was the presence of heterogeneous metals that, with the help of a moist material, conducted electricity—not animal spirits. Volta replaced the talismanic fluids of Galvani's battery with other (less fetishistic) wet materials, initiating a
chain of material displacements that make it harder to discern how
animal signs and substances are encrypted in technology's very "stuff
of inscription," in the words of Lisa Gitelman.[43] As I continue to track
the promise of telemobility across the twentieth and twenty-first centuries, the pathological will not always be seen to lie in as palpable
proximity to the sympathetic as it did in Galvani's discourse.

Although Volta eventually debunked the scientific credibility of
Galvani's theory of animal electricity, variants of his theory would return alongside revolutions in "mediated communication"[44] in the nineteenth century, reappearing in the belief in the spiritual telegraph and
in the popular sense that the telegraph and telephone could operate
"both sides of the life-and-death switchboard."[45] As Jeffrey Sconce
notes, early in the twentieth century *Popular Science Monthly* declared
that through the emerging wireless media of communication "the nerves
of the whole world [were], so to speak, being bound together, so that a
touch in one country [was] transmitted instantly to a far-distant one."[46]
This is an image that AT&T would capitalize on with its invitation, in
the 1930s, to "reach out and touch somebody" (subsequently popular-
ized as "keeping in touch" via the technological media). Telemobility
discourse then, as now, has constituted a promise of virtual "touch"
shed of the pathological body. Yet often materially underpinning the
promise of virtual connection, as Galvani's lab drawings reveal, has
been the body of an animal.

Thomas Edison

Galvani's wet battery was in both a literal and a figurative sense an animal "crypt," physically storing the talismanic fluids of what Galvani
believed to be the electric animal as well as encoding a belief in animal
spirits.[47] Thomas Alva Edison was similarly fascinated with the possibility of electrical storage, working for years on the design for an alkaline

battery. However, it is not the battery that encrypts Edison's discourse on the electric animal but another recording-storage apparatus of which he was the father figure: the motion picture.[48]

As I have already mentioned, among the first early subjects to be immured on celluloid by the Edison Manufacturing Company was a sober "actuality"—*Electrocuting an Elephant* (1903). The black and white, single-shot, silent moving picture shows smoke rising up Topsy's elephantine legs as she is administered a bolt of alternating current through electrodes attached to her feet (see Figure 8). Smoke and her slowly teetering body are the only signs of the technological communication of death captured by Edison's movie camera; the smell of burning flesh and the sounds of the Coney Island crowd that gathered on a Sunday to watch her electrocution are outside of its scope. A New York newspaper reported that Topsy died without "a trumpet or a groan," bereft of the animal cry that might have negatively scored her physical trial as she was being suspended in a silent reproduction of her death.[49]

In *Electrocuting an Elephant,* the narrative arc consists solely in the electrical felling of an animal. The seemingly transparent monstration of animal death was in fact calculated by Edison to communicate several ideologically pointed messages: the deadliness of the Westinghouse current coursing through Topsy, the ability of Edison's moving picture camera to mimetically capture reality (appearing to passively record rather than actively render the "actuality" before it), and finally, the painless immediacy of both electrical and cinematic affect. In his study of the technological relays linking bodies and machines around this period in American culture, Mark Seltzer draws attention to the mixed sympathetic and pathological promise of electrical current or, as he puts it, "the violent immediacy promised by communication and control technologies operated by the electric signal or button": "The electric switch, ready to hand, promises to reconnect the interrupted links between conception and execution, agency and expression. Such a violent immediacy posits an identity between signal and act and an identity between communication and execution—'execution' in its several senses."[50] The "violent immediacy" of Edison's electrical and cinematic execution of Topsy, like Galvani's experiments on frog legs, makes visible the often overlooked fact that animal sacrifice constituted something

Figure 8. Film stills from one of the Edison Manufacturing Company's earliest moving pictures, Electrocuting an Elephant *(1903).*

of a founding symbolic and material gesture of early electrical and cinematic culture. At the same time, it served to normativize the spectacle of animal death as a means of monstrating the powers of the new technological media. Lippit writes: "Modernity sustains . . . the disappearance of animals as a constant state. That is . . . animals never *entirely* vanish. Rather, they exist in a state of *perpetual vanishing*. Animals enter a new economy of being during the modern period, one that is no longer sacrificial in the traditional sense of the term but, considering modern technological media generally and the cinema more specifically, *spectral*."[51] In *Electrocuting an Elephant*, however, the cinematic apparatus is glimpsed not as a sympathetic preserver of the trace of vanishing animal life, as Lippit later formulates it, but as an active agent in the sacrifice of an animal and her encryption within cinema's spectral "economy of being."

The historical plot thickens when we recall that the celluloid physically supporting *Electrocuting an Elephant* was first developed by the Celluloid Manufacturing Company in the 1870s as a substitute for ivory and only subsequently developed by George Eastman into the stuff of flexible film. As I noted in chapter 2, onto the celluloid of flexible film, Eastman machines then applied a see-through photographic gelatin emulsion derived from the remains of industrial slaughter, an emulsion necessary to the literal development of early cinematic images. The film stock supporting *Electrocuting an Elephant* thus bears a *sensible* trace of cinema's contingency on animal sacrifice. It was onto the translucent animal gelatin of film stock that the electrocuted image of Topsy was seared, trebling the film's convoluted relationship to animal rendering. The sympathetic "alliance between animals and cinema" that Lippit theorizes is further troubled by this sensible trace of sacrifice (25).

Edison had associated death by electrocution with cinematic communication prior to the ten seconds of silent footage composing *Electrocuting an Elephant*. In "Execution of Czolgosz" (1901), Edwin S. Porter's camera work had probed the walls of a penitentiary and pulled viewers toward the terrible vanishing point of the freshly instituted electric chair. Yet "Execution of Czolgosz" was a special-effects restaging of the electrocution of President William McKinley's assassin rather than an "actuality"; inasmuch as it did not stake a cultural ideology of technological communication on the transparent body language of an animal, it was not a monstration in the sense in which I have been using Gaudreault's term. Nevertheless, the attraction of cinematic and electrical power to the crux of discipline and punishment helps me to mutually implicate them in the emergence of biopower theorized by Foucault.

While modern punishment remains corporeal, writes Foucault, "in its most severe forms [it] no longer addresses itself to the body" but to the soul.[52] Because the effects of electrocution were designed to be contained within the invisible interior of the subject's body, ideally leaving no visible mark of violence, it promised to take the disciplinary accomplishments of the guillotine and the noose to a heightened level of subtlety. Lethal injection was appealing for the same reason and was already under consideration in the Edison era. In accordance with the productive impetus of biopower, moreover, the electrocution of Topsy would also generate a series of "positive effects" for the agencies that collaborated in staging it.[53] Her death would demonstrate that capital punishment could be administered in a humane, sensitive manner, supporting Foucault's contention that the sovereign power to sentence subjects to the "pain of death" was shifting to a model of biopower in which the state was increasingly interested in subtracting pain from the operation and delivering a sentence of death only in the positive cause of optimizing "life in general."[54] If Lippit is right in suggesting that "technology becomes a subject when it gains an unconscious" and that an "artificial unconscious is established by the incorporation of vanishing animals," cinema also fetishistically came to life through Edison's deadly exchange with Topsy.[55]

Turning Topsy into the sacrificial subject of a technological monstration nevertheless proved a risky—and far from smoothly executed— modern project. By killing three abusive trainers, Topsy had asserted her own willful subjectivity and earned herself something of a reputation; she was a subordinated but not wholly subordinate body caught in the webs of nature, race, and labor in the "electric Eden" where she lived.[56] The 250,000 incandescent Edison lightbulbs that lit up Coney Island's Luna Park when it opened in the early 1880s attracted visitors to a wonderland in which displays of exotic animals, capital, and electricity blurred into a metaphorical excess, generating the spiritualistic and libidinal promise in which Luna Park trafficked. The unprecedented shows of electric light, the symbolic and somatic thrills of riding on the back of an Indian elephant such as Topsy or spending the night in the hind leg of the Elephant Hotel, of riding a roller coaster or being strapped into "the electric chair" for a mock fatal shock, constituted some of the park's dizzying mimetics.[57]

The owners of Luna Park, Frederick Thompson and Skip Dundy, used Topsy and other elephants in their private herd to haul and hoist materials during the park's monumental construction. Yet they were not content to capitalize on the physical strength of the captive animals; elephants worked double duty for amusement capital both as labor power and as phantasmatic support. Topsy was therefore also presented as an animal spectacle on whom paying visitors could take a ride, sitting in a tasseled pagoda astride her back that was a piece of colonial aesthetica capping the fantasy of foreignness cultivated by Luna Park. In her double exploitation as labor and as spectacle, Topsy was subject to the violent contradictions and historical predicaments of the black picaninny-minstrels whose generic name she had been given, a name that racially typecast African American slave laborers as natural entertainers whose antics were more animal than human.[58] Though she was an elephant from India, giving her the name Topsy (the name of the black slave girl in Harriet Beecher Stowe's *Uncle Tom's Cabin*) allowed Thompson and Dundy to present her as an African specimen and to capitalize on familiar racist stereotypes in American culture. Topsy, the ill-tempered elephant of Luna Park, was expected to embody a fantasy of animal otherness that could not be configured without a supplementary fantasy of racial difference, racism and speciesism relying on each other's phantasmatic supports as intercalated discourses of difference. Thompson and Dundy's original plan to lynch their disobedient charge—though rejected due to opposition from the American Society for the Prevention of Cruelty to Animals (ASPCA)—would have consummated the interactivating imaginaries of species and race preyed on by amusement capital. Topsy's electrocution managed, nonetheless, to make a spectacle out of both an impudent animal and a racial chimera.

As animals like Topsy were being transfigured, through the fantastic convergences of money and electrical power reified by Luna Park,
into a valuable symbolic as well as material resource, they were subjected to new ethological treatments training them to be the obedient
body content of circuses, public zoos, amusement parks, and photographic and filmic events. Animals were becoming subject to biopower,
to forms of positive economic and emotional investment designed to
mold them into docile, willing performers of capitalist spectacles. The
elephant with possibly the most symbolic currency in this period was
Jumbo, purchased by P. T. Barnum from the London Zoo for $10,000
in 1882. (Jumbo would be accidentally hit by the Northern Trunk freight
train in Canada in 1885 at another fatal intersection of technological
mobility and animal life.) Elephants like Jumbo and Topsy had to be
materially trained not only to physically labor for capital but to perform new symbolic functions demanded by the cultural exhibits and
amusements of the Edison era. However, Topsy was what a journalist
in New York's *Commercial Advertiser* called a "Bad Elephant" in a story
covering her execution.[59] By killing two handlers, Topsy showed her
resistance to the pressures and often brutal prompts used to physically
adapt her to serve the symbolic economy of the Forepaugh Circus,
whose owners had first brought her to North America as captive animal capital. After being sold to Thompson and Dundy, Topsy continued to express agency and animosity by trampling a third handler,
who peppered her daily training with vicious acts such as feeding her a
lit cigarette. His act suggests that Topsy's handlers may themselves
have been "bad," that is, not yet in line with emerging ethological sciences of animal behavior and communication, with new principles of
sympathetic animal management, and with the fervor for interspecies
intimacy that would make primatologists such as Dian Fossey and
Jane Goodall popular heroes in the latter half of the twentieth century.
Only the handler responsible for Topsy directly before her electrocution
modeled the properly modern love of the animal trainer by refusing to
lead her to the platform where she would be executed.

One hundred years after Topsy responded with agency to her cruel
taunts, captured wildlife seems to have far fewer reasons for repaying

the care of human trainers with seemingly unwarranted violence. In 2003, when Roy Horn of the renowned Siegfried and Roy magic show was attacked by one of his white Bengal tigers during a Las Vegas performance, Siegfried assured the media that the two had only gotten their telepathic signals crossed.[60] As methods of animal handling over the twentieth and early twenty-first centuries have become increasingly invested in principles of genuine interspecies communication and respect, attacks by well-trained animals are harder to read as possible symptoms of biopower applied to animals, that is, as symptoms of a logic of power that goes unrecognized as such because it denounces physical violence and operates, instead, through sympathetic investments in animal communication. Rather than an expression of cynicism, to suggest that animal love is never disinterested in its expectation that emotional investment will be returned with animal fidelity and compliance is to begin examining the extension of modern biopower into the domain of animal life. The case of Siegfried and Roy hints at the inescapable complicity of emotional and economic investment in the biopolitics of animal training insofar as it reveals the contingency of the trainers' stupendously lucrative "show" on the earning of animal trust and obedience.

It is arguably because a sympathetic interest in animal health and welfare was on the rise during Topsy's lifetime that the agents who conspired to execute her—backed by electrical, cinematic, and amusement park capital—also used her execution as an occasion to demonstrate electricity's power to render death humane. The fact that Topsy was criminalized and sentenced to public execution granted that she was, paradoxically, a subject of the law, and hence made her an exception among animals. Topsy was among the last publicly executed animals in North American modernity.[61] Though she had not been prosecuted in a court of law as had myriad animals called to trial in premodern Europe, her public execution nevertheless mimicked a ritualized procedure of legal punishment.[62] In this sense, the execution of Topsy constituted an exception—and a confusion—in the smooth "institution of speciesism" that, by the turn of the century, had routinized both the "non-criminal putting to death" of livestock and the euthanization of unwanted animals.[63] Even if the public execution of an animal was designed as a publicity stunt, in announcing the event Thompson and Dundy reawakened the idea that animals were socially answerable subjects bound to the same judiciary processes as humans. The potential confusion that Topsy's execution introduced into a humanist culture stemmed not only from the murderous intent attributed to her actions (contradicting the Cartesian doxa that animals were no more than a bundle of preprogrammed instincts and involuntary reflexes)[64] but also from the implied suggestion that an animal like Topsy could in fact suffer a sentence of death. In animals' philosophical construction as undying energies "recycled constantly throughout the world,"[65] the anticipation and finality of death were, after all, what they were said to be incapable of suffering. The electrical rendering of Topsy thus betrays a tension in a culture that was willing to pretend that Topsy shared the same symbolic order as humans, yet the culture fell back on species difference as justification for sacrificing her to a demonstration of technological power. Her electrocution substantiates Derrida's contention that animals are the "sacrificed foundation . . . of the symbolic order," negatively defining the field of "human order, law and justice" from which they are excluded.[66]

Topsy was sacrificed to a culture debating, among other things, a historic shift in the state's technologies of death. If the pain of animals had been barely legible in Galvani's time (as the animal welfare discourses that would enable its recognition were only just taking shape), it had certainly become intelligible by the time Edison began plotting Topsy's death. Unlike in premodern trials in which the torture of human and animal bodies was expected and accepted, Topsy's execution had to be "humane." In the 1780s, although Luigi Galvani was still preparing animal bodies according to the understanding that they were unfeeling automata, the first glimmers of an animal welfare movement were stirring in Europe.[67] Jeremy Bentham not only designed a Panopticon that signified, at least for Foucault, the advent of modern institutions and techniques of power; he also inspired a movement against animal cruelty that would compel reforms in the corporeal treatment of animals and a new attitude toward the violence of killing. As Bentham declared: "The question is not, Can they reason? Nor Can they talk? But Can they suffer?"[68]

His words shifted "the question of the animal" to an emotional register that threw corporeal maltreatments of animal bodies into visible relief and arguably pressured power into new biopolitical shapes. As Derrida puts it, Bentham opened "the immense question of pathos and the pathological, precisely, that is, of suffering, pity, and compassion."[69] His outspoken recognition of animal suffering would inspire Britain's SPCA, founded in 1822, to push for parliamentary acts punishing cruelty to animals, as well as for slaughterhouse reforms. It would also inspire the founding of New York's ASPCA in 1866 by Henry Bergh. In 1892, the American Humane Association would pass laws "prohibiting the repetition of painful experiments [on animals] for the purpose of teaching or demonstrating well-known or accepted facts," a motion that was, however, not opposed to an exemplary delivery of death without pain such as Edison planned for Topsy.[70] Rather than contesting the speciesist institutions underpinning capitalism, the animal welfare movements inspired by Bentham demanded, in the end, only that animals be "manage[d] . . . in a more humane way."[71] The indexes of animal suffering raised by Bentham were thus strategically folded back into efforts to develop new technologies of death designed to eliminate physical suffering.

Electricity (and soon cinema, through documentary footage of abattoirs, among other things) had in fact become a key technology in the biopolitical project of rendering death humane. The first aim of the Humane Slaughter Association of Britain (founded in 1928) was to replace the pole axe with a mechanically operated stunner. In Europe as well as in the United States, it subsequently became mandatory to use stunners on all cattle and calves and an "electrolethaler" on pigs and smaller animals, introducing a series of disjunctions into the act of slaughter analyzed by Noëlie Vialles in *Animal to Edible*. Just as the pressing of the electric switch by state officials was designed to remove pain and recrimination from the administration of capital punishment, Vialles argues that the humane act of stunning animals similarly enabled a displacement of the violence of slaughter.[72] In other words, the noncriminal putting to death of both humans and animals found a new institutional grounding in the deliverance from pain promised by electric shock:

Who kills the animal? The person who stuns it, or the person who bleeds it? Not only is such a doubt formally possible; it exists in reality. . . . What we have here is not a sequence of operations but a disjunction— and even a *double disjunction:* between bleeding and death on the one hand; between death and suffering on the other. Indeed, the first man does not really kill, he anaesthetizes. The second (or third) does not really kill either; he bleeds an animal that is already inert and, in the terms that are in constant use, "as if dead." The result of dissociating death from suffering in this way is as follows: since anaesthesia is not really fatal and since painless (or supposedly painless) bleeding is not really killing, we are left without any "real" killing at all.[73]

Electricity was not only useful in displacing the charge of killing from the act of slaughter; it was equally productive of an ensemble of tasteful side effects. Benjamin Franklin—among the first to recommend electrocution as a method of humane slaughter—discovered not only that the discharge from a battery of two Leyden jars was "sufficient to kill common Hens outright" but that "electrical slaughter" improved the taste of the meat. "I conceit that the Birds kill'd in this Manner eat uncommonly tender," he wrote.[74] In the 1950s, animal carcasses were electrically stimulated in accordance with Benjamin's idea that electricity had a tenderizing effect on meat. Although by the 1980s this idea had fallen out of vogue, meat was still being electrified to achieve "improved lean color, firmness, texture, and marbling score" according to the shifting aesthetics of "dressed" meat.[75]

However, although the ASPCA and other humane societies had denounced hanging, they were not yet convinced that electrocution was the painless solution Edison claimed it to be. In the opinion of some of the public witnesses to William Kemler's electrocution in 1890, it was a traumatically inexact technology of death, "far worse than hanging," as a headline in the *New York Times* put it (August 6, 1890). Determining how much voltage was needed to kill the average human proved a messy science; Kemler had to be administered an impromptu second bolt when it became apparent that the first had not communicated instant death after all. If Edison could definitively monstrate that even the massive body of an elephant could be electrically felled in a single lightning stroke, North Americans would find it easier to accept capital punishment by the switch. Thus Edison sought to prove

that a jolt of alternating current was fatal (in order to ruin Westinghouse) yet painless (in order to appease new conditions of sympathetic
treatment pressured by humane societies). Further, he sought to position
the motion picture camera as a documentary eye impassively capturing
an "actuality" rather than as a medium complicit in staging the animal
passion it was recording. Over the body of Topsy in *Electrocuting an
Elephant*, cinema and electricity emerged as supplementary technologies
of communication. The ability of the first to excite a new degree of
sympathetic identification with the animal was contingent, paradoxically, on the pathological ability of the latter to bring about her "quick
and painless death."[76]

The explosion in the Edison era of new technological media based
on the electrical signal—telegraphy, telephony, radio—excited a popular sense that long-distance communication was no longer contingent
on any earthly structures of transmission. An understanding of the
technological media's physical workings and their embeddedness in
political economy was eclipsed by widespread belief in electricity's metaphysical current. To appreciate the extent to which the technological
media appeared to have transcended the material logistics of transmission one need only recall that even the electricians who designed them
often expressed a spiritualist belief in their unearthly powers of communication. Mr. Watson, Alexander Graham Bell's assistant, wrote in his
autobiography that the telephonic apparatus he and Bell were building
"sometimes seemed to me to be possessed by something supernatural."[77]
Nikola Tesla, the electrical genius whose theory of alternating current
was rejected by Edison (but not by Westinghouse), believed in extra-
terrestrial transmissions and invented an early system of wireless communication with which he claimed he could channel signals from
outer space.

By contrast, Edison choreographed an event that promised to give
a concrete demonstration of electrical power by way of its transparent
effects on a terrestrial body. Topsy's death would communicate once and
for all the "actuality" of alternating current's deadliness to Westinghouse
supporters, its efficiency as a technology of death to penal authorities
in New York State, and its painlessness to humane societies. Yet in

claiming to deliver the raw "truth" of technology through the visceral event of an animal sacrifice, Edison's monstration itself invited fetishistic belief in the seeming animus of the electrical current that struck Topsy down, and it mystified his own motivated part in her death.

Telus Mobility Inc.

At the dawn of the twenty-first century, "old dreams of magic communication" are being revived once again by an advertising campaign that presents the act of telecommunication as animal—mesmerizing, affective, and "electric."[78] This time, however, it is the wireless technologies of the Telus Mobility corporation that are identified with the "communicative powers of animal magnetism."[79] If automobility discourse fetishizes the physical mobility of animals, in telecommunications culture the "act of communication," as Régis Debray notes, is represented as a pure bolt of code, one which I've been working to show is recurringly fetishized as animal.[80] With markets in telecommunication emerging as powerful forces of globalization, it is significant that Telus stages communication as an *"animalséance,"* to borrow from Derrida, that is, as a telepathic exchange of animal affect that appears utterly "other" to political economy.[81]

In the case of Telus Mobility Inc., the logic of monstration that I have traced through Galvani and Edison takes the shape of a concerted marketing campaign designed to "show" that the act of telecommunication is animal. The Telus corporation is careful to assure the public that their "spokescritters" are "never forced to perform in any way they do not want to."[82] Moreover, it claims that its "most successful footage is often of the animals simply being themselves.... Digital imaging is sometimes used ... but it is rarely needed to enhance the natural actions of the animals."[83] The desired message of the telecommunications corporation has become biopolitically one, ostensibly, with the unprogrammed desires of animals and is transparently expressed by animals "simply being themselves." A little digital touching up is all that is needed to correct any slight divergences that may arise between how animals choose to act and the marketing agenda of Telus; nature and capital now function in harmless unison. Or so it would appear unless, as I argue, the pathological conditions and effects of telecommunication have only been spatially displaced from view by a neoliberal discourse that excites magical belief in the possibility of communication without cost, consumption without production.[84] Telemobility is a potent articulation of this neoliberal fantasy, given that in the figure of the electric animal long-distance communication appears to be a charismatic gift of nature rather than a product of human labor. However, even as Telus ads fetishize long-distance communication as an animal faculty, they inadvertently provide clues as to where the material labor and nature of telecommunications culture have been displaced.

On the Web page for Taxi Advertising and Design of Toronto, the agency behind Telus Mobility's prolific ad campaigns, one reads, "Learn how frogs, bugs and ducks transformed a wireless company into one of the most valued brands in the telecommunications industry."[85] Indeed, a seemingly infinite visual string of flora and fauna thread together the ads in the Telus campaign, ads unified by their hallmark "nature": crisp, colorful, and often comical animal and plant species on clinically white backgrounds, with the Telus tagline "the future is friendly." Telus's brand ecology regularly enlists exotic species associated with southern latitudes, species imported into the decontextualized white space of technological culture. Frogs, chameleons, monkeys, parrots, turtles, and penguins by turn enliven a range of telecommunications wares and services. In Telus's parade of species, global biodiversity arguably functions as an allegory for multiculturalism and the celebration of species diversity as a coded expression of the company's multicultural message: that beneath cultural difference one discovers sameness in the universal joy of communication.

One particularly evocative ad in the Telus campaign recalls the grisly experiments of Galvani (see Figure 9). The ad consists of a photograph of a neon-green frog sitting down to table with a starched, digitally rendered napkin tied around its neck, anticipating a dinner plate. As in every Telus ad, the background is astringently white; the production and consumption of technological media is bloodless. "Why pay more for à la carte?" the ad asks, pitching a telecommunications package deal. "Order a Value Bundle."

Figure 9. "Why pay more for à la carte?" Flyer advertising a telecommunications package deal (c. 2001). Telus Mobility Inc.

If the frog in the ad is a tool of commodity fetishism, described by Marx as a table-turning séance in which use values are stood on their heads, it is important to recall that the table turns both ways when it comes to the life of the animal.[86] For the double entendre of the Telus ad cleverly implies that frog legs are the order of the day in a telecommunications marketplace in which animal signs feed on their own carnalized parts. Animals become exchange values—or, as Derrida puts it, they become "animal Thing[s]" that "get up on their hind legs to the laborer and confront him as 'capital'"[87]—by cannibalizing their own sensible supports. In the case of the overdetermined frog, the complicity of telemobility's fetishistic effects and pathological means is glimpsed in the quip with which Telus humors its clients: in the wireless world one can order a virtual "Value Bundle" and eat it, too.[88]

Other ads in the Telus campaign humorously dramatize the technological fidelity promised by the company's telecommunications media, a fidelity that is tested against an animal's sensory acuity in the style of the infamous RCA Victor logo that I glanced at in chapter 2. That logo, "His Master's Voice," depicts a dog quizzically listening to a phonograph transmitting a recording of his master's voice, fooled by the virtuosity of the sound reproduction into believing its owner must be present inside the machine. Similarly, in a fifteen-second television spot for Telus—"Introducing photo caller ID"—a hedgehog carefully approaches a Sanyo 5000, the first mobile phone with a full-color screen.

The phone's screen is upright, facing away from the viewer and toward the hedgehog. Suddenly the hedgehog bristles, stops, and retreats; the ad cuts to the phone's screen, where Telus's photo ID feature shows that the caller is a skunk. The live hedgehog is daunted by the superlative fidelity, or "liveness," of the image confronting it on the screen.[89] The phone's technological virtuosity promises more than just visual and auditory transmissions; it promises virtual *presence*, in this case a presence that threatens to materially spray the receiver with nature's sensorium. In the arena where animal and technology are put to such a biological test of verisimilitude, the hedgehog cedes to the overpowering mimetic fidelities of telecommunications media.[90]

More than a "monstration" of technological fidelity is at stake in the animal ads of Telus, however. The other sense of fidelity—the affective bond of faithfulness between dog and master that Michael Taussig discusses in his reading of the RCA Victor logo—is also at play. Here, however, the bond of fidelity between animal and human arguably models the larger affective relationship to capital that branding and advertising strive to create through their control of mimesis. If the biopolitical object of corporate branding is to generate bonds of identification with and loyalty to a culture of capital that rival or supplant those between human and animals, the marketing discourse of Telus suggests that a discourse of species constitutes a particularly potent technology of branding insofar as it generates affection for capital *as and through* affection for animals.

A closer analysis of Telus's animal advertisements confirms Cary Wolfe's remarkable statement that "the discourse of species . . . is rearticulated upon the more fundamental ur-discourse of the 'organization of mimesis' by the world system of global capitalism in its postmodern moment."[91] It is notable, first of all, that in its campaign Telus favors mimetic species, whether chameleons who chromatically blend in with their environment or species such as parrots and monkeys who embody the originals of the cultural tropes of "parroting" and "aping." Telus's discourse of species is often patently a discourse of mimesis. One of the political effects of its advertising campaign is arguably to naturalize mimesis by articulating it to and through a biological discourse of species and thus to obscure recognition of "the 'organization of mimesis' by the world system of global capitalism in its postmodern moment." Yet if the mimetic species that regularly feature in Telus ads are rearticulated by a system of branding and advertising that controls mimesis in the interests of reproducing capital, they were also previously a mainstay of colonial discourses that mapped figures of "aping" and "parroting" onto the ostensibly primitive other. Taussig contends that colonial discourses sought to keep mimesis in "some sort of imperial balance" by portraying colonized subjects as prone to "primitive" acts of copying, then using their primitive mimesis as justification for imposing a civilizing culture on them.[92]

Although species are presented as innocent and universally readable pictographs in the Telus campaign, the company's "spokescritters" in fact carry virulent histories and connotations. While Telus operates as though animals are biologically transparent bodies rather than social signifiers burdened with history, it tacitly banks on the historical connotations evoked by the species enlisted in its dramas of telecommunication. For instance, to render performing monkeys a comic staple of its ad campaigns, as Telus does, requires *denying* the racist tropes that monkeys historically encode while contradictorily *depending on them* to achieve the clever effects of its campaign. On the one hand, the success of the Telus campaign plays to a public that takes monkeys at their biological face value and "forgets" that in Western culture they are historically racialized signs overdetermined by nineteenth- and twentieth-century discourses of colonialism and biological racism that systematically portrayed Africans as "simianlike."[93] On the other hand, the humorous appeal of Telus ads accrues to the fact that they routinely show monkeys and other species performing acts of mimicry and thereby consciously reactivate tropes of "aping."

Consider, for example, a 2002 Telus ad that explicitly evokes the racist trope of the performing monkey even as it works to ironically distance contemporary telecommunications culture from it (see Figure 10). Above the caption "Avoid the re-gift. Ask for a cool phone" sit a pair of squirrel monkeys, a biological original beside a cheap reproduction. The latter appears in the petrified shape of a lamp stand, a frozen caricature of a performing monkey who is abjectly trying to please, an artifact that bears historical traces of black minstrelsy in its brightly

Avoid the re-gift.
Ask for a
cool phone.

X Phones from as low as $24.99*
Let everyone know what you really want. Ask for a
TELUS Mobility phone with 1X capability, the latest
in wireless technology, and other cool things like:

■ Colour screens
■ Games
■ Access to fun downloads like ringtones and images*
■ 2-Way Text Messaging capability

Available at TELUS Mobility stores, authorized
dealers and retailers. To find out more visit
telusmobility.com/student or call 1-866-810-5555
The future is friendly.*

TELUS
mobility™

Figure 10. "Avoid the re-gift. Ask for a cool phone." Ad recirculating racially saturated signs of simian mimesis (c. 2001). Telus Mobility Inc.

painted red tongue and matching toenails. The live monkey looks with dismay at its kitschy sidekick, less than ecstatic at receiving a gift that nobody wants. The garish lamp represents an embarrassing mode of mimicry out of sync with the ostensibly postracist, neoliberal multi-culture represented by the Telus species. Yet while the ad seeks to distinguish Telus spokescritters and the culture of capital they represent from the antics of the performing monkey, it nevertheless betrays an awareness that Telus's simian signifiers all too easily convoke racist tropes.

The ad is also designed to distinguish new technologies of reproduction from old. The clunky lamp, belonging to an outmoded era of stationary goods tethered to fixed power outlets, is no longer a fit, the Telus ad suggests, for the effortless, wireless mobility of the animal. The "age of mechanical reproduction" has become the ironic content of the new media of communication and of a post-Fordist order of technological mimesis that claims to no longer have anything to do with the crass factory of mass reproduction.[94] Rather than the tacky "re-gift," a Telus "cool phone" is a better mimetic match with the monkey, ostensibly sharing a subtler kinship with the animal than one based on outer physical resemblance. The hidden kinship posited by the ad, the deeper likeness that constitutes mobile phone and monkey as kin, involves their shared faculty for wireless communication. As Telus self-consciously makes mimesis itself the overt subject of its species discourse, the animal tropes of telemobility are at their most witty and persuasive, as well as at their most precarious. Precarious because, as I will shortly show, Telus's simian signifiers can be turned against telemobility culture to implicate it in ongoing histories of racism structuring the material relations of production that it claims to have transcended.

Telus repeated the scenario involving the monkey, with a difference, in a 2003 holiday season ad for its new camera phone, a multimedia mobile phone coupling photographic with telephonic capabilities (see Figure 11). Instead of the mismatch of a squirrel monkey and an imitation lamp, however, this ad depicts a live piglet next to a pile of piglet imitations (a piggy bank, stuffed toy piglets, and so on), with the caption "The perfect gift for those who have everything." Whereas the earlier ad with the monkey brought the Telus ur-discourse on aping into view in a way that the ad with the piglet does not (because pigs do not canonically connote mimesis the way monkeys do), Telus's periodic deployment of North American domestic animals such as pigs, goats, and rabbits in place of its usual fare of exotic species arguably also encodes a discourse of mimesis. Once again distinguished from the friendly reproductions next to it, the piglet embodies a power of mimesis that appears to have moved beyond the mere imitation of life to become, instead, constitutive of it, to become the "perfect gift" of

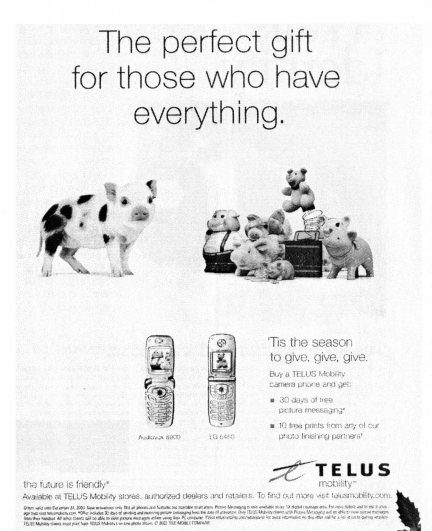

Figure 11. "The perfect gift for those who have everything." Ad advertising the capabilities of the camera phone (c. 2001). Telus Mobility Inc.

new life itself.[95] The little farm animal is a fetish for the virtual presence and charismatic immediacy birthed by the camera phone.

Yet even as Telus ads turn imitation into their ironic content in order to demarcate the superlative powers of new tele-technologies, the piglet almost too easily evokes its own double: the bacon breeder or gene machine subjected to unprecedented degrees of material and reproductive management in late capitalist culture. The dewy piglet's material twin mediates the meat life of capitalism to the tune of 402,233 pigs per week in Canada alone.[96] Rather than posing a problem for its discourse, however, Telus's camera phone ad seems to confidentially invite the realization that in the new biopolitical world order, capital's conditions of production have fused with the conditions of life itself. Aesthetics and genetics have become one double-sided currency of advanced capital via its iconic control of animal code.

Telus organizes and mobilizes mimesis in the service of its culture of capital through a discourse of species. This is perhaps nowhere more clear than in a 2004 series of ads for its camera phone. The mimetic species that feature in this series are vivid lizards, chameleons whose photosensitive skin becomes the spitting image of its surroundings. In each ad, a lizard is shown blending in with the object next to it, an object that is often, but not always, a camera phone. In one exception, a chameleon is shown "becoming" a blue-swirl lollipop in time-motion stages, stages recapitulated in the hyphenated caption "Inexplicable? Send-a-pic-able." The thing-likeness of the animal and the animism of the thing are also posited in a camera phone ad sharing the same caption (see Figure 12) but this time showing a chameleon humorously attempting to "pass" as a wooden Russian nesting doll. Here the chameleon mimics woodenness to fit in with and into the classic *mise-en-abyme* structure of the nesting dolls while at the same time revealing the life ostensibly secreted inside the inanimate body of the doll and, by extension, the Telus camera phone. These Telus ads cry out to be read in the context of the theory of "*le mimetisme*" elaborated by Roger Caillois in his 1938 essay "Mimicry and Legendary Psychasthenia." As I described in chapter 1, Caillois turned to the study of mimetic insects to theorize the "pathology" of animal mimicry.[97] Insects mimicking the appearance of leaves, twigs, or stones demonstrated, for Caillois, an animal death wish ("*le mimetisme*") compelling them to approximate inanimate nature, stasis, and even death.[98]

Telus ads reveal a similar fascination with the notion that mimetic animals are instinctively compelled to become thinglike, whether in stages, like the lollipop lizard, or instantly, like a chameleon in a different

Inexplicable?
Send-a-pic-able.

Some things just can't be described with words. So why not send a pic instead? With camera phones from TELUS Mobility, it's as easy as See, Snap, Send. The future is friendly®

Samsung A670   Audiovox 8920   LG 5450   Samsung A600

TELUS
mobility®

Figure 12. "Inexplicable? Send-a-pic-able." Ad representing reification as biological desire (c. 2007). Telus Mobility Inc.

ad, which has become of a piece with shards of colorful porcelain lying around it. In reading the Telus discourse alongside the work of Caillois, it becomes apparent that it similarly dramatizes the idea of *"le mimetisme,"* and to powerful effect. Indeed, Caillois's theory is one that lends itself dangerously well to hegemonic forces in the current moment, a moment in which mimesis is increasingly subsumed into the service of capital *through* a discourse of species. The drama of *"mimetisme"* at play in the progressive thingification of the Telus lizard serves, in this instance, to frame the becoming-capital of animal life and the becoming-animal of capital as a biological compulsion, as a force of nature rather than an effect of power. According to Telus, species are compelled to become things; they *want* to become identical with the dead labor and dead nature of capital. Through its own popular rendition of *le mimetisme*, Telus is able to suggest that it is animals who desire and drive reification and that its mobile phones are only biological species in their wished-for commodity form.[99] Here Telus fetishistically encourages us to believe that capital is innocently compelled by an animal nature seeking to realize its secret goal.

The Telus campaign invariably returns, however, to the species most productive of its mimetic discourse: monkeys. The telecom model of sending and receiving poles across which signals effortlessly bounce—a model that edits out the *"violent* collective process" of material transmission[100]—is recurringly configured by two monkeys. Shown crouching behind a cluster of bananas or tossing bananas back and forth between them, the monkeys play on the ludic resemblance of banana and telephone until they themselves evolve into the cool phones of the caption titles. The consumption of mobile phones takes on the quality of a subsistence diet through the association encouraged by Telus ads between the monkeys' "prehensile" grab for a banana and the purchase of a mobile phone.[101] Via this "aesthetics of consumption," a neoliberal enjoyment of telecommunications culture is equated with the biological need to eat.[102] The suggestion, moreover, is that in the culture of telecommunication, consumption is no longer contingent on production and cell phones do indeed grow on trees.

The "primate ethograms" favoured by Telus can be pressured to speak, however, to the violent neocolonial relations of production they occlude from view.[103] For the company's deployment of simian code inadvertently links Telus to a global resource economy on which telecommunications culture is in fact contingent and marks a site where its "friendly" culture of consumption can be implicated in the politics of Congolese coltan, civil war, and bushmeat. The material contradictions of telemobility in the twenty-first century, unlike the discourses of Galvani and Edison, are not played out directly on animal flesh. It is indirectly, through the artisanal mining of coltan in the Democratic Republic of Congo, that animals, land, and laborers suffer the pathological costs of telemobility's promise of *"painless transmission."*[104]

Coltan is the thread that I follow into the material labyrinth of production supporting telecommunications culture. The mining of coltan extends the history of Belgian colonialism in the Congo (from the 1885 Berlin Conference to the Congo's independence in 1960) into neocolonial economies related to telecommunications capital. Coltan extraction in the Congo is artisanal in that mining methods, through the throes of civil war, have been deinstitutionalized from state controls, resulting in an ad hoc series of volatile camps run by shifting military groups and rogue armies. Coltan, short for colombo-tantalite, is a highly conductive mineral ore found in soils three billion years old. The tantalum derived from coltan is a corrosion-resistant precious metal used in the manufacture of microcapacitors, electronic components that control current flow inside the miniature circuit boards of computers and electronic gadgets such as cell phones, BlackBerries, iPods, pagers, and game consoles. Coltan, not "animal conductors," makes telecommunication possible. Revitalized geopolitical interests in the eastern Congo as resource colony and provider of precious minerals for a global telecommunications empire have supplanted former colonial trades in slaves, ivory, and rubber from when this region of Africa was under Belgian rule. Coltan is legitimately mined in Australia, Brazil, and Canada, but it is more cheaply extracted, by virtue of deeply entrenched neocolonial plunder economies, in the Congo.

A 2002 United Nations Security Council Report indicting the latest pillaging of the Congo's natural resources, *Final Report of the Panel of Experts on the Illegal Exploitation of Natural Resources and Other Forms of Wealth of the Democratic Republic of the Congo,* links telecommunications capitals and multinational mineral corporations to illegal trade in coltan.[105] The electronics industry uses approximately 60 percent of the world's supply of coltan, with mobile phone manufacturers using the bulk of that percentage. Corporations such as Nokia, Motorola, Compaq, Dell, IBM Ericsson, and Siemens are primary users of capacitors made of tantalum (a black powder derived from coltan) that invariably lead back to the Congo.[106] A material genealogy of Telus Mobility "cool phones" links them to giants such as Nokia, Samsung, and AudioVox (the maker of the Telus camera phone), manufacturers whose tantalum is supplied by multinational mineral corporations such as H. C. Starck (Germany). Mineral multinationals such as H. C. Starck are in turn supplied by myriad illegal traders opportunizing on "a variety of forced labor regimes" working in artisanal mining camps controlled either by Rwandan and Ugandan armed groups who invaded eastern Congo in 1998 or by Congolese militants operating under the rationale of the "war effort" to loot natural resources.[107]

An overvaluation of technology markets spurred by a new genera-tion of mobile phones and "a rush on computer games (Sony Play-station II)" triggered a coltan boom from 2000 to 2002, allowing rebel groups in eastern Congo to haul in as much as $20 million a month for weapons purchases and private profit.[108] While the soaring market value of coltan made it a lucrative source of funding for military fac-tions invested in the economics of permanent war in the Congo (as claimed by the UN report), further along the commercial chain global demand for coltan kept Sony from releasing its PlayStation II on sched-ule, a minor sign within electronic consumerism of its contingency, after all, on material histories of production.[109] Even with a fall in coltan prices in late 2001, the use of child and convincible labor working under the omnipresent threat of violence continues to make the eastern Congo the cheapest and most attractive global source of coltan; in the vast difference between the "costs" of Congolese nature and labor and the enjoyment of electronic and digital culture, capital makes the most of itself.

In 2001, a group of Belgian nongovernmental organizations initi-ated a worldwide campaign—"No blood on my mobile! Stop the plun-dering of Congo!"—with the aim of pressuring multinationals into certifying (legalizing) coltan production so that benefits would return to the people of the Congo as opposed to being expropriated by the "elite networks" named in the UN report.[110] At the same time, inter-national wildlife groups such as the Dian Fossey Gorilla Fund (DFGF) mobilized international concern for the lowland gorillas that Fossey had helped to make virtually synonymous with wildlife conservation in Africa. During the coltan boom, miners in the numerous artisanal coltan camps in eastern Congo came to rely heavily on bushmeat for food, including species living within national park boundaries. Concerned with the effects of illegal mining on gorilla, elephant, and other wildlife populations in the Kahuzi-Biega National Park, the DFGF (with the Born Free Foundation) prepared a report titled "Coltan Boom, Gorilla Bust: The Impact of Coltan Mining on Gorillas and Other Wildlife in Eastern DR Congo" (2001). Its call for "gorilla-friendly" coltan production, more than the UN documentation of illegal economic networks and human rights alerts of the atrocities of war in the Congo, aroused popular support in North America.[111] Moved by the sign of endangered animal life, Hollywood film star Leonardo DiCaprio gave his high-profile endorsement to the DFGF.

In a television documentary titled *Gorillas under Threat,* a narrator says: "There is a sinister link between cell phones and the last remaining gorillas in central Africa."[112] Most media coverage of coltan mining in the Congo has, following the strategy of the DFGF, employed the lowland gorilla as an affective technology to awaken concern in cosmopolitan subjects. As an affective technology, however, the gorilla risks reviving racist sentiment against Africans despite—or rather, *because*—of its efforts to arouse sympathy for African animals. Coltan campaigns are in danger of reinscribing a sense of white supremacy even as aspects of a dominant, consumerist culture are being called to account. In response to the damning linkages made between cell phones and the loss of the lowland gorilla (more than any other living species, perhaps, bound up with the hegemony of Western culture across colonial and neocolonial eras and overdetermined by evolutionary discourses, anthropological knowledges, and ecological emotion), multinationals such as Motorola, Ericsson, Nokia, and the manufacturers of their components sought to reassure a global public that their products do not use tantalum from the Congo. In an open letter to the DFGF offices in London (and cross-posted on Leonardo DiCaprio's web site), Motorola nevertheless easily displaces the blame:

> On your website, you ask that companies "simply not turn away from raw materials mined in the region, but rather demand gorilla-friendly tantalum mined in a way as to benefit the environment and provide better

economic returns to peasant miners." The solution that you request is a difficult and immeasurable one to achieve. The roots of the conditions in the Congo are steeped in political and social unrest and guerilla fighting between warlords who profit from illegal mining. If we buy materials from the region, we have no way to ensure that the warlords will not profit and continue to perpetuate the lawlessness and despicable actions that we condemn.[113]

By suggesting that the fate of innocent African "gorillas" is at bottom in the hands of lawless African "guerillas," Motorola effectively absolves itself of the "roots of the conditions" in the Congo, presenting itself as a law-abiding corporate entity that has no control over lawless black "warlords who profit from illegal mining." New configurations of familiar racist slippages between *gorilla* and *guerilla* emerge in the Motorola letter (and in the context of the coltan campaigns, more broadly) to deflect the terrorizing economics of a global trade in telecommunications off of the transnational corporation and onto the "despicable" black warlord. African guerillas are depicted as driven only by the law of the jungle, their violence and greed removed from historical contexts of colonialism and neocolonialism. The easy slippage between *guerilla* and *gorilla* returns the conflicts in the Congo to a state of nature outside of civilized history, where alpha males periodically terrorize their monkey families. With such guerillas, suggests Motorola, rational exchanges are not possible, a racist rhetoric belied by the very effective business associations between multinationals and "warlords" detailed in the UN report.

If, under the pressure of campaigns calling for "gorilla-friendly" coltan mining, Motorola reactivates what Donna Haraway terms "simian orientalism" to disavow the incommunicable violence of a guerilla-terrorized Congo as one of telecommunication capital's material conditions and effects, the conservationist politics that exposes the blood on the mobile in the name of twentieth-century primatologists such as Dian Fossey are themselves historically imbricated in the violence— and the fantasy—of global telecommunication.[114] As Haraway argues, Western primatology is ultimately a fantasy of communication. She contends that the stories of Dian Fossey, Jane Goodall, and other white women scientists making contact with monkeys in the "vanishing forest gardens" of Africa (or Western ethology labs)—stories made famous by *National Geographic* articles and television specials—are emphatically "about modes of *communication*, not history" (149). By popularly narrating white women's love for allochronic African nature, that is, for a nature "existing in a time outside the contentious, coeval time of history," primatology stories had the effect, Haraway contends, of displacing the material histories and social struggles of decolonization (149). The dramas of touch linking female primatologists to apes in Africa "are played out in a nature that seems innocent of history" (156). The fact that while Jane Goodall was setting up her research camp Patrice Lumumba was leading a "successful revolution against colonial rule in the Belgian Congo" (164) and "dozens of African nations [were] achieving their national independence, 15 in 1960 alone," was erased from the *National Geographic* portrayals of interspecies intimacy in a timeless Eden.[115]

Haraway believes that the model of communication advanced by primatology stories is one in which primates and humans communicate across species difference via a direct sign language, consummated by the primate's "'spontaneous' manual gestures towards the white female man."[116] "The fantasy is about language," writes Haraway, "about the immediate sharing of meanings" (135). This fantasy crystallized, for Haraway, in a 1984 Gulf Oil ad supporting *National Geographic*'s coverage and showing the high-contrast image of a dark animal hand touching a white female hand. Text fleshes out the image: "In a spontaneous gesture of trust, a chimpanzee in the wilds of Tanzania folds his leathery hand around that of Jane Goodall" (134). The primate gesture arguably mediated the historic moment at which Gulf Oil, the image of resource capitalism, made itself over in the image of postindustrial modes of production, that is, in the image of communication (not to mention the moment at which capitalist ideology touched hands with conservationist ideology).

While the Gulf ad historically predates the Telus campaign, it nevertheless predicts the monkey signs and "primate ethograms" staged in the achieved postindustrialism of the Telus ads, whose white spaces are resonant, for Haraway, of research labs in which apes are tutored in technologies of communication (139). The primatological dream of trans-species signaling in a suspended state of timeless contact meshes with the promise of telemobility excited by the ads of Telus Mobility. Indeed, an international conservationist network founded on the work of women such as Fossey and Goodall risks functioning as an ally of telemobility even as it protests the blood on the mobile. After all, it, too, is premised on a fantasy of unmediated (animal) communication and mobilizes the affective sign of animal life in protection of the African species that embody this dream. "Communication is the foundation and goal of the whole innocent-transgressive enterprise," as Haraway writes (146).

Moreover, because "European culture for centuries questioned the humanity of peoples of color and assimilated them to the monkeys and apes," as Haraway writes, tales of bushmeat disseminated via gorilla-friendly cell phone campaigns easily connote cannibalism (154). News of Africans eating gorillas affectively reactivates colonial imaginaries of primitives consuming their own kind in an animal state of nature. While international coltan campaigns overtly aim to make Western multinationals culpable for the pillaging of the Congo's wealth so as to trouble electronic consumerism, on a covertly affective level the campaigns strongly invite the racist allegation that Africa's nature—which for international institutes such as the DFGF constitutes a global birthright transcending nation-state boundaries—is being gobbled up by Africans.[117] While the campaigns ostensibly tell the latest segment of a postcolonial, self-reflexive story about the West ransacking the Congo, they nevertheless reinstall the rights and concerns of a universal humanity anxiously watching Africans devour gorillas that are a living evolutionary link to the "origins of 'man.'" If coltan campaigns alert the world to the continued pillaging of Africa, the stories they tell of rare gorillas being reduced to bushmeat also evoke the image of an enmired Africa literally consuming the threatened resources of a global humanity. The pillaging of mineral resources such as coltan or diamonds pales beside the "raw" act of eating an animal that embodies humanity's genetic prehistory. Thus, even in their attempt to incriminate Western corporations, coltan campaigns enable an affective displacement of the pathologies of telecommunications consumption onto a bushmeat-eating Congo.

The material violence subtending the virtual mobility promised by Telus must be willfully developed, for the Canadian corporation convincingly conducts its business at a vast remove from the embroiled politics of nature, race, and labor being lived out in the Congo. Telus has been unable to remain as remote from its immediate labor force in Canada, however. Dissatisfactions of its Canadian employees, triggered by outdated contracts and poor customer service ratings related to dramatic downsizing, carry little of the incommunicable weight of centuries of compound exploitation suffered by the Congolese. One measure of the great material differences in the international division of labor is the communications agency enjoyed by the Telecommunications Workers Union, exercised in the media campaign it mobilized in January of 2004 to pressure Telus to heed its demands. Because of its access to communications media, the efforts of the union to air three mock television ads parodying Telus's "spokescritters" managed to briefly disrupt the corporate composure of Telus.

The three mock ads featured a parrot, a pig, and dalmatian dogs, all performing in the recognizably white space of Telus brand culture yet brazenly complaining about poor customer service. "Telus wants to use animals to sell its services but even the animals know that things aren't right at the telephone company," a voice declares at the beginning of one union ad.[118] Unlike the animals in Telus television spots, whom viewers watch physically "behaving" in time with catchy popular tunes, the union animals are less manicured vehicles of the message; bluntly rather than subtly anthropomorphized, they talk. The piglet complains that "Telus customers are getting the shaft," and the parrot squawks "Telus customers are getting plucked," whereupon a suited man suggestive of a shadowy Telus executive yanks it off-screen and does (audible) violence to it. The ventriloquized animals of the union ads deploy metaphors of material maltreatment (even rendering) to capture the elusive violence perpetrated by a private corporation that profits from denying that communication is a "*collective* process."[119]

No sooner had the union ads begun airing, however, than the apparent freedom enjoyed by informational laborers in the global North was quickly constrained by Telus in a rare show of legal force, making momentarily visible its tight control of mimesis. The mock ads aired on television channels in the western provinces of British Columbia and Alberta for a mere ten days before Telus succeeded in obtaining a court injunction prohibiting further airing of the union spots on grounds that their use of animals infringed on the copyrighted image of the company and poisoned its popular brand identity. Brief and barely noticed, the mimetic excess that broke out in its symbolic economy was quickly sealed off by Telus, which resumed vigorous publicity stints drawing on a seemingly infinite reserve of animal signs.[120]

"The struggle for ideological and political hegemony," writes Slavoj Žižek, is "always the struggle for the appropriation of the terms which are 'spontaneously' experienced as 'apolitical,' as transcending political boundaries."[121] While the ads of Telus and of its union have antagonistic content, they are alike in that they agree to conduct a struggle for hegemony over the mediatized sign of animal life; in this sense, they are complicit monstrations. The particular content spoken or behaved by animal signs seems to come, after all, from a place of spontaneous and apolitical life. Because animals arguably most encode the innocent place of "life itself" in biopolitical times, even ironic discourses fed through the mouths of animal signs risk appearing to make propositions from a position of unpower. Telus and its union mark just two antagonistic agendas among many striving for hegemony over animal signs; environmental and animal rights movements as much as corporate capitals and their unions struggle to make their particular ideologies into the universal, innocent content of animal signs. That said, the strategically ironic mimesis mobilized by the union's ads at least made momentarily visible capitalism's unofficial and official economy of mimesis: a competition to occupy "spontaneous" signs of life in which the most powerful players can resort, when necessary, to copyright law, a property logic that in the final event protected Telus's brand image and managed against mimetic excess.

Chapter 4

Biomobility: Calculating Kinship in an Era of Pandemic Speculation

Along with the common celebrations of the unbounded flows in our new global village, one can still sense also an anxiety about increased contact and a certain nostalgia for colonialist hygiene. The dark side of the consciousness of globalization is the fear of contagion.
—HARDT AND NEGRI, *Empire*

In the guerrilla rescue operation composing the opening scene of the movie *28 Days Later* (directed by Danny Boyle, 2002), British animal rights activists break into a London laboratory to release its captive simian subjects. They find live chimpanzees locked inside glass and metal cages. The only chimp not contained inside a cage is strapped down by its arms and legs onto a medical bed cum sacrificial altar inside a ring of television sets shown incessantly playing and replaying grainy media footage of human executions, violent riots, and wars. Among the cruel experiments to which the lab animals appear to have been subjected is that of forcing them to consume a continuous visual loop of traumatic images, using them as test subjects to study, as it were, the psychosocial effects on humans of exposure to endless hours of television violence.

As the animal liberationists are soon to fatally discover, this exposure indeed produces effects that are directly, disturbingly mimetic: their media diet has infected the chimpanzees with viral "rage." When one of the activists unwittingly frees the first of the caged chimps, it attacks and infects her with its tainted blood, unleashing a potential pandemic of contagious violence that will ravage the human population of the United Kingdom over the next twenty-eight days. The movie's second scene opens onto the aftermath of the near-pandemic, in which a mere smattering of infected and still uninfected human survivors scavenge in the eerily empty, postapocalyptic landscape of London.

The plot of *28 Days Later* helps to illuminate the trope of "biomobility" that frames this chapter. With biomobility, the "rapid movement of affect" constituting the spiritualistic currency of telemobility discourse shows its obverse face in the biological threat of zoonosis, or species-leaping disease.[1] If telemobility traffics in the promise of a "painless transmission" of affect through seemingly ethereal global networks, with biomobility the *substance* of virtual communication reappears in the pandemic potential of communicable disease.[2] Biomobility names, in other words, the threat of telecommunications' pathological double, the potential of infectious disease to rapidly travel through the social flesh of a globally connected life world. This pandemic potential is one sign of what Arturo Escobar calls "the irruption of the biological" in a neoliberal culture given to celebrating globalization as a feat of time-space transcendence over nature, exciting belief in a metaphysics of capital.[3] Alongside other global-scale events such as climate change and loss of biodiversity, pandemic discourse signals that "the survival of biological life" itself is reemerging as an object and project of biopower.[4]

In tracing the modern emergence of biopower, Foucault writes that "the pressure exerted by the biological on the historical had remained very strong for thousands of years; epidemics and famine were the two great dramatic forms of this relationship that was always dominated by the menace of death."[5] As Foucault contends, modern European states sought to relieve the pressure of the biological by making it an explicit object of political calculation according to a new logic of power invested in optimizing the health and welfare of its human populations. Foucault neglects to address a significant discrepancy in the operations of biopower, however, insofar as colonial populations were often deliberately exposed to epidemics and famines that were being successfully managed, if not wholly averted, in Europe.[6] The reappearance, with the current specter of pandemic disease, of a biological "menace of death" that had been alleviated only for some populations, in the first instance, suggests at least two things. First, it suggests that we may have arrived

at a historic conjuncture in which pandemic, by posing an indiscriminate threat to human species life on a global scale, levels the uneven
distribution of exposure to disease previously accommodated within the
history of biopower. Those dominant countries, classes, and populations
once able to secure relative immunity from the pressure of the biological are suddenly confronted with the fact that their historical immunity
may have expired as disease threatens to irrupt out of or exceed those
techniques of biopower that managed to contain it. Second, as the scale
of biological menace graduates from epidemic to pandemic proportions under conditions of globalization, a universal or whole humanity
is constituted as the new object of biopower. As this chapter will seek
to show, however, both its leveling and unifying effects need to be interrogated as just that, *effects* of a cultural discourse of pandemic that
produces and protects its own material contradictions. For in the biopolitical constitution of a global humanity united by the threat of pandemic, what also gets constituted are those populations, both human
and animal, perceived as compromising its survival and therefore at
risk of being socially ghettoized or materially sacrificed.

The trope of biomobility draws attention, moreover, to a relatively
undertheorized feature of globalization: in a world compressed by the
movements of immigrants, laborers, refugees, tourists, and a transnational business class, it is not only interfaces and encounters between
different ethnic and cultural groups that dramatically proliferate but also
interfaces and encounters between humans and other "communicable"
species. More than economic and cultural boundaries are volatilized in
an era of globalization; so are material and imaginary boundaries between species. Biomobility notates a condition in which, by virtue of
the "radically changing time-space relations that epitomize postmodernity," interspecies exchanges that were once local or "place-specific"
are experienced as global in their potential effects.[7] Yet just as globalization cannot be said to have a uniform effect of dissolving national
borders (as evidenced by numerous resurgences of nationalist sentiment), it would be a mistake to equate biomobility solely with an increased permeability of human-animal boundaries. While biomobility
is suggestive of a radical ontological breakdown of species distinctions
and distance under present conditions of global capitalism, it also brings

into view new discourses and technologies seeking to secure human health through the segregation of human and animal life and finding in the specter of pandemic a universal rationale for institutionalizing speciesism on a hitherto unprecedented scale.

If interaction between species has always, historically speaking, exposed human populations to zoonotic disease, biomobility names the fear of a pathological communicability that can no longer be contained in its source population, as well as discourses and technologies of would-be containment. When a zoonotic disease has, as pandemic origin stories portray it, made a seemingly impossible leap across the human-animal divide only to threaten to piggyback on the material flows of a globalized economy to the four corners of the earth, the virtual mobility that is so valorized in neoliberal discourses of telecommunication and global finance reveals its biological underbelly. Because globalization unwittingly supplies the conditions for disease to travel rapidly and because a future pandemic will by all accounts be zoonotic (animal) in origin, the species line emerges as a prominent material stress line in neoliberal culture.

Yet, as I have suggested, there is also a productive dimension to the politics of biomobility, a dimension of biopower. This chapter engages with the cultural discourse of a coming pandemic disseminated by the World Health Organization (WHO), the mass media, and the prominent "ecology of fear" social critic Mike Davis in the context of recent global outbreaks of avian influenza.[8] Unlike AIDS, an avian flu pandemic currently exists only as a matter of fearful speculation. However, it is as a phantasmatic or speculative currency that the coming pandemic is most productive of animal capital (which names both material traffics in biological life and cultural discourses that metaphorize capital as animal). Speculation, as Jean and John Comaroff theorize it in relation to what they term "millennial capitalism," is the very modus operandi of neoliberal culture.[9] Stock market speculation drives virtual flows of capital and yields staggering bonanzas of wealth without, it would seem, any material links to labor and nature. Yet in their analysis of the rise of "worldwide speculation, in both senses of the term, provoked by the shifting conditions of material existence at the turn of the twentieth century," the Comaroffs also trace how perplexity, desire, and panic provoked by the disconnect between virtual capital and material production drive speculations of another sort (7). The Third World "occult economies" studied by the Comaroffs, including enterprises that capitalize on a resurgence of belief in zombies and zombie masters in parts of postcolonial South Africa, respond to the neoliberal gospel of prosperity without labor, consumption without production, with their own "locally nuanced fantasies of abundance without effort" (6).

While an avian flu pandemic is predicted to have catastrophic effects on the global economy and community, awaiting its disastrous coming is also productive of worldwide speculation, in both senses of the term. At first glance, pandemic speculation would seem to represent the antithesis of the occult economies theorized by the Comaroffs. Rather than gambling on the chance of a miraculous windfall of wealth without work, pandemic discourse speculates in the coming of an event that threatens to precipitate the collapse of the global economy and a hard reckoning with materiality. Yet although pandemic discourse speculates in dark rather than bright "futures," it is arguably no less implicated in reproducing neoliberal culture.[10]

Consider, for instance, how pandemic speculation conjures "the global" itself as an imagined community, a *global village* harboring what Mike Davis calls the "bioterrorist" threat of the H5N1 avian flu virus.[11] The once enticing fusion of cosmopolitan and peasant worlds in the oxymoron of the global village, of the technologically advanced First World and quaintly developing Third World, turns sinister under the medical gaze of pandemic discourse.[12] The "small world" of the global village no longer popularly connotes an ideal of multicultural mingling in a world marketplace. Instead, in pandemic discourse the "village" re-emerges as a breeding ground of disease that must be quarantined from the space of liberal cosmopolitanism to which it had been intimately articulated but that it now threatens to infect. The village retracts in scope to connote recalcitrant cultures incarcerated in traditional or "backwards" life ways, cultures lacking clear boundaries between their human and animal populations and therefore signifying sickness for the universal subject of the global. In recasting the global

village as a too-intimate space containing a single contiguous humanity vulnerable to zoonotic disease, pandemic speculation at once works
to biologically unify and culturally divide a global humanity through fear.

Pandemic discourse is, to borrow from Brian Massumi, an agent of
"biofear production."[13] Positing an epistemic shift, after World War II,
in the "social landscape of fear,"[14] Massumi argues that fear can no
longer be thought of as just an emotion privately experienced by individuals but instead must be seen as the very "subject-form of capital,"
as the constitutive affect of "late capitalist human existence."[15] It is in
the fearful state of awaiting "an unspecifiable may-come-to-pass," suggests Massumi, that humans are constituted as capitalist subjects (11).
Although the productivity of speculation around a potential avian flu
pandemic appears to be more affective and social than economic—
even at times at the expense of the economic, if one takes into account
tourism losses resulting from advisories against traveling to areas re-
porting an outbreak of disease—such speculation is not economically
unproductive, either. Among other things, pandemic speculation has
spawned offshoot economies in emergency preparedness, as well as
generated astronomical returns for multinational pharmaceuticals as
the world gambles in the high-stakes hope of a universal cure.[16] Later
in this chapter, I show that the profit-driven business of making antivirals provides an all too literal example of the logic of the pharmakon
as the promise of immunological security itself threatens to trigger an
autoimmune attack.

My immediate concern in this chapter, however, is the violent effects
that pandemic speculation can have on animal and human populations
long before it materializes—if ever—on the scale that is predicted.
While discourses of the coming pandemic are, in the first instance,
productive of a ruthless species hierarchy that rationalizes the segregation and sacrifice of (nonhuman) bodies suspected to be infected so
that others (human) may live, they simultaneously distinguish racial
ontologies in the global species body of humanity. Donald S. Moore,
Anand Pandian, and Jake Kosek argue that race and nature are invariably co-constructed as "historical artifacts"; instead of treating them
separately, they urge the importance of tracking the "recombinant muta-

tions" and "articulated effects" of discourses of race and nature across colonial and neocolonial terrains of power.[17] In pandemic discourse, it appears increasingly futile to trace the biopolitical vicissitudes of the species line without simultaneously tracing those of ethnicity and race: in the specter of zoonosis, they are inextricably entangled. If on the one hand pandemic discourse seems to unify a global humanity on the basis of its irreducible biological vulnerability to disease, on closer inspection it can be seen to effect racialized reinscriptions of cultural difference within the "bare life" of the biologically continuous humanity it invokes.[18]

After all, pandemic discourse pathologizes those members of the global village who live in "unhygienic" intimacy with other species and with one another, positioning them as needing to be enlightened about the new sanitary standards of global citizenship that alone hold hope of averting the leap of disease across species lines. As Roger Keil and Harris Ali contend in their study of the 2003 SARS outbreak in Toronto, in an ostensibly postracist and globalized multicultural city such as Toronto, in which "biologistic references to difference" have been banned from public official discourse, one way racism is culturally rearticulated is through stories of "*infectious disease and the bodies allegedly carrying it.*"[19] The discourse of the coming avian flu pandemic similarly appears postracist in its pleas for pandemic preparedness and in the concern it expresses for a whole humanity seemingly without distinction. Yet as the SARS precedent suggests, pandemic speculation functions as a form of liberal racism insofar as it pathologically articulates fear of zoonotic disease to images of cultural difference (unhygienic intimacy with animals, exotic taste for animals), conjuring a deadly combination of ethnic-animal alterity that ostensibly "threatens to destroy the global."[20] Moreover, as I suggest later in this chapter, it is deeper assimilation into a neoliberal marketplace as the universally mediating principle of human-animal coexistence that appears to effectively sanitize and redeem unhygienic subjects for global kinship.

In the previous chapter I linked the monkey signs rendered in a contemporary telecommunications ad campaign to the material politics of nature, race, and labor in the eastern Congo. Here it is the pathologization of animal and ethnic alterity effected by the discourse of a coming pandemic that compels analysis. However, rather than devoting this entire chapter to the politics of "biofear" raised by pandemic discourse, I am interested in exploring how a liberal *longing* for interspecies intimacy circulates concurrently, and in productive contradiction, with pandemic discourse, complicating Massumi's suggestion that fear is the constitutive "subject-form of capital." To this end, I pursue an idiosyncratic route into the politics of biomobility, one that mimics the confrontation dramatized in the opening scene of *28 Days Later* between the ethical idealism of animal liberationists determined to free their simian cousins and the horrifying zoonosis their idealism unwittingly releases. This chapter likewise confronts two "structures of feeling" in late liberal culture, to borrow from Raymond Williams, two affective dispositions that, while seemingly contradictory, arguably function in tandem to structure the possibilities and limits of kinship in the global village.[21] Indeed, the contention informing this chapter is that pandemic discourse is not solely constitutive of the politics of biomobility; in the current era of globalization, the crossing of species lines is produced not only as a pathological object of fear but also as an object of intense desire.

Before engaging more closely with pandemic speculation, then, I want to first examine a contemporary love exhibit for animals, one that exemplifies a liberal longing for posthuman kinship as the affective flip side of pandemic discourse. Gregory Colbert's photographic spectacle of interspecies intimacy in his *Ashes and Snow* exhibit is a portrayal of posthuman kinship physically touring the globe inside his "nomadic museum" as well as virtually circulating on the World Wide Web. While there are numerous cultural discourses that could exemplify the growing desire in neoliberal culture for a reenchanted life in kinship with animals, Colbert's explicitly evokes, like pandemic speculation, the space of the global as the theater of human-animal contact. Moreover, the fetishization of the museum's mobility or nomadicity in the *Ashes and Snow* discourse is a provocation to confront it with the material politics of biomobility explored in this chapter.

The nomadic museum's popular reception is indicative of a larger liberal longing for contact with animals that would seem to run counter to the medical rationalization of human-animal commingling that pandemic speculation universally mandates. However, just as it can be argued that the biofear produced by pandemic discourse at least partially constitutes the "subject-form of capital," the love of animals that Colbert offers as an *antidote* to late capitalism is arguably also constitutive of it. Moreover, the liberal ideal of interspecies intimacy visualized by Colbert is productive of a new species of orientalism, or orientalism encoded in a discourse of species. And because it is a purely *contemplative* relationship to animal life that is framed as an ecological ideal in the nomadic museum, the materiality of the relationships embodied by other global subjects who out of need and desire continue to live with, use, and eat animals is almost calculated to offend that ideal and risks becoming the new basis for racialization.

Among other things, my analysis of *Ashes and Snow* will examine how the love of difference yet loathing of its "real" substance that Slavoj Žižek discerns in multicultural discourse is also at play in cultural discourses of biodiversity, indeed how multiculturalism and biodiversity may function as intertwined ideologies of late capitalism. Yet, as I have noted, the love and loathing that viscerally accrue to the species line are not so much ideologies as they are *affects* disposing liberal subjects toward some, and not other, possibilities of collective coexistence. Horror of zoonosis and longing for interspecies intimacy do not calculate the conditions of universal kinship in any ideologically deliberative or intentional sense. It is in constituting liberal subjectivity and collectivity at the micropolitical level of felt fear and desire that they regulate the possibilities and limits of living together with (human and animal) others in the global village.

I write out of my own susceptibility to both of these affects but also from my conviction that the fetishization and pathologization of interspecies kinship are twin expressions of power that do violence to existing and future collectivities of humans and animals. Those who scheme for alternative futures from within a neoliberal culture of speculation can no longer proceed without acknowledging the intimate enjambments of human and nonhuman lives—and, even more, the irreducible contingency of human lives on those of other species. An ethics of "precarious life," as Judith Butler formulates the "'common' corporeal vulnerability" of humans in an era dominated by America's imperial rhetoric and machinery of security, needs to extend to a recognition of this ontological contingency, profound in its implications.[22]

Specific kinds of animal capital are bound up in the politics of biomobility, from Colbert's efforts to manage the symbolic capital of animal signs through his Animal Copyright Foundation to the economic pressure placed on peasants and villagers outside of the Western world to sanitize or slaughter their fowl under the new global health imperative of averting an avian flu pandemic. Animal rendering, likewise, is historically embroiled in the cultural and carnal politics of biomobility. Indeed, a transnational traffic in animal remains emerges as a visceral link between East and West in one racializing tale of zoonosis examined in what follows.

Visions of Kinship: A New Species of Orientalism

From March to June of 2005, more than five hundred thousand visitors flocked to New York's Pier 54 to view Gregory Colbert's "nomadic museum," a reception rarely logged in the postmodern art world. The museum, traveling under the name *Ashes and Snow,* houses a collection of animal photographs shot by Colbert on numerous global expeditions and first put on display in a Venice shipyard in 2002. Custom designed by the high-profile architect Shigeru Ban (a finalist among post-9/11 contenders to design a new World Trade Center), the museum is a portable structure assembled out of more than 150 recycled shipping containers and paper-tube columns. The self-conscious example of sustainable architecture structurally reinforces the exhibit's ecological message while also serving the more functional purpose of easy disassembly and reassembly along what Colbert calls the museum's "migratory journey" to "ports of call around the world."[23]

While the traveling patterns of elephants is the organic model with which the migratory journey of the nomadic museum is most often conflated in the *Ashes and Snow* discourse, the museum's mobility is also identified with the migrating bodies of whales and birds. The insinuation is that the museum's itinerary is dictated by an internal (biological) compass and that it has no more motivation than a V formation of birds for touching down in Venice, New York, Santa Monica, and Tokyo. These are the global cities charted by the nomadic museum between 2002 and 2007, cities in which Colbert has cumulatively drawn over a million people to view his spectacle of animal kinship.

Even before considering the contents of the kinship vision disseminated by the nomadic museum, even in approaching the museum at the level of an architectural artifact whose mobility is innocently identified with the biological law of animal migration, the contradictory conditions of Colbert's discourse can be glimpsed in the shipping containers used in its construction. That containerization is a material condition of possibility of economic globalization has been recognized at least since the 1950s. "Today," as a recent news article titled "The Box That Makes the World Go Round" states, "some 18 million containers are constantly crisscrossing the seven seas. These standardized receptacles have become the building blocks of the global village."[24] Indeed, the intermodal, universally standardized boxes that slip equally well onto trains, planes, ships, and trucks are key to the accelerated movement of goods and bodies that materially underpins the politics of biomobility. Yet shipping containers, the "building blocks" of globalization, are emptied of their economic freight and used to house what Colbert describes as "a world that is without beginning or end, here or there, past or present."[25] The space fashioned out of interlocking steel containers and paper tubes (one of Shigeru Ban's signature materials)[26] is represented as a sanctuary from material history, as a high temple of culture standing apart from political economy. In other words, in Colbert's private museum containerization is turned into an empty signifier, a postmodern architectural aesthetic framing an ostensibly timeless spectacle of human-animal communion.

Although human-animal kinship is idealized in the nomadic museum as a timeless relationship transcending material relations and histories of power, *Ashes and Snow* inadvertently reveals that the containers voided of economic content have effectively been refilled with new *cultural* content and returned to circulation. Far from being removed from the global economy, the nomadic museum exemplifies how culture—

and Colbert's animal kinship discourse in particular—can come to constitute globalization by other means. The recycled containers are a first hint that the mobility of Colbert's exhibit, contrary to its fetishistic effects, is at once materially contingent on and culturally constitutive of a global empire of capitalism.

What is carried inside this postmodern ark? Photographic tablets, if you will, performatively uttering a universal covenant between humans and animals. *Ashes and Snow* constitutes a complex performance of posthuman kinship that I will not try to comprehensively analyze. Instead I limit my discussion to those aspects that most help to elucidate the politics of biomobility, including the affective articulation of race and nature in Colbert's images of a kinship beyond speciesism. What also makes mine a necessarily partial analysis is the fact that, being neither willing nor able to buy into the museum experience itself (for an impure mix of reasons including both economic constraints and political reservations), I have sought to negotiate a compromise by confining my analysis to the *Ashes and Snow* Web site, to interviews with Colbert and reviews of the exhibit, and to Colbert's pronouncement of a related initiative, the Animal Copyright Foundation.[27]

Colbert, as narrated on the *Ashes and Snow* Web site, "has spent 13 years filming and photographing elephants, whales, birds, and other animals in India, Burma, Ethiopia, Sri Lanka, Kenya, Namibia, Egypt, the island of Dominica, Tonga, and Antarctica." From his neoimperial expeditions to a range of former colonies, he has produced the spectacle of more than fifty large-scale photographs on display on the Web site and in the museum. Alongside highly exoticizing photos of the "extraordinary interactions" of animals and brown-skinned humans, the multimedia exhibit of *Ashes and Snow* includes a 35-mm film (continuously projected on a screen inside the nomadic museum), two nine-minute film "haikus," and an accompanying novel in letters. Virtual visitors to the Web site can read exegeses of Colbert's vision of.posthuman kinship and of his ongoing, *National Geographic*–style expeditions to collect object matter for his museum. The "ashes and snow" mantra, projected through speakers inside the nomadic museum, encapsulates the faux Zen mysticism manufactured by Colbert, one that I am not alone in challenging.[28] Indeed, an at once familiar and altogether new species of orientalism is at work in Colbert's liberal vision of posthuman kinship. It is a vision that hinges on two pivotal tropes: that of a "universal bestiary" and a "family of animals."

Before engaging with these potent tropes, allow me to draw attention to the orientalism insinuated in those signs of materiality that *are* fetishistically foregrounded in the *Ashes and Snow* discourse (as opposed to those that are occluded). Colbert's valorization of "the East" as a timeless place apart from capitalist postmodernity and as the source of the images that appear in his photographic bestiary is reinforced at the level of material production. To begin with, his "mixed media photographic works marry umber and sepia tones in a distinctive encaustic process on handmade Japanese paper."[29] The distance and difference the exhibit seeks to inscribe between itself and the current neoliberal culture is communicated by handicraft techniques and handmade textiles signifying a precapitalist time of artisanal craftsmanship and authenticity uncorrupted by market-driven modes of production. Consider the description, posted online, of the Tokyo exhibition catalogue: "Printed and bound in Italy on Italian deckle edge paper; hand-sewn binding; covers from handmade paper from Nepal sealed with natural beeswax; tied with thread stained with hibiscus tealeaves and a Nepalese bead." In one of the first incarnations of the *Ashes and Snow* Web site, the museum's migratory journey was mapped on a simulation of old parchment paper, a cartographeme connoting strong nostalgia for Europe's imperial age of discovery via ocean travel. Indeed, the "umber and sepia tones" of Colbert's photographs aesthetically encode an earlier era of both imperial exploration and image production, exciting what Renato Rosaldo calls "imperialist nostalgia"[30] (a notion to which I will return).

Colbert's heroic claim to protect global species diversity by means of its photographic collection and aesthetic appreciation is publicized on the *Ashes and Snow* Web site. "So far," according to the site, "Colbert has worked with twenty-nine different species. While it is unlikely that he will cover anything more than a small fraction of the entire spectrum of life forms, given that this is a lifetime project, he hopes that *Ashes and Snow* will eventually include most of the keystone animal species in the world." While Colbert's cultural discourse of biodiversity generates an aura of scientific legitimacy, the deeper goal of *Ashes and Snow* is to shift *species* from a scientific to an emotional register. His project can be best described, as Colbert states in an interview, "with a word that has fallen into disuse. It's a bestiary."[31] Fond of all things anachronistic or ostensibly prior to the time of capitalist postmodernity within which his project is in fact embedded, he expounds: "A bestiary is an expression of man's emotional relationship with nature and the wonders of nature. For the Egyptians it would be the falcons, for the Mayans the jaguar, the elephants would be for the Indians, for the Native American Indians it would be the eagle and the buffalo. Every culture had a bestiary, and this culture has none."[32] Aside from the temporal insinuation that Egyptian, Native American, and Mayan cultures once "*had* a bestiary" (emphasis mine), implying that indigenous cultures exist only in the past tense, Colbert's remark reveals his mission as a deeply problematic one. It is that of collecting signs of species diversity from a timeless global culture pool in order to create a bestiary for "this culture" that has none; "this culture" is arguably white neoliberal culture as the unmarked universal.

Problematic though Colbert's liberal love of species biodiversity may be, "this culture" appears to be lapping it up.[33] Colbert was acclaimed as among "the world's most inspired thinkers" when he was invited, in 2006, to deliver a speech at an annual TED (Technology, Entertainment, Design) conference in Monterey, California. The elite conference is "an invitation-only event where the world's leading thinkers and doers gather to find inspiration" among the likes of Bill Clinton and Al Gore.[34] For those not among the select one thousand invited to the event, the inspirational talks have been videotaped and posted online through TED's "clearinghouse of ideas."[35] In his videotaped TED presentation, Colbert reiterates that a bestiary "attempts to inspire an emotional understanding of nature and our place within it." He adds that, until now, "a universal bestiary has never existed that gathers all of the totemic species of the planet."[36]

The global collecting of species diversity is thus represented as a spiritual rather than a scientific mission in the rhetoric of the nomadic museum. In the neoprimitivist evocation of totemism as a form of animal worship innocent of political economy—and in Colbert's hubristic vision of creating a universal bestiary containing "all of the totemic species on the planet"—is it not possible to discern biodiversity being emptied of political force and affectively repackaged as an universal religion? If animal signs are potently *literal* expressions of capital as a "species of fetish," as I contend in the Introduction to this book, could not Colbert's globalization of animal love in the form of a universal bestiary be read as an organized form of commodity worship?[37]

It gets more complicated, however. For what becomes disturbingly apparent when one studies Colbert's photographs is that the rhetoric of the universal bestiary does not account for the exoticized *human* others shown communing with animals in every shot. Along with the "40 totemic species" displayed in the museum by the time it had traveled to the Santa Monica Pier in 2006 (up from the initial 29 on display in New York) appear an array of ethnically diverse humans. With the exception of narcissistic shots of Colbert himself (shown swimming in the company of sperm whales), they are brown-skinned "others" of the West's cultural imagination. Colbert is the only white person, as well as the only adult male, to appear in the Web site portfolio, and his presence is linked to the virile symbology of the sperm whale, a biological metaphor of disseminatory power. Otherwise only women and children appear, seminude or sumptuously draped in sartorial signifiers of a colonial era, such as white cottons and linens (no T-shirts and jeans here, no signs of corrupt coevalness with modernity and the West). They are shown either erotically or prayerfully entwined with animal bodies, as in the photo of a young South Asian boy reading to an elephant or that of an Asian child sitting in a meditative pose beside a leopard. Another photo of a young South Asian woman waist-deep in water, rapt in the phallic embrace of two elephant trunks, is an unabashed rendering of imperialist desire. Reiterating well-worn orientalist tropes, the East is both feminized and infantilized, semiographed as a terrain awaiting sexual discovery by the white male explorer. In virtually every photo, the eyes of the languid other are closed, enabling viewers of Colbert's exhibit to reproject imperialism's primal scene of intercourse with a passive virgin territory.

During his TED talk, Colbert recites a claim also made on the *Ashes and Snow* Web site: "I want to remind you that none of the images are computer generated or digitally collaged. This is exactly what I saw through the lens of my camera." In view of the elaborately choreographed images displayed on the Web site, Colbert's claim to mimetic authenticity appears truly incredible. More perniciously, the claim to photographic transparency serves to naturalize a powerful new species of orientalism. I call it a species of orientalism because the essentializing and othering stereotypes of the East that Edward Said claimed are discursively produced by Western knowledges have been cannily rearticulated, in Colbert's work, to and as a challenge to speciesism. This challenge is explicitly pronounced by the second seminal kinship trope mobilized by Colbert's discourse, that of a "family of animals." Colbert says that his vision is "to lift the natural and artificial barriers between humans and other species, dissolving the distance that exists between them." In a pivotal statement, he declares, "No longer shown as merely a member of the family of man, humans are seen as a member of the family of animals."[38] Yet the humanity that is fetishistically visualized inside the animal family is almost exclusively composed, as I have noted, of racialized figures long the object of a Western gaze.

The oneness with flora and fauna through which colonizing imaginaries framed non-Europeans as having a surplus of nature and therefore a deficit of culture is recalculated as a credit in Colbert's new species of orientalism, partly by virtue of the role that biodiversity discourse has come to play in valorizing an ecological ideal of species interconnectedness in a sensual and sacred web of life. In the nomadic museum, ethnic others are arguably racialized on the "positive" rather than the negative grounds of their presumed embeddedness in life's ecological web. In Colbert's discourse it now counts as a compliment rather than a slur to be considered closer to animals, to belong to the greater family of animals rather than to the family of man. Nevertheless, this compliment is racially reserved—with the exception of Colbert himself—for visibly ethnic others who exist, as one admiring reviewer of *Ashes and Snow* put it, in "a parallel, yellow-brown pigmented universe."[39]

The presence of human others from "the East" in Colbert's family of animals raises troubling questions. Do Third World humans fall under the classification of "totemic species" in the museum's discourse? After all, the diversity they represent appears, like the diversity of animals, to be based solely on the fetishistic criteria of visible, exoticized difference. Moreover, the humans who appear in Colbert's images are not acknowledged in the section of the Web site titled "Gregory Colbert and Collaborators," in which three equal partners in the project are recognized: "Gregory Colbert," "The Animals," and "The Architect." While he liberally acknowledges his animal collaborators by species name—Cheetahs, Elephants, Ocelots, Baboons, Tapirs, and so on—Colbert makes no mention of his human collaborators. The suggestion is that there is no need to make a "speciesist" distinction between Third World humans and animal species, given that they now constitute one global "family of animals."

Colbert's liberal-minded acknowledgement of his animal collaborators has potentially pernicious effects. On the one hand, it anthropomorphizes animals by attributing to them a subjectivity and an agency that are ostensibly readily transparent (versus potentially inscrutable), enabling Colbert to play up their willing participation in the drama of interspecies intimacy he has staged. Agency is configured, in other words, as a universally readable body language that transcends not only the potential aphasias posed by cultural, class, and linguistic differences but also, Colbert suggests, those posed by species difference. On the other hand, Colbert demotes the human subjects appearing in his photos to a dumb animality by excluding them from the rhetoric of collaboration and the possession of subjectivity that it connotes.

The "Family of Animals": Loving Imperialism

Around fifty years prior to Colbert's exhibit, in 1955, Edward Steichen's landmark photographic exhibit *The Family of Man* opened at New York's Museum of Modern Art. The 503 photos of diverse humanity in his family album were meant to be emblematic, as Steichen himself wrote, "of the essential oneness of mankind throughout the world."[40] In *Mythologies*, Roland Barthes accuses Steichen's work of a reductive "sentimentality," one that works to "suppress the determining weight of History: we are held back at the surface of an identity, prevented precisely by sentimentality from penetrating into this ulterior zone of human behavior where historical alienation introduces some 'differences' which we shall here quite simply call 'injustices.'"[41] Steichen's exhibit might be seen as having marked the end of the humanist career of the figure of the family of man, as its last burst of universalizing sentiment prior to the eruption of the injustices of history into a sentimental world picture with the decolonizing movements of the 1960s.

However, Colbert's claim that in his work a global humanity appears no longer "as merely a member of the family of man" but instead "as a member of the family of animals"[42] suggests that the canonical figure of the family of man went underground rather than expired, resurfacing in a new form to continue its universalizing work in the early twenty-first century. Colbert's rearticulation of the "biological humanism" of the family of man at once illustrates that colonial kinship taxonomies persist, after decolonization, in new guises, *and* suggests that the terrain of power has significantly extended since Steichen to involve species other than "man" and to include posthumanist means and ends.[43]

Prior to the cosmopolitan currency of Steichen's portrayal of the family of man in the Cold War era, it circulated as a key trope in colonial discourse. Tracking the figure of the family of man back through its discursive career in the nineteenth century, Anne McClintock writes, "According to the colonial version of this trope, imperial progress across the space of empire is figured as a journey backward in time to an anachronistic moment of prehistory."[44] Significantly, Colbert describes the photos in his bestiary "as a direct connection to ancient man and his Paleolithic cave paintings," to a period of prehistory in which "humans coexisted with their fellow beasts."[45] That Colbert's "journey backward in time" also gets spatialized as traveling to the East for his photographic object matter suggests that the trope of the family of animals performs similar ideological functions to those of its canonical predecessor. Yet the colonial figure of the family of man, which, McClintock argues, encodes a narrative of progress framing non-Europeans as perpetually belated in their humanity, receives a temporal twist in Colbert's rearticulation.

In Colbert's posthumanist rendition of kinship, European humanity no longer represents the evolutionary goal and upright standard toward which all other cultures are cast as perpetually slouching. Universal man appears to have relinquished his imperial right to represent the ideal family (or to have been forced to by decolonizing movements), shifting that ideal onto the animal kingdom and the goal of living in ecological harmony with other species. That is, Colbert's kinship vision suggests that while it is politically fraught in the early twenty-first century to represent (European) humanity as the telos of history, it is more than acceptable—in fact, it is environmentally desirable—to cede that place to the animal. Paradoxically, the new, universal goal of history that has reappeared after the upheavals of decolonization, at least the one enciphered in Colbert's kinship trope, is to become animal, to evolve *back into,* rather than out of, our animal prehistory. Yet once again the prehistoric posthumanism of becoming-animal is represented as equivalent, in Colbert's logic, with traveling East. His kinship ideal reappraises the colonial discourse of the other's belated humanity by investing it with ecological value, but at the same time his vision of kinship presupposes that the brown-skinned non-Westerner is closer to animals than the white Westerner, who, after all these twists and turns, remains in imperial position as the universal subject.

Colbert's "family of animals" subsumes the appreciation of global human diversity represented by Steichen's work into a yet *more liberal* appreciation of species biodiversity. One might say that Colbert's work collates the logics of multiculturalism and of biodiversity within a larger kinship optics of family life. Against the essentialism of both Steichen and Colbert's kinship visions, it is helpful to recall how Slavoj Žižek ideologically implicates the multicultural appreciation of diversity in the logic of capital's globalization. Žižek contends that the appreciation of diversity enshrined in multiculturalist ideology constitutes the "cultural logic of multinational capitalism."[46] In the celebration of ethnic particularity, he claims, can be seen the "form of appearance of its opposite, the massive presence of capitalism as universal world system" (44). Multiculturalism, pursues Žižek, "is a racism which empties its own position of all positive content . . . but nonetheless retains this position as the privileged empty point of universality from which one is able to appreciate (and depreciate) properly other particular cultures" (44). His prognosis is apropos to the late liberal interest in biological as well as cultural diversity. The exhaustive inventorying and appreciation of nature's particularity in the cause of saving biodiversity equally deserves to be interrogated, alongside liberal multiculturalism, as "the form of appearance of its opposite": the universalizing force of capital (44). In Colbert's discourse, it is "this culture" (the one ostensibly lacking a bestiary) that inhabits the position of the "privileged empty point of universality" from which the greater family of animals is appreciated in all of its diversity.

When cultural and biological diversity are aesthetically detached from the realm of political struggle, as they are in Colbert's private museum, they turn into floating signifiers purified of what Žižek calls "pathological" substance. Rather than a psychiatric diagnosis, for Žižek the pathological indexes a world composed of material bodies posing a threat of "real" alterity in their excessive *jouissance,* or unassimilable "kernel of Otherness."[47] "Liberal 'tolerance,'" writes Žižek, "condones the folklorist Other deprived of its substance—like the multitude of 'ethnic cuisines' in a contemporary megalopolis; however, any 'real' Other is instantly denounced for its 'fundamentalism'" (37). The model of human-animal kinship idealized in the nomadic museum is one of contemplative coexistence and interspecies civility: monklike boys bow humbly before wise elephants; young girls sit reverently next to cheetahs. The right relationship toward our animal kin, Colbert's photos intimate, is one of aesthetic appreciation. What is not permitted within the frames of Colbert's vision are signs of Third World subjects working with and consuming animals. Any material labors and visceral pleasures of human-animal relationship exceeding the pure language of kinship he claims to represent are excised from view, at risk of being measured against his sympathetic ideal and found to be not only lacking but "sick." I will return to the pathological shortly in tracking how the sick substance of ethnic and animal alterity has returned, with a vengeance, in pandemic discourse.

First, however, let me zoom in on just one of Colbert's family photos and on that scene of human-animal contact that is contradictorily charged with so much desire and so much menace in the current era of global capitalism. In the sequence of photographs posted on the *Ashes and Snow* Web site, this image appears immediately after another one

showing an orangutan perched on the tip of a slim wooden boat, keeping vigil over a sleeping Asian girl whose hand trails in the water. The
orangutan in this shot is looking backward. While one of its hands
gently grasps the boat just next to the girl's head, the other reaches out
with its slender, graceful arm to something behind it. The following
photograph focuses on the hand of the orangutan, now touching another hand that could be its mirror image except that it is white and
attached to a man submerged in the water. The man, we can safely
assume, is Colbert. A distortion effect caused by the water makes Colbert's arm appear blurry and surreal; the point of clarity in the dream-
like state of nature is the high-contrast connection and caress of hands.
In this posthuman rendition of Michelangelo's "The Creation of Adam"
in the theater of the Orient, it is no longer a transcendent God but an
immanent, animal god who touches the white man into existence.

This photograph of Colbert's bears an uncanny resemblance not
only to "The Creation of Adam," but to a 1994 Gulf Oil ad studied by
Donna Haraway in her analysis of primatology stories. Haraway draws
attention to the Gulf ad in her study of *National Geographic*'s popular
coverage of female primatologists who ventured into Africa at the moment of its decolonization, in search of animal kinship (this same ad is
discussed in chapter 3). Gulf publicized its sponsorship of the *National
Geographic* stories with an image capturing what it described as "a
spontaneous gesture of trust" as "a chimpanzee in the wilds of Tanzania
folds his leathery hand around that of Jane Goodall."[48]

Haraway notes that the Gulf Oil image depicts the encounter between the female primatologist and the African animal as *allochronic*,
that is, as "existing in a time outside the contentious, coeval time of
history" (149). The dramas of touch linking female primatologists to
apes in Africa "are played out in a nature that seems innocent of history," effectively displacing material histories and social struggles of
decolonization from political view (156). Like the Gulf Oil ad, Colbert's photo also appears to capture a "spontaneous gesture of trust" as
a Third World animal reaches out, with a soft, wise gesture of inclu-
sion, to the white man. The orangutan is inviting white man into the
timeless family of animals, into the family composed of himself and
the sleeping South Asian girl. While race, gender, and species remain

crucial codes in this echo of the *National Geographic*–Gulf Oil system of signs, it is no longer a female primatologist but rather a white, male photographer who mediates an allochronic drama of interspecies intimacy. With the time of decolonization ostensibly safely past, white man can again venture forth in the cause of reconnecting with nature. Yet the question that Haraway broadly poses in *Primate Visions*— "What forms does love of nature take in particular historical contexts? For whom and at what cost?" (1)—is the question that also needs to be asked of this photograph. For the "contentious, coeval time of history" is once again being effaced by a timeless spectacle of human-animal kinship. This time around, what is deflected from view are the new forces of imperial power that evolved, as Hardt and Negri argue, precisely in response to the decolonizing struggles of the latter half of the twentieth century.[49]

Despite their disavowal of history, the ostensibly timeless scenes of human-animal intimacy depicted in Colbert's photos in fact semiotically encode a very specific historical period—that of European empire. Colbert's denial of history can be read, in fact, as a longing for empire's eternal recurrence. The "umber and sepia" tones of his photographs, the colonial cottons gracefully draping the human subjects appearing in them, the imperialist rhetoric of global adventuring and collecting all bespeak nostalgia for empire's lost "elegance of manners," in the words of Renato Rosaldo.[50] Like the late twentieth-century films that Rosaldo says spurred him to theorize "imperialist nostalgia," the nomadic museum excites longing for a time of culture and nature prior to the present.[51] "Curiously enough," writes Rosaldo,

> agents of colonialism—officials, constabulary officers, missionaries, and other figures from whom anthropologists ritually dissociate themselves—often display nostalgia for the colonized culture as it was "traditionally" (that is, when they first encountered it). The peculiarity of their yearning, of course, is that agents of colonialism long for the very forms of life they intentionally altered or destroyed. (107–8)

However, rather than nostalgia for a traditional culture as it was prior to *colonization*, Colbert's discourse evinces imperialist nostalgia for the world as it was prior to *decolonization*. It is a colonial, rather than precolonial, time that his photographs render natural and nostalgic.

When *Ashes and Snow* left New York's Pier 54 to continue on its "migratory journey" to Los Angeles (Santa Monica) in January of 2006, the Web site celebrated the effect its arrival had of "transforming an area adjacent to Santa Monica's historic pier into a timeless realm in which animals co-exist with humans." The effacement of history, as I have noted, is incessant in the *Ashes and Snow* discourse. Yet Colbert has made the mistake of condensing his disavowal of historical time into a signature refusal to wear even a wristwatch, a gesture that catches him in a blatant contradiction. "Though he moves around the world, living in Paris and Scotland," relates one reviewer of *Ashes and Snow*, "he eschews the Internet, cell phones, even watches."[52] Colbert's renunciation of "even watches" too intimately contradicts the material conditions of his own exhibit, given that none other than the Rolex corporation purchased *Ashes and Snow* after it first opened in Venice and currently sponsors the museum on its migratory journey. The irony of Colbert's eschewal of wristwatches is profound: his rendering of a timeless spectacle of interspecies kinship is backed by a company whose empire has been built on the commodification of time, a company that represents "the ultimate luxury brand worldwide."[53] Indeed, the Rolex empire can surely be implicated in the "real subsumption" of time theorized by Antonio Negri (and discussed in chapter 1).[54] Behind the eternal ideal of human-animal kinship visualized by Colbert lies the imperial claim that capitalism now transcends history, in the form of Rolex's assurance that "impervious to the hands of time, a Rolex watch is made to last."[55]

On this note, let me turn to the speculative discourse of pandemic that circulates in productive contradiction and in real time with Colbert's exhibit. It will circuitously lead back, by the end of this chapter, to Colbert's latest initiative, the Animal Copyright Foundation.

Zoonotic Disease: The Sick Substance of Interspecies Intimacy

If an opportunity is inadvertently provided by the *Ashes and Snow* discourse itself to implicate it in the domain of material history that it disavows, I locate it in the coincidence that the Hudson Street district around New York's Pier 54 was formerly a meatpacking district containing as many as 250 slaughterhouses and packing plants. By the

1980s, the postindustrial makeover of the Gansevoort market had displaced packing plants with an influx of niche shops and nightclubs. Traffics in sides of beef yielded to traffics in images of biodiversity around Pier 54 when the nomadic museum opened there in 2005. Yet, as global "crises" of mad cow disease and avian flu in the present make clear, the animal capital of industrial slaughter has not disappeared with the postindustrial production of animal signs but rather persists as its "pathological" supplement.

Colbert's zoo-love for bare sacred life (in all of its ethnic and animal diversity) has become deeply appealing at the same historical moment that its seeming opposite, panic at the possibility of species-leaping disease, is brewing in neoliberal minds and bodies. In fear-mongering discourses of global disease, images of ethnic and animal life are entangled to seemingly opposite, yet arguably supplementary, effect. The Janus face of the longing for interspecies intimacy is the horror of breached species barriers, a horror closely bound up with intolerance for the pathological substance of ethnic alterity that Žižek sees lurking in the ideal of multiculturalist tolerance.

Around the same period that slaughter was being displaced from urban space in New York, peasant bone collectors in India were gathering animal remains for export to Britain, where they usually ended up in livestock feed. These Indian bone collectors in the second half of the twentieth century were just one material segment in the global chains of nature and labor supporting mass monocultures of capitalist livestock. However, this "ethnic" segment in the material chain of animal capital was isolated out as pathological in September of 2005 when two British scientists, Nancy and Alan Colchester, published an article in the prestigious medical journal the *Lancet* tracing the mad cow epidemic in Britain back to bone collectors on the Indian subcontinent.

The Colchesters speculate that human remains from corpses floated down the Ganges after Hindu funerals—"infected cadavers," in their words, carrying the human variant of mad cow[56]—were indiscriminately mixed with the flesh and bones of animals collected for export to Britain from the 1950s to the 1970s. Their idea challenges the general scientific opinion that mad cow disease is caused by the practice of "animal cannibalism," that is, the agroindustrial practice of feeding rendered remains of ruminants back to livestock. In the Colchesters' view, it was ethnic flesh mixed with animal remains and exported to Britain that infected European cattle being fattened for market on high-protein meals.

The ugly limits of multiculturalism risk being aroused by what the Colchesters admit is still just scientific speculation; there is virulent potential for reading their origin story of mad cow disease as a metaphor for Europe's infection by ethnic others. Here, scientific justification for reasserting the biological boundaries of "species," "race," and "nation" appears as the contradictory supplement to Colbert's fantasy of a global "family of animals." Moreover, the Colchesters' scientific speculation absolves "the market" of the pathology of mad cow disease by racially linking the disease to darkly imagined ethnic rites and the unsanitary miasma of the Ganges.[57]

Many multicultural theorists have noted that, along with female genital surgeries, Hindu funerary practices of *sati* (widow self-immolation) have constituted an ur-limit of liberal understanding. As Elizabeth Povinelli describes the limits of Australian multiculturalism in tolerating indigenous difference, "No matter the heroic rhetoric of enlightenment understanding, 'their ways' cannot cease to make 'us' sick."[58] Here, in the context of a global traffic in animal material, widow immolation as a limit of multiculturalist empathy and mad cow disease as a limit of zoo-love are twisted together in the gut feeling of being made sick. Racist intolerance reemerges as a visceral, seemingly "preideological," and thus permissible, response to the excessive alterity of culture and nature.[59]

The panic inspired by mad cow disease, AIDS, SARS, and most recently, avian flu accrues to the fact that they are zoonoses, diseases capable of leaping species barriers between animals and humans. A fixation on zoonotic diseases in the last decades of the twentieth century and the first decade of the twenty-first suggests that human-animal intimacy is one of the most ideologically and materially contested sites of postmodernity as formerly distinct barriers separating humans and other species begin to imaginatively, and physically, disintegrate. HIV/ AIDS, arguably *the* defining disease of postmodernity until its recent displacement by concern over the H5N1 avian flu virus, was recently declared to be of zoonotic, or animal, origin. The 2003 SARS epidemic that afflicted Toronto and Hong Kong, among other global cities, has likewise been attributed to a species-leaping virus carried by the civet cats that many Chinese consider a delicacy. However, since the outbreak of a deadly strain of avian influenza in China in 2003, it has been the H5N1 virus that has riveted global attention to the species line and to its ominous permeability. It is around avian flu that the ugly limits of the liberal ideals of multiculturalism and biodiversity have again come into view.

Carriers of avian flu, migratory wild ducks and birds have come to represent a form of biological mobility, or biomobility, that appears no longer benign (in contrast to the "migratory" tropes of the nomadic museum) but rather all too malignant. The avian flu virus lodges asymp-tomatically, or harmlessly, in the intestines of wild geese and fowl. Yet in species that have not built up immunity to a new viral strain such as H5N1, including humans, it can be lethal. When a young Chinese girl died of avian influenza in 2003, medical doctors discovered that a new virus had leapt directly from infected bird to human victim, "a stagger-ing, paradigm-shifting discovery," as Mike Davis writes in *The Monster at Our Door: The Global Threat of Avian Flu* (2005), given that the species barrier "was believed to be insurmountable."[60] Since then, with subsequent outbreaks of avian flu in poultry, animals, and humans, the possibility of a mutation in the virus that would enable it to be transmit-ted rapidly and directly from human to human has ignited a discourse of pandemic that currently grips the global village. Or, more accurately, as I suggested in the opening section of this chapter, a discourse of the coming pandemic partially *constitutes* as well as restriates the global village through the affect of fear.

Pandemic predictions intensified over the course of 2005 and 2006 as the Western media tracked incidents of avian flu in Asia, the Middle East, Africa, and finally Europe. Despite outbreaks and mass poultry cullings in Canada and the Netherlands, the disease was narrated as a threat emanating from the East, originating in the ostensible epicenter of disease, China's Guangdong province.[61] The nearly daily coverage of newly infected or dead ducks, chickens, and humans in the East

was accompanied by growing consternation at countries' underprepared-
ness or their unwillingness to ready themselves for a pandemic that
many scientists claimed was not "simply imminent" but in fact "late."[62]

Before continuing, let me reemphasize that my purpose here is not
to stake a wager on whether pandemic is an empty rather than a real
threat or to treat its possibility at all lightly. Rather, what concerns me
is the seriousness of its effects even though it exists only as a virtuality.
At stake is the power of pandemic speculation to infect subjects like
myself—well-intentioned, white, liberal-minded, middle-class subjects
living in relative security in affluent pockets of the globe—with fear
for our own survival, that of our close relatives, and, by extension, that
of the "family of man." What more compelling reason than fear for
"human species survival" itself could there be to justify growing intolerance toward dangerously entwined ethnic-animal populations?[63]

Pandemic speculation invokes avian flu as an indiscriminate, generic
threat to the species life of humans. As former WHO director Jong-
Lee Wook declared, in words ostensibly designed to excite solidarity
on the grounds of the bare species life of an endangered humanity, "An
influenza epidemic will not discriminate between those who live in
mansions and those who live in slums."[64] Yet arguably a pandemic
would in fact severely discriminate between immiserated multitudes
and an affluent global class; rather than irreducible, human species life
is deeply striated by differential vulnerabilities to disease and death
along the political lines of class, race, gender, nationality, age, and so
on. Despite its persuasive effect of smoothing over material differences
and leveling all humans within a shared state of vulnerability, pandemic speculation works, as I have already noted, to reinscribe racial
difference in the global village.

The possibility of a pandemic requires that human and animal populations be biologically monitored and managed on a scale surpassing
that of the nation-state, authorizing institutions such as the WHO to
place "life" under global surveillance. Through pandemic speculation,
a logic of biopower associated by Foucault with the practices and technologies of the state expands to include supranational institutions and
techniques devoted to tracking global human and animal health, and
accelerates as a nanoproject working, under the pressure of time, to

achieve greater knowledge of and control over microbial nature. The threat of a pandemic also supplies an imperative for more intensively capturing the contingencies of biological life in the calculus of the political.

As my interest in the speculative function of pandemic suggests, it is not only communicable disease itself that is at stake but how communicable disease itself is infectiously communicated as imminent. Charles L. Briggs has devised the neologism "biocommunicability" to draw attention to "the political economy of communicability," that is, to the question of who does and who does not possess the institutional power and symbolic (as well as material) capital to communicate authoritative biomedical knowledge of disease in the first place.[65] The racialization of disease operates, Briggs suggests, not only at the level of the storied content of pandemic discourse but at the level of the political economy of disease communication itself, which positions some subjects as "experts" relaying ostensibly transparent knowledge about the origins and outbreaks of disease and others as ignorant victims tied to cultural geographies represented as both on the receiving end of knowledge and as innately prone to infection. "In grasping how epidemics seem to distinguish sanitary citizens from unsanitary subjects naturally," Briggs writes, it is important to consider "how access to the production and reception of authoritative knowledge about disease is distributed, and . . . how this communicative process is ideologically constructed in such a way as to make some people seem like producers of knowledge, others like translators and disseminators, others like receivers, and some simply out of the game" (274).

While Briggs contends that "spheres of communicability, like publics, are multiple, competing, overlapping, and shifting" (274), he also claims that in the case of epidemic and pandemic disease it "becomes possible to place the entire world within a single biocommunicable sphere and signal the WHO's status as its center" (278). Following Foucault, Briggs views biocommunicability as productive insofar as public discourses of disease "help create the publics they purport to address," which in the case of the WHO involves the constitution of a global public sphere (275). Moreover, biocommunicability shifts attention away from the political conditions that make some regions of the globe more prone to outbreaks of disease than others (through neocolonial regimes of capital, structural disparities in health care, and so on) by fostering the sense that microbes spontaneously erupt in some (usually nonwhite) populations and not others. "That 'their' bodies should be diseased just seems natural" in the global public sphere created by pandemic discourse (277). "Herein lies the tremendous value for neoliberal globalization of producing inequalities with the help of biocommunicability," contends Briggs, because "this move draws attention away from global patterns of health and political economy and onto how the losers in health disparities seem to be incarcerated in culture" (277).

Biocommunicability repeatedly represents China's Guangdong province as the breeding ground of zoonosis by virtue, significantly, of the region's imagined excess of interspecies intimacy and, in the eyes of the West, its "sick" intermingling of human and animal flesh. This is the flip side of the human-animal intimacy fetishized in the nomadic museum. A bird flu story published in a 2005 issue of *Newsweek* magazine is typical in its view that China's mixed human-animal population is excessive:

> If the virus makes the leap to human-to-human transmission, the odds are that it will happen in China. The place is home to 1.3 billion humans— three quarters of them still living on the farm—and more than 10 times that number of chickens, ducks, and other domestic poultry. Those farmers keep 70 percent of the world's pigs, which can be walking Petri dishes for mutating strains of flu. To top it all off, the public-health system is in ruins.[66]

In Guangdong, as Mike Davis reiterates, "an extraordinary concentration of poultry... coexists with high human densities."[67] "Guangdong is also a huge market for wild meat," he notes, adding that "the Chinese predilection for exotic animals stems from ancient homeopathic beliefs; the demand is inexorable" (60).

Indeed, Asian "wet markets"—markets selling live poultry and sometimes wild animals—are racially pathologized as zoonotic hotbeds in pandemic discourse. They deeply offend Western sensibilities by virtue of the seemingly superstitious and callous consumption of the exotic and even endangered animal life they supply. Davis's own claim that this consumption is driven by "ancient" beliefs and therefore "inexorable" demand risks incarcerating an idea of Chinese consumption as irremediably traditional. Just as SARS origin stories involve an Asian "predilection" for eating civet cats, evoking in the West the worst imaginings of their preparation and consumption, in the case of avian flu it is again ethnic constituencies living in close quarters with the animals they eat that are identified as the source of disease.[68]

Mei Zhan notes that popular and scientific discourses around the SARS outbreaks of 2003 were laced with orientalist stereotypes of visceral consumption, stereotypes evoking an "exoticized bodily continuity between the wild animal and the Chinese people who readily consume it."[69] Writes Zhan, "European, North American, and many Chinese newspapers and websites were replete with narratives linking the 'age-old tradition' of eating wild animals with SARS. These sensational reports portrayed the strange entanglements of human and animal bodies, and the deadly filthiness of such entanglements" (37). Identifying the Chinese with the visceral consumption of "wild" animals produces the image of "a traditional, exotic Chinese culture out of sync with a cosmopolitan world" (33). As Zhan argues, however, "It is precisely through encounters generated by transnational projects and [neoliberal] processes of marketization... that such an imaginary is sharpened and given a visceral form" (33). Rather than the sign of an atavistic subjectivity locked in tradition, contends Zhan, the visceral consumption attributed to the Chinese in SARS discourses requires that we break down the opposing signs of the traditional and the modern in order to trace how neoliberal subjectivity is discrepantly constituted in China through heterogeneous and contested forms of consumption (34). Given Davis's conflation of wet markets, "ancient homeopathic beliefs," and "inexorable" demand for wild meat in his portrayal of the breeding grounds of the coming pandemic, Zhan's analysis of SARS discourses is instructive. She claims that "while mass media and scientific representations constructed a visceralized ancient epicurean tradition of China as the 'real origin' of the SARS outbreak, they also did so by locating narratives of excess squarely within the sphere of the market and mass consumption, which is not an emblem of 'ancient Chinese culture' but a product of recent economic, social, and political transformations in China" (38). Tracking related contentions that "excessive" Chinese consumption

begins to appear in post-Mao China (partly in response to the "defi-
ciency" of the Mao era and partly through "large-scale marketization"),
Zhan notes that rather than traditional, "visceral practices of consumption in China today are intimately entangled in the emergence of
an urban middle class" (38).

Zhan's argument supports Žižek's claim that multiculturalist ideology celebrates the difference of ethnic cultures and cuisines on the
condition that they be emptied of their substance, their kernel of *jouissance.* It is the visceralization of consumption, she suggests, that racially
links Asians to zoonotic disease and to forms of "sick" alterity that
cannot be stomached by the universal subject protected in multiculturalist ideology. But Zhan also draws attention to how those signs of
visceral alterity that expose the racist limits of multicultural tolerance
themselves are racially construed through discourses of zoonotic disease. Rather than a "kernel of Otherness" (37)—which implies that
the excessive substance of cultural alterity is a "real" essence preexisting
discourse—Zhan suggests that "the visceral is already discursive" (32).

Hardt and Negri claim: *"Disease is a sign of physical and moral cor-
ruption, a sign of a lack of civilization. Colonialism's civilizing project,
then, is justified by the hygiene it brings."*[70] Pandemic speculation can be
seen as a civilizing project that works, specifically, to correct ethnic
others' unhygienic intimacy with animals in an era of globalization. As
the animal entanglements of ethnic constituencies are filtered through
the hygienic mask of pandemic discourse, it is the legitimacy of these
ethnic subjects as global citizens and their place within the kinship
structure of global capitalism that is being biopolitically calculated.
This civilizing project extends to the role the WHO plays in teaching
certain nation-states a lesson in the global civility of transparently
sharing biomedical information. China's defensive Communist Party
bureaucracy, for instance, repeatedly appears in the WHO's discourse of
global public health as a serious obstacle to the biomedical transparency
required to effectively guard against a pandemic.[71]

In the pandemic stories disseminated by the Western media, formerly quaint scenes of ethnic life suddenly appear disquieting. Scenes
of Chinese, Indonesian, or Turkish children playing in their yards and
even sleeping in their beds with pet chickens or geese now appear in

the dark frames of a discourse of disease that threatens human species life. Global biosecurity is breached by a Thai villager who is unwilling to report possible signs of avian flu in his flocks due to a "national obsession" with fighting cocks,[72] by another Thai man caught trying to smuggle two infected hawk eagles (endangered species) into Brussels,[73] and by a medically unenlightened Indonesian who, down with the flu, seeks out a witch doctor rather than checking himself into the hospital. Indeed, in a news article titled "Indonesia Bird-Flu Victim Sought Witch Doctor, Shunned Hospital," the story of Dowes Ginting, who died of bird flu in May of 2006 on the island of Sumatra, is tinged with racist paternalism.[74] Although a representative of the WHO recommended that Ginting "be isolated and treated in the hospital with the Roche Holding AG antiviral drug, Tamiflu," the story relates how Ginting "fled local health authorities and sought care from a witch doctor."[75] The suggestion is that Ginting not only was dangerously backward in failing to place his trust in advanced Western medicine but lacked proper kinship sensibilities insofar as, by evading doctors for three days, he ended up infecting "at least six of his relatives, including his son."[76] Because the deaths of Ginting and his relatives raised the serious possibility that the H5N1 virus had achieved the dreaded mutation into a strain capable of being transmitted from human to human, his infection of family members was metaphorical for the potential infection of the entire global village by his ignorance.

Even though advanced biomedicine has proven itself largely useless in determining the causes and in developing reliable cures for SARS and avian flu, pandemic stories routinely racialize non-Western subalterns as backward primitives who need to be enlightened to the new demands of global hygiene, civility, and kinship to be prevented from communicating disease and mass death to the larger family of man. Significantly, this racializing discourse displaces the pathological nature of global capitalism—and of animal capital, in particular—onto the figure of the ignorant "villager." Without confronting its racist connotations, Mike Davis nevertheless suggests that the fixation of many influenza experts on South China as a disease epicenter constitutes "a near-dogma" that blinds them to "compelling evidence [that the] environmental preconditions for the rapid interspecies evolution of

influenza are now found elsewhere."⁷⁷ Indeed, the breeding grounds of
avian influenza may not be Guangdong province, relates Davis, but
rather sites of large-scale industrial animal capital following from a late
twentieth-century livestock revolution that has globally rationalized
poultry and livestock production, either destroying peasants and family farmers or incorporating them into the machinery of multinational
agribusiness (83).

Rather than the sickening crush of humans and animals associated
with Guangdong, in this alternate origin story it is the "extraordinary
population concentrations of poultry" resulting from the highly rationalized profit logic of multinational animal capital that constitute
the possible breeding grounds of bird flu (84). As Davis notes, "There
are now regions in North America, Brazil, western Europe, and South
Asia with chicken populations in the hundreds of millions—in western Arkansas and northern Georgia, for example, more than 1 billion
chickens are slaughtered annually" (84). He also notes, moreover, that
instead of suffering from global outbreaks of avian flu, multinational
animal capitals are often strengthened by it. The racist (and class)
dogma that views interspecies intimacy on small-scale and family farms
in the East as the primal scene of disease has resulted in devastating
demands on subalterns and small producers to cull entire flocks, ra-
tionalize their operations with expensive flu-monitoring systems and
vaccination programs, or integrate into an already rationalized global
livestock industry that, unlike them, is purportedly the model of hygiene. In tracing the case of Pranee Thongchan, an eighteen-year-old
Thai woman who died of avian flu in 2004 in Thailand, Davis relates
how the response of the Thai prime minister played right into the
hands of powerful poultry producers: "More than chicken exports were
now endangered: tourism, the source of 6 percent of the nation's GDP,
was under threat. Prime Minister Thaksin responded with a tantrum
in which he blamed the 'ignorance' of villagers for the persistence of
the outbreak and—music to the ears of corporate poultry producers—
threatened to ban farm families from raising fowl in their yards" (121).

Alongside its racializing effects, then, pandemic speculation arguably
drives new forms of primitive accumulation in the present. Members
of the Retort Collective⁷⁸ are not alone in working to revise Marx's

original notion that primitive accumulation—which Marx theorized
as a force of enclosure and proletarianization splitting workers off
from the land and their own means of production and turning them
into a class that can survive only by selling its labor power—is a one-
time precondition of capitalism. "For in practice," they write, "it has
turned out that primitive accumulation is an *incomplete* and *recurring*
process, essential to capitalism's continuing life."[79] The new intolerance for "farm families . . . raising fowl in their yards" suggests that it is
tenacious forms of subsistence and small-scale production that are being
enclosed as governments, anxious about tourism economies and striving
to take visible preventive action in demonstration of their conformance
to the new ethical imperative of global hygiene, demand that poultry
raised outside of corporate facilities be sold or slaughtered. "As of March
2006," notes a Canadian guide to avian flu, "the WHO estimated that
the culling of poultry in Asia and other places has affected over 300
million subsistence farmers with an estimated economic impact of over
US$10 billion, much of this borne directly by poor rural farmers."[80]

Pandemic speculation becomes an alibi for primitive accumulation,
providing incontestable grounds (with human species life itself hanging in the balance) for splitting subsistence producers off from their
own protein sources and rendering them reliant on a globalized food
industry. Primitive accumulation extends beyond the proletarianization of humans, moreover, to the enclosure of the reproductive labors
and lives of chickens and other species. Yet primitive accumulation
goes deeper than the enclosure of animals as food sources; it involves
splitting apart relationships and knowledges forged out of the everyday living together of humans and animals and segregating them into
separate populations who live and die for abstract capital rather than
for and with one another.

Autoimmunity

Yet counterhegemonic potentials also reside in the specter of pandemic. Indeed, one sign of resistance to pandemic speculation springs,
perversely, from inside its own logic. A year after I first began writing
this chapter, during a lull in the media hype over avian flu, a startling

joint announcement was issued by the U.S. Food and Drug Administration (FDA) and the Swiss drugmaker Hoffman–La Roche Ltd.
(manufacturer of the antiviral drug Tamiflu, or oseltamivir). In light of
its review of 103 reports of bizarre ill effects and even deaths caused by
Tamiflu, the FDA stated that the drug would thenceforth require a
product label indicating the possible risk that Tamiflu itself might pose
to human health. Shortly afterward, Health Canada issued a similar
statement concerning the potentially adverse effects of Tamiflu. In its
news bulletin, Health Canada alerted the public that "people in other
countries, particularly children and teens in Japan, exhibited strange
behavior, including hallucinations and self-injury, after taking the
drug."[81] (Even this biomedical caution inserted in the discourse of pandemic is arguably productive of a racialized global cartography.) Moreover, between the lines of the Health Canada bulletin is a suggestion
that the hallucinatory and psychiatric effects of the drug may have induced more than just irrational "self-injury" and that some of the deaths
caused by Tamiflu may have been suicides: "A majority of the cases involved people under age 17 in Japan and involved three people who fell
to their death after taking the drug. One 14-year-old boy fell to his
death after climbing on the railing of his family's condominium."[82]
Indeed, in its coverage of the story, the *Los Angeles Times* explicitly
stated that suicide was among the "neuropsychiatric adverse events"
provoked by oral consumption of the drug.[83] Why these individuals
were consuming Tamiflu in the first place is left open to speculation,
but there are hints that in many cases the drug may have been taken
either as treatment for the seasonal flu or under the prophylactic logic
of preemptively protecting against a coming pandemic.

   With tragic irony, the potential threat to life posed by avian influenza is mimicked in the material effects of its ostensible cure. In the
effects of the antiviral drug currently being emergency stockpiled by
the WHO, by wealthy nation-states, and by panicked individuals, there
is a revelation that the threat of a pandemic can no longer be solely attributed to the bioterrorism of viral nature. A potential pandemic is also
immanently produced by health security discourse itself in the shape
of a drug-induced autoimmune disorder, a sick surplus of disease-
fighting activity leading bodies to turn on and attack themselves. If

"Sales of Flu Drug Soar amid Pandemic Worries," as one news headline in the Canadian media put it, so, concomitantly, does the possibility of a mass prophylactic consumption of the antiviral.[84] In retrospect, the WHO's gratitude at receiving a donation from Hoffman–La Roche of two million treatment courses of Tamiflu in 2006, contributing to its stockpile of three million courses of Tamiflu to be distributed to "first affected areas" of disease, is darkly ironic.[85] In light of the strange reports around the effects of Tamiflu, is it not possible to imagine a global course of preventive medicine that would simultaneously augur a boon for pharmaceutical capital *and* trigger a global wave of autoimmune violence potentially rivaling the death toll predicted for an avian flu pandemic itself? Although there has always been a concession that, while Tamiflu is one of the only effective antivirals available, it might prove useless against a rapidly mutating avian flu virus, there has been little sense that it might itself be virulent.[86]

While it is undoubtedly a speculative exercise on my own part to conjure up a global autoimmune disorder as the immanent logic of pandemic speculation, I do so finally to raise some of the ethical ramifications of the imperialist rhetoric and machinery of "global health security" that responds to the condition of biomobility I have introduced—the inescapability of living together in a tight space—with efforts to ontologically segregate human and animal lives. First, however, let me sum up the two "constitutive affects" of late liberal life that I have been exploring in this chapter by way of two images. The first image consists of the book cover of Mike Davis's *The Monster at Our Door: The Global Threat of Avian Flu* (see Figure 13). The second is a symbol devised by Gregory Colbert for the Animal Copyright Foundation, his latest environmental initiative (see Figure 14). Together they pictorially condense the new animal enclosures operating, under the affects of love and fear, to circumscribe possibilities of kinship safely (and not so safely) within the neoliberal universe of capital.

Consider, first, the cover of Davis's book. It pronounces, with alarmist typeface, a gothic horror genre whose monster slot is now semiotically filled by a rooster with threatening red cockscomb and beady alien eye, the figure of a newly hostile nature. *The Monster at Our Door* seeks to alert its readers to a looming public health crisis whose origins,

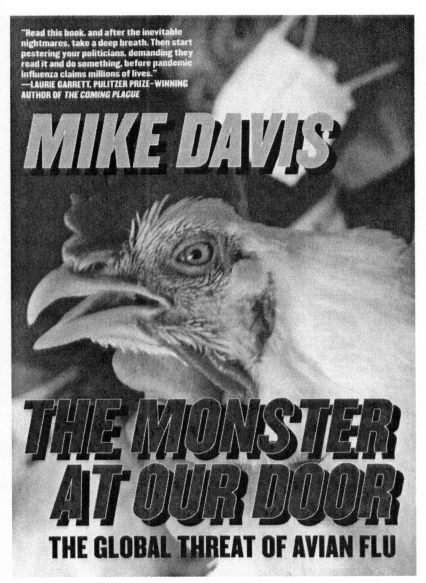

Figure 13. Avian nature in the monster slot. Book cover of Mike Davis's
The Monster at Our Door: The Global Threat of Avian Flu *(New York:*
New Press, 2005).

ANIMAL COPYRIGHT

Figure 14. Placing universal copyright under the protection of nature. Revised symbol of the Animal Copyright Foundation (2008). Reprinted with permission.

Davis argues, are political rather than natural, lying in the profit-driven control of antivirals by pharmaceutical companies such as Hoffman–La Roche as well as in "ecologies of disease resulting from globalization."[87] Nevertheless, the book perpetuates a terrorist rhetoric mobilized by the WHO, governments, and the media in response to the threat of avian nature. In deploring the lack of funding allocated within the United States' "Project Bioshield" for fighting the threat of avian influenza, Davis reinforces the idea that bird flu has usurped the position of even Osama Bin Laden as the world's "'most wanted' terrorist" (13). When it is not the horror genre, it is the rhetoric of the Western deployed by George W. Bush in the U.S.-led war against terrorism that infuses Davis's own pandemic politics.

Indeed, chilling resonances between a discourse of pandemic preparedness and the imperial rhetoric and machinery of the war against terrorism again give us a glimpse into the dangerous conflation of constructions of racial and species alterity in biopolitical times. In the discourse of the WHO, pandemic preparedness is a matter of biosecurity and requires a global "surveillance network" and "epidemic intelligence" around the bioterrorist threat of avian flu.[88] Moreover, the WHO's Epidemic and Pandemic Alert and Response system, a "real time alert" system designed to communicate current levels of pandemic threat posed by avian flu, bears an uncanny resemblance to the U.S. Homeland Security Advisory System, which similarly monitors levels of terrorist threat coded green ("low"), blue ("guarded"), yellow ("elevated"), orange ("high"), or red ("severe"). Pandemic discourse prepares us, in other words, for a new imperial war against nature.[89]

The elephant symbol for Colbert's Animal Copyright Foundation condenses a very different affective disposition vis-à-vis animal life in the present. It is a simple, abstract logo that brands an idea announced by Colbert at the end of his 2006 TED talk in Santa Monica, California: "Every year corporations spend billions of dollars in advertising their products using nature and animals," he stated there. "But unlike humans, nature is not paid for its contribution. This practice reveals our failure to understand a basic principle of nature. One must give back what one takes to preserve and sustain the world in which we live."[90] This makes sound ecological sense. Yet it renders nature and capital tautologous through the ethical rubric—reminiscent of the rhetoric of industrial ecology deployed by the modern rendering industry (see chapter 1)—of "giving back." It is the taking and giving back to nature as *"incarnate capital"* that is reified as a natural principle.[91] "Until now," continued Colbert,

> because they've had no representation, animals have been used without compensation. It is for this reason I'm founding ... the Animal Copyright Foundation, a non-profit entity that exists to serve and preserve

species and habitats around the world. Starting January 1, 2007, the foundation will collect 1 percent of all media buys, including print, broadcast,
and internet that use animals. These payments will go to the Animal Copyright Foundation. These funds will be distributed, each year, to different
conservation projects around the world.[92]

Again, rather than posing a challenge to the universal rule of capitalism, in this instance an ecological ethics serves to biopolitically extend
the logic of capital more deeply into nonhuman nature, turning animal
life into a symbolic stakeholder in the universe of capital, with Colbert
as its representative and fund manager. The current trademark replaces
an earlier, discarded symbol for the Animal Copyright Foundation
that consisted of an "A" encircled within a "C"; the earlier symbol bril-
liantly mimicked the universal copyright symbol itself, but at the risk
of exposing how the foundation in fact rendered a capitalist logic of
intellectual property and an ethic of saving nature tautologous. That
is, the circle encapsulating the "A" revealed that the protection of animal life would be achieved by subsuming the family of animals within
the universal domain of capital and its intellectual copyright laws. The
foundation's current logo marks an attempt to correct its telling earlier
design by instead placing the "C" within the curl of an elephant's trunk
as a form of graphic reassurance that "copyright" and "capital" serve
the public domain of nature rather than the other way around. In effect,
the revised trademark works to more cleverly conceal how the ethical
discourse of the Animal Copyright Foundation itself operates as a force
of enclosure in the service of capital.

In between the expedient ecological ethics of the Animal Copyright Foundation, the fetishistic spectacle of entangled ethnic-animal
life touring the world in Colbert's nomadic museum, and the pandemic
discourse of global health security that seeks to remaster the pathological substance of ethnic and animal difference, the possibility of
posthuman kinship seems hopelessly overdetermined. Yet it is precisely a refusal to relinquish the possibility of posthuman kinship that
I want to seize, finally, in retort to the tautological time of global capitalism. For abandonment of the hope of a mutually benefiting material
coexistence with other species is possibly the most terrifying prospect of all.

How can we critically seize this possibility? Renato Rosaldo prescribes a course of critical treatment for "imperialist nostalgia" that is particularly interesting in relation to this chapter's discussion of biomobility. Recognizing the weakness of "a classic perspective which asserts that ideologies are fictions (in the sense of falsehoods)" which can simply be unmasked, Rosaldo proposes instead to "immunize" readers against imperialist nostalgia.[93] While he grants that "demystifying approaches have proven their value," Rosaldo contends that "they all too often short-circuit their analyses by rushing to reveal the 'real' interest involved and failing to show how ideology convinces those caught in its thrall" (110). His analytical strategy, by contrast, "attempts to infect the reader, so to speak, with a case of the ideology's persuasiveness in order to provide immunity against more pathological episodes" (110).

Immunization is, for Rosaldo, a figure of immanent critique that recognizes that ideology operates as constitutive affect rather than as a superstructural illusion that can be pulled back to expose an underlying reality. Yet read in the historical context of the antiviral drug Tamiflu and reports of the autoviolence it has triggered, immunization arguably divulges its own weakness as a critical and ethical model. Tamiflu gives a concrete example, in Derrida's words, of the "perversion by means of which the immune becomes auto-immunizing," that is, of the logic of the pharmakon.[94] The logic of immunization involves injecting a "sick" bit of an animal's body into one's own in order to *build immunity* in the event of future contamination. Derrida links the defensive logic of immunization to the act of autobiography, which marks a desire to inscribe the individual as a distinct, self-same subject. He points to the immanent dangers of an immunological logic of self-defense at work in attempts to secure both the *autos* of the individual and that of the species:

> Autobiography, the writing of the self as living, the trace of the living for itself, being for itself, the auto-affection or auto-infection as memory or archive of the living would be an immunizing movement (a movement of safety, of salvage and salvation of the safe, the holy, the indemnified, of virginal and intact nudity), but an immunizing movement that is always threatened with becoming auto-immunizing, as is every *autos*, every ipseity, every automatic, automobile, autonomous, auto-referential movement.[95]

Derrida has examined the "autoimmunitary process," that is, "that strange behavior where a living being, in quasi-*suicidal* fashion, 'itself' works to destroy its own protection, to immunize itself against its own immunity" in relation to the events of 9/11.[96] Similarly, in *Precarious Life*, Judith Butler also argues against a dominant logic of self-defense in the political context of a post-9/11 American culture awash in discourses of terror and security. Heightening security measures only generates a closed immunological loop in U.S. culture, suggests Butler, because "the violence it fears is the violence it engenders."[97] Opposed to an immunization program against terror that is itself terrorizing, Butler draws on the work of Emmanuel Levinas to formulate an ethics of corporeal vulnerability for the current era.

Corporeal vulnerability, Butler writes, accrues to the fact that "we are not only constituted by our relations but also dispossessed by them as well" (24). The fact that one's very life is constituted in relationship with others is what also makes it, precariously, vulnerable to violence at the hands of others. Butler's formulation of ontological vulnerability in the face of the current violence of "indefinite detention," extreme rendering, and war in the Middle East bears closely on the precariousness of the species line in an era of globalization, particularly given the sinister overlap of the imperial rhetoric and machinery of the war against terrorism and the war against the bioterrorist threat of the H5N1 virus (24). However, under the moral obligation that weighs on the humanities to speak to the times, Butler herself renders a state of exception by taking it as self-evident that, in critical times such as these, there is no question that the human names the ethical priority and proper object of the humanities. Butler writes, "I propose to start, and to end, with the question of the human (as if there were any other way for us to start or end!)" (20).

Rather than "following" on the question of the animal, as Derrida urges, Butler reproduces an autobiography of the humanities, albeit with a difference. "If the humanities has a future as cultural criticism, and cultural criticism has a task at the present moment," she writes, "it is no doubt to return us to the human where we do not expect to find it, in its frailty and at the limits of its capacity to make sense" (151). Butler herself fails to perceive how species is presupposed as self-evident in her own discourse and how it operates as one of the "schemes of intelligibility" that constitute "what will be a livable life, what will be a grievable death" in the present era (146).

The "depopulation" of millions of fowl, wild geese, and ducks in the biopolitical defense of global human health—and the hyper-rationalized conditions under which other species increasingly live and die in order to reproduce capitalism without, ideally, communicating disease or death to humans—suggests that accepting both the responsibility and the vulnerability of living together with other species is also the task of the humanities if it hopes to politically and ethically address the times. Derrida has helped to orient the humanities in this direction by countering (auto)immunizing forces with the notion of a "zoosphere," that is, "the dream of an absolute hospitality" that extends to other species.[98] Like Butler's formulation of an ethics emerging out of a common vulnerability to violence, the zoosphere emerges out of a shared ability to suffer—or rather, a shared "not-being-able" to suffer (396). "Being able to suffer is no longer a power, it is a possibility without power, a possibility of the impossible," writes Derrida (396). "Mortality resides there, as the most radical means of thinking the finitude that we share with animals" (396).

Far from immune to the effects of pandemic speculation on the body, however, the possibility of such a hospitality must be continuously negotiated at the level of the visceral in an era of biomobility. That is, hospitality involves resisting the "gut" instinct to secure ourselves against the perceived animal and human carriers of disease and recognizing the constitutive workings of biofear without perverting an ethics of corporeal vulnerability into the extreme passivity of abandoning the pragmatics of protecting individual and collective health by becoming "hosts" to disease.

Animal Cannibalism in the Capitalist Globe-Mobile

Globalization popularly connotes a swirling *mise-en-abyme* of mobiles inside mobiles, of media inside media. Zooming in from the "globe-mobile"— from an earth that is in its entirety now subsumed, albeit unevenly, by the flows and forces of capital—one narrows in on arteries coursing with automobiles and airplanes carrying subjects who, if they are sufficiently affluent to own a mobile phone, BlackBerry, or personal laptop, can dial up digital connections and virtually spiral back out to the World Wide Web. Yet as the previous chapter suggested, alongside neoliberal promises of effortless auto- and telemobility, globalization also poses a threat of biomobility, or the pandemic spread of zoonotic disease. What loom with the proliferation of virtual and biological mobilities in the current era are the increasingly closed loops of global capitalism, its involuted conditions of existence, and its abysmal effects.

As the ability to distinguish between animal and capital dwindles in the globe-mobile of market culture, or as animal life ceases to mean and matter in ways capable of challenging its symbolic and carnal currency as capital, market discourses themselves fetishize animal alterity. Neoliberal cultures speculate in signs of noncapitalized life even as they effectively render it incarnate capital. In this speculation, global capitalism enacts on a macro scale the paradox that the automobile enacts on a micro scale, materially displacing the "first nature" that is in part its fetishistic destination. Yet even when nature is "gone for good," in the words of Fredric Jameson, capitalism cannibalizes itself to ensure a future.[1] Through its semiotic as well as its material recycling, a perennially undead nature can be kept in "interminable survival," as Derrida puts it in relation to current conditions of animal life.[2] If cannibalism of its symbolic economies gives rise to simulacra and a perpetual reprocessing of mimetic effects, cannibalism of its material resources makes global capitalism into a giant rendering industry, into the sorting and reconstitution no longer of any so-called first nature but of nature as by-product, capitalized in advance.

Capitalist culture's convoluted turning in on itself spawns unpredictable and disturbing forms of "mimetic excess," to borrow from Michael Taussig, in its linked economies of rendering.[3] Global outbreaks of mad cow disease or BSE over the past two decades have been attributed to the practice of "animal cannibalism," that is, the practice of feeding the remains of ruminants back to livestock in order to speed animals to market, provoking a material crisis in the protein chains of advanced capitalism. At the same time, in the symbolic economies of global culture, digital technologies of rendering have provoked a different crisis of mimesis through their unrestrained cannibalism of representational effects, a crisis of simulacra. In the semiotic closed loops of simulacra, "nature" is recycled as a signifying effect detached from any external material referent, while in the closed loops of animal cannibalism, it is recycled as mere material. Animal cannibalism could even be seen as the pathological flip side of the culture of simulacra and simulacra as the spectral double of animal cannibalism. Although mad cow disease and simulacra both began to erupt in the latter decades of the twentieth century as symptomatic crises of postmodernity, I am not suggesting that their historic appearances are causally linked. Rather, they are related as contradictory yet complicit effects of a terrain of capitalist biopower, a terrain in which the reproduction of capital has become one with the symbolic and biological reproduction of "life itself."

Animal Capital opened with an image of the animal nation in an advertisement for *Maclean's* magazine, an ad presenting the anatomy of a beaver as a metaphor for the national geography and "imagined community" of Canada.[4] The normally generative identification of "Canada" with the biological sign of animal life was threatened, however, when a dead cow from an Alberta farm was diagnosed with BSE in 2003. Canadians rallied together to exorcize the taint of bad meat suddenly staining the nation. Canada's prime minister at the time, Jean Chrétien, and Alberta's provincial premier, Ralph Klein, made dramatic public displays of cooking, serving, and consuming Canadian beef, modeling a metabolic commitment to the health and "carnophallogocentrism" of the nation through patriotic displays of meat eating.[5] Not only is the purity of a nation's meat representative, on a deeply affective level, of its domestic economy; meat also enciphers ideological investments in the masculinist virility and racial purity of the national body. The act of consumption asked of Canadians (and of Albertans in particular) through the public barbecues of prominent figures was disseminated through the rousing calls of the mass media to "Eat Beef for the Sake of Our Farmers, and Our Province."[6]

Although the nation was metabolically modeling trust in the purity of its meat in the hope of averting a crisis of animal capital, the United States immediately closed its border to Canadian beef and livestock. Animals became one of the pathological populations justifying the resurrection of discriminating national borders in terrorizing times. In the desire to contain the pathological products of a global traffic in rendered material, the U.S. FDA led the effort to trace a second diseased cow, this time found in Washington State, back to Canada, exonerating itself of the excesses of rendering. The U.S. border remained closed to Canadian cattle over the age of thirty months until November 2007, a drawing of national lines productively contradicted by the fact that the Canadian beef packing industry is largely controlled by the U.S. multinationals Cargill and Tyson Foods Inc., which have been making quantum profits off of animal capital by "transcending" national differences to operate out of Mexico and Canada.[7] Around the recent North American crisis in animal capital, it became apparent that in the empire of global capitalism the power to lift trade barriers between nations is calibrated with the alternate power to strategically reentrench national and cultural differences in the name of policing against pathological impurities.

Mad cow disease holds something of a privileged place among the material symptoms of rendering's logic, given that it springs from the carnal business of industrial rendering itself, from that recycling of animal remains that I historicized in the first chapter of this book. When mad cow disease first erupted as an epidemic in Great Britain in 1985, exposing the widespread practice of feeding rendered brains, spinal cords, and nervous tissues of ruminants back to livestock to facilitate the rapid turnover of animal capital, the kind of "mimetic excess" created by capital's closed loops began to loom large. Mad cow disease is caused by a novel infectious protein, christened a "prion" by the scientist who discovered it,[8] which is an uncannily mimetic product of the protein recycle from which it springs. Prions slowly consume the brains of animals stricken with mad cow disease (and of people stricken with its human variant, Creutzfeldt-Jakob disease), eating holes in the brain until it is reduced to "mere jelly."[9] In the mimetic vengeance of the disease—repaying the profit-driven practice of feeding cortical and nervous tissues back to animals with an abnormal protein that "wastes" the brain—mad cow disease is indeed suggestive of what Michael Taussig calls "the mimesis of mimesis," or "mimesis made aware of itself."[10] When a disease mimics its material conditions, as mad cow disease does, it holds the potential of bringing those conditions to historical and political consciousness. As Jean and John Comaroff recall, consumption (tuberculosis) "was the hallmark disease of the eighteenth and nineteenth centuries, of the First Coming of Industrial Capitalism, of a time when the ecological conditions of production, its consuming passions ... ate up the bodies of producers."[11] Similarly, mad cow disease can be counted among the new wasting diseases that, like consumption, are at once a material symptom and a powerful metaphor of the current ecological conditions of capitalism. Described by scientists as "misfolded" proteins, in their very biological structure prions mimic the involuted logic of animal cannibalism and of what I more broadly historicized in chapter 1 (following Antonio Negri) as the "tautological time" of nature's real subsumption.[12]

The rogue proteins causing mad cow disease assume a monstrous aspect in their resistance to being "cooked" by culture. Studies in the wake of Britain's epidemic reported that prions pass unaffected through the tremendous heats and sterilizing treatments of the industrial rendering process. Rather than reading in the monstrous character of prions an indigestible kernel of animal alterity, however, it is crucial to read them as immanent products of animal capital. If there are forms of alterity haunting cultures of capital, they demand to be understood less as a primal surplus of animal life that evades cooking than as a species of stomach trouble symptomatic of the churning insides of biopolitical culture.

In chapter 2 I suggested that, rather than obvious or given, counterhegemonic histories and signs of animal protest must themselves be actively "rendered." Is it possible, beyond highlighting how mad cow disease materially mimics the protein recycles of late capitalism, to metaphorically articulate that mimicry to counterhegemonic effect? One way of doing so might be to self-consciously elaborate the pathetic fallacy of the vengeful prion, to deliberately attribute to sick nature a capacity for symbolic protest. To turn such a pathetic fallacy to political purpose, moreover, might a comparison be drawn between the symbolism of the prion, which in attacking the brains of its victims mimetically protests the tautological production of animal capital, and the 9/11 strikes on the World Trade Center, in which the U.S. center of global finance capital became a symbolic target of attack? In likening the symbolism of these two attacks I do not mean to suggest, as Mike Davis does in relation to the H5N1 avian flu virus, that the prion is a "bioterrorist." On the contrary, my intent is to challenge a rhetoric of terrorism that repudiates both attacks as material symptoms of neoliberal culture by attributing them to pathogenic nature, a rhetoric that also deploys *rendering* as a euphemism for the illegal transfer of suspected terrorists to countries where they can be tortured (as noted in the Introduction to this book). It is because *rendering* simultaneously euphemizes the violence of animal recycling and that of reducing so-called human pathogens to a state of bare life that politically articulating the symbolism of these different protests is perhaps justified.

As Bruno Latour recognizes, prions serve to politically "stir up the collective" only so long as they do not "become *natural*," that is, so long as they are not reduced to knowable essences or "matters of fact."[13] Latour invokes the excessive prions in arguing for a shift from "matters of fact" to "matters of concern" as a basis for political ecology. "The famous prions," he writes, "symbolize these new matters of concern as much as asbestos symbolizes the old risk-free matters of fact" (24). However, whether the "mimesis of mimesis" posed by pathological prions is capable of provoking an actual crisis of animal capital or simply an emergency that will be folded back into its continued hegemony is the pressing question of the moment. The answer will in part depend on whether the mimetic vengeance of mad cow disease can be seized as an occasion to politically antagonize the biopolitical terrain of capitalism or whether it will serve as an opportunity for powerful forces to further extend and tighten their biopolitical management of life. Subsequent to the mad cow epidemic in the United Kingdom two decades ago, it was just such a biopolitical heightening of control that strove to settle the question, restoring normalcy to capitalist food chains. Britain legislated that every livestock animal had to be given a "passport," stapled to its ear, so that its movements from farm to farm could be tracked. Just as nations now screen for terrorists at increasingly discriminating national borders, livestock is now placed under tight national and international surveillance as a potentially pathological population whose movements threaten infection. Animal passports, genealogical charts, genetic profiles, and BSE testing bespeak an attempt to manage mad cow disease within the intensifying life markets of biocapitalism. In 2006, moreover, a group of scientists announced that they had cloned cattle with a genetically built-in resistance to the disease, quelling the disturbing mimicry of prions while extending the biotechnological means of reproducing animal capital.[14]

If the BSE crisis in the United Kingdom was managed in ways that allowed animal capital to return to normalcy, the crisis was nevertheless reopened by North American incidents of mad cow disease in the first years of the twenty-first century. Yet almost immediately, the power to turn crisis into capital was everywhere in evidence. In Canada, for instance, a provincial auditor general's report investigating allegations that multinational meatpackers had benefited from the BSE crisis confirmed that their profits had, astoundingly, trebled in

2003.[15] As Bill Brown writes in a different context, "The dynamics of capital have a history of converting any such excess into surplus."[16] In the incitement to eat beef, in government subsidies for ranchers and meatpackers, and in the determination to build up national slaughtering and rendering facilities to lessen Canada's dependence on U.S. meatpackers, the currency of animal capital in North America has been reorganized but not structurally challenged. Before normalcy resumes in North American cultures of animal capital, however, I hold out hope that there is an opening in which to develop the mimetic vengeance of rogue proteins into a politics of rendering capable of protesting our biopolitical times.

It has long been imagined and hoped, beginning with Marx, that the internal contradictions of capitalism will eventually lead to its undoing (a hope that also underpins critical discourse analysis and immanent critique). Even Jean Baudrillard hints that capitalism will ultimately deteriorate in the merciless "desert of the real"[17] created by its own logic of simulacra:

> Hyperreality and simulation are deterrents of every principle and every objective, they turn against power the deterrent that it used so well for such a long time. Because in the end, throughout its history, it was capital that first fed on the destructuration of every referential, of every human objective, that shattered every ideal distinction between true and false, good and evil, in order to establish a radical law of equivalence and exchange.[18]

While the aim of *Animal Capital* has been to provoke productive contradictions into unproductive antagonism for cultures of capital by confronting symbolic and carnal economies of rendering, it has also complicated the hope that capital's contradictions might be turned against it, sobering that political optimism. For the sinister prospect accruing to the double logic that *rendering* describes is that of capitalism's potential interminability, a perpetual existence supported by the ability to materially and semiotically recycle its conditions of possibility ad nauseum. Those living in the globe-mobile of market culture have to contend with the possibility that capitalism may not necessarily bump up against the limit of finite resources or unravel from its own immanent contradictions. On the contrary, it appears all too capable of infernally surviving.

Caught in the double binds of animal capital, there seem to be few modes of political intervention capable of breaking its material-semiotic loops to produce other signs of nature and culture. Irregularities and recrudesences of animal rendering—unpredictable, pathological products of the closed loop itself, such as mad cow disease—expose the harrowing tautology of animal capital, but they are not yet a formulation of political struggle. The genealogies of animal capital and the theory of rendering this book has elaborated thus begin, and hopefully will persist, as a question asked from within a double bind and addressed to a heterogeneity of protesting subjects struggling to articulate livable alternatives to the present.

Notes

Introduction

1. The beaver was one in a series of "dissection" ads published inside *Maclean's* magazine, as well as appearing on posters at public transit sites in Ontario, among other places. I came across it in *TransCanada Trail* 8, no. 1 (Fall–Winter 2002). Other ads in the campaign depicted equally charged if less visceral symbols of the nation, including views of the dissected Canadarm (a mechanical arm used on the Space Shuttle) and the insides of a female hockey player's bag.

2. The beaver had been transubstantiated into a symbolic currency long before its "official" signing-in in 1975. In 1678, the Hudson Bay Company imprinted the beaver on the shield of its coat of arms. An eighteenth-century silver Canadian trading token valued at 10 beaver pelts was smelted in the totemic shape of a beaver. In 1851, the first Canadian postage stamp, the "Three-Penny Beaver," was put into circulation. And in 1920, the Hudson Bay Company published a magazine titled *The Beaver*, which remains in circulation today.

3. For a recent critical engagement with the entwined colonial tropes of the "vanishing" native and "vanishing" animals, see Pauline Wakeham's *Taxidermic Signs: Reconstructing Aboriginality* (Minneapolis: University of Minnesota Press, 2008).

4. Daniel Coleman, *White Civility: The Literary Project of English Canada* (Toronto: University of Toronto Press, 2006), 3; Dennis Lee, "Cadence, Country, Silence: Writing in Colonial Space," in *Unhomely States: Theorizing English-Canadian Postcolonialism,* ed. Cynthia Sugars (Peterborough, Ontario: Broadview, 2004), 54.

5. Slavoj Žižek, "Multiculturalism, or the Cultural Logic of Multinational Capitalism," *New Left Review* 225 (1997): 44.

6. Well-known for the ranking of Canadian universities it publishes each year, in this sense *Maclean's* subscribes to institutions of "knowledge" and articulates with academic cultural capital.

7. I borrow the notion of "wry" self-reflexivity from Daniel Coleman's *White Civility.* There he claims that the onus of dismantling hegemonic discourses of "white civility" falls "to cultural critics and scholars" who can counter it "by means of a critical or wry civility," one whose key feature is self-reflexivity around the structural ambivalence of civility itself (239). What the *Maclean's* ad suggests, as does the Bell Mobility ad that I examine later in this Introduction, is that the critical edge of wry civility may itself be preempted by discourses of capital whose strategy also appears to be that of turning stereotypes of national culture into the self-reflexive content of their discourse.

8. Homi K. Bhabha, ed., *Nation and Narration* (London and New York: Routledge, 1990), 3.

9. Homi K. Bhabha, *The Location of Culture* (London and New York: Routledge, 1994), 67. Emphasis in the original. Throughout the book, all italics in quotes were in the originals unless otherwise indicated.

10. Ibid., 74–75. "For fetishism is always a 'play' or vacillation between the archaic affirmation of wholeness/similarity—in Freud's terms: 'All men have penises'; in ours: 'All men have the same skin/race/culture'—and the anxiety associated with lack and difference—again, for Freud 'Some do not have penises'; for us 'Some do not have the same skin/race/culture'" (74).

11. William Pietz, "Fetishism and Materialism: The Limits of Theory in Marx," in *Fetishism As Cultural Discourse,* ed. Emily Apter and William Pietz (Ithaca, N.Y.: Cornell University Press, 1993), 125.

12. Cary Wolfe, ed., *Zoontologies: The Question of the Animal* (Minneapolis: University of Minnesota Press, 2003).

13. Pierre Bourdieu, "Structures, Habitus, Power: Basis for a Theory of Symbolic Power," in *Culture/Power/History: A Reader in Contemporary Social Theory,* ed. Nicholas B. Dirks, Geoff Eley, and Sherry B. Ortner (Princeton, N.J.: Princeton University Press, 1993), 173.

14. Michel Foucault, *The History of Sexuality*, vol. 1, *An Introduction*, trans. Robert Hurley (New York: Vintage, 1980), 144.

15. Michael Hardt and Antonio Negri, *Empire* (Cambridge, Mass.: Harvard University Press, 2000), 24.

16. Foucault, *History of Sexuality*, 143. Michel Foucault, *The Order of Things: An Archaeology of the Human Sciences* (New York: Pantheon, 1970), 278. Foucault clearly maps the notion of biopower in "Right of Death and Power over Life," the last chapter in *The History of Sexuality*, vol. 1. As he writes there, "the beginning of an era of 'biopower'" can be discerned in a historical shift in modernity from the sovereign power to administer death to "a power that exerts a positive influence on life, that endeavors to administer, optimize, and multiply it" (140, 137).

17. Foucault, *Order of Things*, 277.

18. Hardt and Negri, *Empire*, 23.

19. Michel Foucault, "La naissance de la médecine sociale," in *Dits et Écrits*, vol. 3 (Paris: Gallimard, 1994), 210, quoted by Hardt and Negri in *Empire*, 27.

20. Hardt and Negri, *Empire*, 25.

21. As Hardt and Negri write in *Multitude: War and Democracy in the Age of Empire* (New York: Penguin, 2004): "Even though immaterial labor is not dominant in quantitative terms, our claim is that it has imposed a tendency on all other forms of labor, transforming them in accordance with its own characteristics, and in that sense has adopted a hegemonic position" (141).

22. Giorgio Agamben, *Homo Sacer: Sovereign Power and Bare Life*, trans. Daniel Heller-Roazen (Stanford, Calif.: Stanford University Press, 1998), 1.

23. Hardt and Negri, *Empire*, 30.

24. Ibid., 25.

25. Hardt and Negri, *Multitude*, 192.

26. Ibid., 29.

27. Foucault, *History of Sexuality*, 139.

28. Agamben, *Homo Sacer*, 4.

29. Ibid., 8.

30. Jacques Derrida, "'Eating Well,' or the Calculation of the Subject: An Interview with Jacques Derrida," trans. Peter Connor and Avita Ronell, in *Who Comes after the Subject?* ed. Eduardo Cadava, Peter Connor, and Jean-Luc Nancy (New York: Routledge, 1991), 112.

31. Cary Wolfe, *Animal Rites: American Culture, the Discourse of Species, and Posthumanist Theory* (Chicago: University of Chicago Press, 2003), 8.

32. It is both because the force of animalization presupposes the abjection of animals and because the struggle for "humanity" is a goal deeply structured by Eurocentric discourses of humanism that cultural geographers Glen Elder, Jennifer Wolch, and Jody Emel call for a "rejection of 'dehumanization,' as a basis for cultural critique" in "Le Pratique Sauvage: Race, Place, and the Human-Animal Divide," in *Animal Geographies: Place, Politics, and Identity in the Nature-Culture Borderlands,* ed. Wolch and Emel (New York: Verso, 1998), 88. They argue that "the connotations of the very term 'dehumanization' are deeply insidious. They imply human superiority and thus sanction mastery over animals and nature, and also suggest that violent or otherwise harmful treatment is acceptable as long as the targets are nonhuman beings" (88).

33. Michel Foucault, *"Society Must Be Defended": Lectures at the Collège de France 1975–1976* (New York: Picador, 2003), 254–55, emphasis added.

34. Foucault, *History of Sexuality,* 141–42.

35. While Giorgio Agamben's *The Open: Man and Animal* (trans. Kevin Attel [Stanford, Calif.: Stanford University Press, 2004], 38) does engage the zoopolitics, if you will, of the production of human-animal distinctions in the "anthropological machine" of Western culture, it remains primarily a cultural history of animals' representation in discourses of the West that makes little reference to the material history and machinery of capitalism that I am arguing overdetermines the cultural and material currency of "the animal" in Western modernity and postmodernity.

36. Jacques Derrida, "The Animal That Therefore I Am (More to Follow)," trans. David Wills, *Critical Inquiry* 28 (2002): 394.

37. Pheng Cheah, "Given Culture: Rethinking Cosmopolitical Freedom in Transnationalism," in *Cosmopolitics: Thinking and Feeling Beyond the Nation,* ed. Pheng Cheah and Bruce Robbins (Minneapolis: University of Minnesota Press, 1998), 292, 322.

38. Ibid., 301–2. The postcolonial theorists Cheah accuses of "closet idealism" are James Clifford and Homi Bhabha. The phrase appears in the following passage: "My position on hybridity theory can be summed up as follows. First, as a paradigm of postcolonial agency in globalization, hybridity is a closet idealism. It is an anthropologistic culturalism, a theory of resistance that reduces the complex givenness of material reality to its symbolic dimensions" (302).

39. Bourdieu, "Structures, Habitus, Power," 176.

40. Ibid. Writes Bourdieu: "Symbolic capital, a transformed and thereby disguised form of physical 'economic' capital, produces its proper effect in-

asmuch, and only inasmuch, as it conceals the fact that it originates in 'material' forms of capital which are also, in the last instance, the source of its effects" (178).

41. Karl Marx, *Capital: A Critique of Political Economy*, vol. 1, trans. Ben Fowkes (London: Penguin, 1976), 163.

42. Derrida, "The Animal That I Am," 402.

43. David Harvey, *Justice, Nature, and the Geography of Difference* (Cambridge, Mass.: Blackwell, 1996), 183.

44. Derrida, "The Animal That I Am," 399, 402.

45. The ad can be viewed online at http://www.duncans.tv/2006/nissan-animals (accessed February 22, 2007).

46. Bhabha, *Location of Culture*, 86.

47. Antonio Negri, "The Constitution of Time," in *Time for Revolution*, trans. Matteo Mandarini (New York: Continuum, 2003), 27.

48. Writes Foucault in *The History of Sexuality:* "The pressure exerted by the biological on the historical had remained very strong for thousands of years; epidemics and famine were the two great dramatic forms of this relationship that was always dominated by the menace of death" (142). And this: "It is not that life has been totally integrated into techniques that govern and administer it; it constantly escapes them. Outside the Western world, famine exists, on a greater scale than ever; and the biological risks confronting the species are perhaps greater, and certainly more serious, than before the birth of microbiology" (143).

49. Fredric Jameson, *The Seeds of Time* (New York: Columbia University Press, 1994), 16.

50. Ibid., 17.

51. Ibid., 18. Jameson has infamously described the impasse of the political imagination that accompanies capital's end-of-history effect as follows: "It seems to be easier for us today to imagine the thoroughgoing deterioration of the earth and of nature than the breakdown of late capitalism" (xii).

52. James O'Connor, *Natural Causes: Essays in Ecological Marxism* (New York: Guilford, 1998), 12. Hence, in O'Connor's view "capitalist threats to the reproduction of production conditions are threats not only to profits and accumulation but also to the viability of the social and natural environment as *means of life and life itself*" (12).

53. One of the more persuasive proponents of the ideology of "natural capitalism" is Paul Hawken, who argues that neoliberal and environmental ideologies can be rendered compatible without sacrificing a profit logic, and

indeed that the future of profit depends on their reconciliation. See Paul Hawken, Amory Lovens, and L. Hunter Lovens, *Natural Capitalism: Creating the Next Industrial Revolution* (Boston: Back Bay, 2000).

54. Derrida, "The Animal That Therefore I Am," 394.

55. Wikipedia defines *pharming* as "a portmanteau of farming and 'pharmaceutical . . . [that] refers to the use of genetic engineering to insert genes that code for useful pharmaceuticals into host animals or plants that would not otherwise express those genes. As a consequence, the host animals or plants then make the pharmaceutical product in large quantity, which can then be purified and used as a drug product" (http://en.wikipedia.org/wiki/ Pharmaceutical).

56. See Anna Lowenhaupt Tsing's theorization of globalization as a "messy" field of contingencies in which "capitalist universals" can take practical root only through "worldly encounters" with particularity (*Friction: An Ethnography of Global Connection* [Princeton, N.J.: Princeton University Press, 2005], 4). The worldly encounters of capitalist universals with concrete particulars creates "friction," writes Tsing, and this "friction refuses the lie that global power operates as a well-oiled machine" (6).

57. The idea "that we can actually destroy the earth," as Harvey puts it, only "repeats in negative form the hubristic claims of those who aspire to planetary domination" (*Justice, Nature, and Geography*, 194).

58. Pietz, "Fetishism and Materialism," 129.

59. Pietz notes that the word *fetisso* first "came into parlance as a Portuguese trading term associated with 'small wares' and 'magic charms' used for barter between blacks and whites. White merchants, compromising both their religion and their 'rational' economic principles, took oaths on fetishes in order to seal commercial agreements" ("Fetishism and Materialism," 5). In other words, *fetisso* archives the cultural compromise of Europeans in the imperial "contact zone" and the two-way creole of commerce (Mary-Louise Pratt, "'Yo soy la Malinche': Chicana Writers and the Poetics of Ethnonationalism," in *Twentieth Century Poetry: From Text to Context*, ed. Peter Verdonk [London: Routledge, 1993]). In the eighteenth century, however, the French philosopher Charles de Brosse coined "fetishism," classifying it as "the most primitive moment of religion" and fueling an Enlightenment imaginary that positioned Europe at a superior stage of cultural development vis-à-vis 'superstitious' African cultures" (131). E. B. Taylor, the so-called father of cultural anthropology, contributed to the Enlightenment discourse of fetishism with his study of the animism of "primitive cultures" and his developmental hierarchy of cultures,

in which crude animal worshipers appeared at the bottom, enlightened Europeans at the apex.

60. Pietz, "Fetishism and Materialism," 129.

61. Ibid., 139.

62. Marx, *Capital,* 164–65.

63. Pietz, "Fetishism and Materialism," 130–31.

64. "In order... to find an analogy we must take flight into the misty realm of religion" (Marx, *Capital,* 165).

65. Erich Auerbach, *Mimesis: The Representation of Reality in Western Literature,* trans. Willard Trask (Princeton, N.J.: Princeton University Press, 1968).

66. Roland Barthes, "The Reality Effect," in *The Rustle of Language,* trans. Richard Howard (New York: Hill and Wang, 1989).

67. Theodor Adorno, "Culture Industry Reconsidered," in *The Culture Industry: Selected Essays on Mass Culture,* ed. and intro. J. M. Bernstein (London and New York: Routledge, 1991), 100. The "culture industry," writes Adorno, "refers to the standardization of the thing itself—such as that of the Western, familiar to every movie-goer—and to the rationalization of distribution techniques, *but not strictly to the production process*" (100, emphasis added).

68. Michael Taussig, *Mimesis and Alterity: A Particular History of the Senses* (New York: Routledge, 1993), 13.

69. I am grateful to Maisaa Youssef for first drawing my attention to the practice of "extreme rendering" by way of a news story in a Lebanese newspaper (the *Daily Star*) titled "The Perils of 'Extreme Rendering'" (June 11, 2004). As its author, William Fisher, notes, while extreme rendering or "rendition" has gained in currency since September 11, it is not a new practice: "One must note that rendition began before Sept. 11, and was a policy of the Clinton administration after the bombings of the US embassies in Kenya and Tanzania in 1998." Extreme rendering enjoys, along with other U.S. human rights abuses, the status of a public secret: "There is ample evidence that Abu Ghraib–type prisoner abuses were known or suspected by many in Congress and some in the US media long before the photos taken by US soldiers in Iraq created a scandal. The same is true of extreme rendition."

70. Wolfe, *Zoontologies,* xx.

71. Ibid.

72. Cary Wolfe, "*Faux* Post-humanism, or Animal Rights, Neocolonialism, and Michael Crichton's *Congo,*" *Arizona Quarterly* 55, no. 2 (1999): 117.

73. Michel Foucault, "Naissance de la médecine sociale," 210, quoted by Hardt and Negri in *Empire,* 27.

74. Pietz, "Fetishism and Materialism," 120.

75. Ferdinand de Saussure, *Course in General Linguistics,* trans. Wade Baskin, ed. Charles Bally and Albert Sechehaye, in collaboration with Albert Reidlinger (New York: Philosophical Library, 1959), 89.

76. Régis Debray, *Media Manifestos: On the Technological Transmission of Cultural Forms,* trans. Eric Rauth (London and New York: Verso, 1996), 50.

77. Ibid.

78. Mark Seltzer, *Bodies and Machines* (New York: Routledge, 1992), 155.

79. Ibid.

80. "Distortion," in *Oxford English Dictionary,* 2nd ed., vol. 9 (Oxford: Clarendon, 1989), 393.

81. Debray, *Media Manifestos,* 46.

82. Code-switching, Pratt writes, involves moving "fluidly and strategically back and forth between two languages and two cultural systems" ("'Yo soy la Malinche,'" 177).

83. Ernesto Laclau and Chantal Mouffe, *Hegemony and Socialist Strategy: Towards a Radical Democratic Politics,* 2nd ed. (London and New York: Verso, 2001), 111.

84. Ibid., 105.

85. Seltzer, *Bodies and Machines,* 51.

86. Slavoj Žižek argues: "More than ever, Capital is the 'concrete universal' of our historical epoch. What this means is that, while it remains a particular formation, it overdetermines all alternative formations, as well as all noneconomic strata of social life" (*Bodies without Organs: On Deleuze and Consequences* [New York and London: Routledge, 2004], 185).

87. Gilles Deleuze and Felix Guattari, *A Thousand Plateaus: Capitalism and Schizophrenia,* trans. Brian Massumi (Minneapolis: University of Minnesota Press, 1987), 266.

88. Žižek, *Bodies without Organs,* 184.

89. Ibid., 183–84.

90. See Friedrich Nietzsche, *Thus Spoke Zarathustra: A Book for All and None,* trans. Walter A. Kaufmann (New York: Modern Library, 1995).

91. Foucault, *Order,* 387.

92. Deleuze and Guattari, *A Thousand Plateaus,* 275.

93. While Deleuze and Guattari theorize multiplicity by way of the animal pack and swarm, they also posit "a single abstract Animal" as the plane of immanence upon which becomings occur (*A Thousand Plateaus,* 45). That is,

the animal returns as an arch-structure outlining the field of immanence, an organizing figure, ironically, for Nature as a great "body without organs" (270).

94. Michel Foucault, "The Discourse on Language," in *The Archaeology of Knowledge*, trans. Rupert Sawyer (New York: Pantheon, 1982), 231, quoted by Brian Massumi in *Parables for the Virtual: Movement, Affect, Sensation* (Durham, N.C.: Duke University Press, 2002), 4.

95. Ibid., 5. Writes Massumi: "One way of starting to get a grasp on the real-material-but-incorporeal is to say it is to the body, as a positioned thing, as energy is to matter" (5).

96. Deleuze and Guattari, *A Thousand Plateaus*, 248.

97. Žižek, *Bodies without Organs*, 184.

98. Hardt and Negri, *Empire*, 137.

99. Deleuze and Guattari, *A Thousand Plateaus*, 5.

100. Hardt and Negri, *Empire*, 142.

101. Jacques Derrida, *Of Spirit: Heidegger and the Question*, trans. Geoffrey Bennington and Rachel Bowlby (Chicago: University of Chicago Press, 1991), 48.

102. Martin Heidegger, *Being and Time* (1926), trans. John Macquarrie and Edward Robinson (San Francisco: Harper and Row, 1962).

103. Derrida, *Of Spirit*, 54.

104. Ibid., 48.

105. Michael Haar, *Le chant de la terre: Heidegger et les assises de l'histoire de l'etre* (Paris: l'Herne, 1987), 70, quoted by Derrida in *Of Spirit*, 53.

106. George Bataille, *Theory of Religion*, trans. Robert Hurley (New York: Zone, 1992), 19.

107. Derrida, "The Animal That Therefore I Am," 405.

108. John Berger, "Why Look at Animals?" in *About Looking* (New York: Vintage, 1992), 5.

109. If one takes Derrida at his autobiographical word, animals have indeed taken on the status of a first metaphor for every figure of deconstruction that has evolved over his career. For ever since he began writing in "a deconstructive style," remarks Derrida, ever "since I began writing in fact, I have sought to dedicate [the arguments of deconstruction] to the question of the living and of the living animal. For me that will always have been the most important and decisive question. I have addressed it a thousand times, either directly or obliquely, by means of readings of all the philosophers I have taken an interest in" ("The Animal That Therefore I Am," 402).

110. Jacques Derrida, *Specters of Marx: The State of the Debt, the Work of Mourning, and the New International,* trans. Peggy Kamuf (New York and London: Routledge, 1994), 409.

111. Derrida, "The Animal That Therefore I Am," 394.

112. Derrida, *Specters of Marx,* 151.

113. Ibid., 40.

114. Marx, *Capital,* 163–64.

115. Derrida, *Specters of Marx,* 149.

116. While Derrida reads the passage in the original German, as I cannot, it is clear that the evocation of "paws" and of a "prophetic dog" is entirely Derrida's.

117. It would be interesting to link the overturning of the four-legged table as a figure of terrestrial life and use-value with Freud's depiction of the "organic repression" of animality in *Civilization and its Discontents.* Civilization began, Freud suggests, when humans began walking upright rather than on all fours, causing "a shift in the sensorium," as Cary Wolfe puts it, "from smell to sight, the nose to the eye, whose relative separation from the physical environment thus paves the way for the ascendancy of sight as the sense associated with aesthetic, contemplative distance and sensibility" ("*Faux* Post-humanism," 118).

118. Derrida, "The Animal That Therefore I Am," 374.

119. Derrida, *Specters of Marx,* 6.

120. Derrida, "The Animal That Therefore I Am," 372.

121. Like Berger, who also focuses on the fascinated look that passes between human and animal, Derrida privileges the eyes and a transferential gaze over more material, tangible communications of animals, such as a cat's rubbing against a human's leg or purring.

122. Derrida, *Specters of Marx,* 8.

123. Derrida, "The Animal That Therefore I Am," 381.

124. Rey Chow, *Ethics after Idealism; Theory-Culture-Ethnicity-Reading* (Bloomington and Indianapolis: Indiana University Press, 1998), xxi.

125. Derrida, *Specters of Marx,* 27.

126. Derrida, "The Animal That Therefore I Am," 126.

127. Derrida, *Specters of Marx,* 151.

128. Derrida, "Eating Well," 113.

129. Derrida, "The Animal That Therefore I Am," 374.

130. Ibid., 394.

131. Derrida uses the word "survival" to describe both the intolerable conditions of animal life and the paraontology of the specter: it is "neither

dead nor alive, it is dead and alive at the same time. It survives" (*Specters of Marx*, 153).

132. Derrida, *Specters of Marx*, 51.

133. Hardt and Negri, *Empire*, 142.

134. Marx, *Capital*, 169.

135. Hardt and Negri, *Empire*, 47.

136. Akira Mizuta Lippit, *Electric Animal: Toward a Rhetoric of Wildlife* (Minneapolis: University of Minnesota Press, 2000), 1.

137. Derrida, *Specters of Marx*, 8.

138. Lippit, *Electric Animal*, 23.

139. Ibid., 36.

140. Ibid., 196.

141. Jennifer Harding and E. Deidre Pribram, "Losing Our Cool? Following Williams and Grossberg on Emotions," *Cultural Studies* 18, no. 6 (November 2004): 863–83; quote on 873.

142. Raymond Williams, *Marxism and Literature* (Oxford: Oxford University Press, 1977), 30; Lawrence Grossberg, *Bringing It All Back Home: Essays on Cultural Studies* (Durham, N.C.: Duke University Press, 1997), 28, quoted by Harding and Pribram in "Losing Our Cool?" 873; Harding and Pribram, "Losing Our Cool?" 875.

143. Lawrence Grossberg, *We Gotta Get Out of This Place: Popular Conservatism and Postmodern Culture* (New York: Routledge, 1992), 79, quoted by Harding and Pribram in "Losing Our Cool?" 875.

144. Harding and Pribram, "Losing Our Cool?" 876.

145. The reference, once again, is to Daniel Coleman's formulation of "wry" civility, with the suggestion that the critical edge of self-reflexive citizenship it proposes may be foreclosed by agencies of transnational capital, which themselves turn tropes of national citizenship into the ironic content of their discourse (*White Civility*, 239).

146. Jean and John Comaroff, "Millennial Capitalism: First Thoughts on a Second Coming," in *Millenial Capitalism and the Culture of Neoliberalism*, ed. Jean Comaroff and John L. Comaroff (Durham, N.C.: Duke University Press, 2001), 7, 10.

1. Rendering's Modern Logics

1. Michael Taussig, *Mimesis and Alterity: A Particular History of the Senses* (New York: Routledge, 1993), xviii.

2. Ibid., xiii.

3. Taussig does carefully historicize the instrumentality of mimesis for colonial discourses, as well as track important postcolonial reversals in which Western subjects appear as curious objects of representation. As he writes, "The whole anthropological trip starts to eviscerate" when the colonial hierarchy of mimetic power is reversed, that is, when the Western subject finds him/herself becoming the subject, rather than the master, of mimesis (Taussig, *Mimesis and Alterity*, 8).

4. See, for instance, Taussig's *Shamanism, Colonialism, and the Wild Man: A Study in Terror and Healing* (Chicago: University of Chicago Press, 1987).

5. Taussig, *Mimesis and Alterity*, xix.

6. Ibid., xviii.

7. For a comprehensive appraisal of theories of mimesis from Plato to Derrida, see Gunter Gebauer and Christoph Wulf, *Mimesis: Culture, Art, Society*, trans. Don Reneau (Berkeley: University of California Press, 1995), originally published under the title *Mimesis* in 1992 by Rowohlt Taschenbuch Verlage GmbH, Reinbek bei Hamburg.

8. Antonio Negri, "The Constitution of Time," in *Time For Revolution*, trans. Matteo Mandarini (New York: Continuum, 2003), 27.

9. Taussig, *Mimesis and Alterity*, xiv.

10. Michel De Certeau, *The Practice of Everyday Life*, trans. Steven Randall (Berkeley: University of California Press, 1984), xx.

11. I invoke the words of Michel de Certeau because they exemplify the rhetorical gesture of identifying cultural mimesis with biological mimicry. If de Certeau is to this degree implicated in the naturalization of mimesis, however, his theory of *bricolage* as tactical resistance to colonial and capitalist hegemonies is by no means reducible to this gesture.

12. Taussig, *Mimesis and Alterity*, 68.

13. Walter Benjamin, "The Work of Art in the Age of Mechanical Reproduction," in *Illuminations*, ed. Hannah Arendt, trans. Harry Zohn (New York: Harcourt, Brace and World, 1968), 225.

14. Martin Jay provides a helpful definition of *mimetology* as opposed to *mimesis:* "What the poststructuralists call mimetology involves subordinating mimesis to a deadening logic of sameness or sublation." By contrast, most poststructuralists understand mimesis as "an infinite oscillation between original and copy . . . [the] hyperbological antidote to mimetology." Martin Jay, "Mimesis and Mimetology: Adorno and Lacoue-Labarthe," in *The Semblance*

of Subjectivity, ed. Tom Huhn and Lambert Zuidervaart (Cambridge, Mass.: MIT Press, 1997), 46.

15. Walter Benjamin, "On the Mimetic Faculty," in *Walter Benjamin: Selected Writings*, vol. 2, *1927–1934*, ed. Michael Jennings, Howard Eiland, and Gary Smith, trans. Rodney Livingstone (Cambridge, Mass.: Belknap Press of Harvard University Press, 1999), 721.

16. Taussig, *Mimesis and Alterity*, 72.

17. Walter Benjamin, "Doctrine of the Similar," *New German Critique* 17 (Spring 1979): 65–69, 67.

18. Walter Benjamin, "Theses on the Philosophy of History," in *Illuminations*, ed. Hannah Arendt, trans. Harry Zohn (New York: Harcourt, Brace and World, 1968), 263.

19. Negri perhaps too forcefully claims that the dialectical method in which Benjamin invests hope is in fact one with "the immanent productivity of the system" of capitalism ("Constitution of Time," 104): "*Now-time (Jetzt-Zeit)*, innovative precision, utopia: capital considers them as its own" (102).

20. Walter Benjamin, "On the Concept of History," in *Selected Writings*, vol. 4, *1938–1940*, ed. Howard Eiland and Michael W. Jennings, trans. Edmund Jephcott and others (Cambridge, Mass.: Belknap Press of Harvard University Press, 2003), 397. I prefer this translation of Benjamin's famous essay because it translates fashion as having a "nose" (versus "flair") for the topical, linking the tiger's leap into the past more closely to questions of smell and animality.

21. Benjamin, "Theses on the Philosophy of History," 263.

22. Gebauer and Wulf, *Mimesis*, 281.

23. Theodor Adorno, *Aesthetic Theory*, ed. Gretel Adorno and Rolf Tiedemann, trans. and ed. Robert Hullot-Kentor, Theory and History of Literature, vol. 88 (Minneapolis: University of Minnesota Press, 1997), 54.

24. Ibid., 175.

25. Theodor Adorno and Max Horkheimer, *The Dialectic of Enlightenment*, trans. John Cumming (New York: Continuum, 1987), 67.

26. Adorno and Horkheimer, 184, quoted by Taussig in *Mimesis and Alterity*, 66.

27. Ibid., 67.

28. Taussig, *Mimesis and Alterity*, 45.

29. Jay, "Mimesis and Mimetology," 33. As Jay notes, "Mimesis, as Adorno develops it, is not to be understood as the simple opposite of reason, as it sometimes has been. It is closer to what Habermas once called a 'placeholder'

for a 'primordial reason,' which, however, cannot be satisfactorily theorized without betraying its preconceptual status" (33).

30. Roger Caillois, "Mimicry and Legendary Psychasthenia (1938)," trans. John Shepley, *October 31* (Winter 1984): 17–32. Denis Hollier notes, "In French psychiatric language of the time, psychasthenia meant—as its etymology suggests—a drop in the level of psychic energy.... Mimesis is [thus] described in terms of energy, along thermodynamic lines" ("Mimesis and Castration 1937," *October 31* [Winter 1984]: 3–15, 11).

31. Gebauer and Wulf, *Mimesis,* 286.

32. Caillois, "Mimicry and Psychasthenia," 28. Against the rationale that the mimetism of insects functions as a protection against predation, Caillois notes that "one finds many remains of mimetic insects in the stomachs of predators," and he argues that "we are thus dealing with a luxury and even a dangerous luxury, for there are cases in which mimicry causes the creature to go from bad to worse: geometer-moth caterpillars simulate shoots of shrubbery so well that gardeners cut them with their pruning shears" ("Mimicry and Psychasthenia," 25).

33. Gilles Deleuze and Felix Guattari, *A Thousand Plateaus: Capitalism and Schizophrenia,* trans. Brian Massumi (Minneapolis: University of Minnesota Press, 1987), 270.

34. As opposed to Deleuze and Guattari's poststructuralist valorization of "becomings" and schizophrenia, Hollier suggests that "Caillois's description of mimetic behavior is...no praise of psychasthenia; rather, it begins with an argument for distinction" ("Mimesis and Castration," 11).

35. Hollier, "Mimesis and Castration," 13.

36. Gebauer and Wulf, *Mimesis,* 282.

37. Taussig, *Mimesis and Alterity,* 72.

38. *Gates of Heaven,* dir. Errol Morris, Gates of Heaven Production Company, 1978. *Gates of Heaven* ironically juxtaposes the irreverent reduction of the animal body in the boilers of the modern rendering plant with the reverent purchase of the perpetual peace of animal souls in the pet cemetery.

39. Don A. Franco and Winfield Swanson, eds., *The Original Recyclers* (Alexandria, Va.: The Animal Protein Producers Industry, the Fats and Proteins Research Foundation, and the National Renderers Association, 1996).

40. Euphemism, Pierre Bourdieu suggests, is key to symbolic violence, which he describes as "*censored, euphemized,* i.e., unrecognizable" violence ("Structures, Habitus, Power: Basis for a Theory of Symbolic Power," in *Culture/Power/History: A Reader in Contemporary Social Theory,* ed. Nicholas B.

Dirks, Geoff Eley, and Sherry B. Ortner [Princeton, N.J.: Princeton University Press, 1993], 185).

41. Gayle Rubin, "The Traffic in Women: Notes on the 'Political Economy' of Sex," in *Toward an Anthropology of Women*, ed. Rayna R. Reiter (New York: Monthly Review Press, 1975), 157–210, quotes on 157.

42. Noëlie Vialles, *Animal to Edible*, trans. J. A. Underwood (Cambridge: Cambridge University Press, 1994), 15.

43. The National Renderers Association states: "The rendering industry began as an unpleasant-smelling but essential business. While still very essential, technology has changed all this with closed cooking systems and other odor control improvements ... odor [being] ... the primary emission from the rendering process" (*North American Rendering: A Source of Essential, High-Quality Products*, 1st ed., http://www.renderers.org [accessed January 2005], 19).

44. Frank Burnham, "The Rendering Industry—A Historical Perspective," in *The Original Recyclers* (Alexandria, Va.: National Renderers Association, the Animal Protein Producers Industry, and the Fats and Proteins Research Foundation, 1996), 15, 14.

45. The North American rendering industry claims to experience its invisibility as a social stigma even while pursuing social and political anonymity through the erasure of smell. The industry's felt stigmatism is most blatantly announced in the title of a book by Frank Burnham, *Rendering: The Invisible Industry* (Fallbrook, Calif.: Aero, 1978).

46. Michael Taussig, *Defacement: Public Secrecy and the Labor of the Negative* (Stanford, Calif.: Stanford University Press, 1999), 2.

47. Vialles, *Animal to Edible*, 28. For a theorization of the public secret as a "knowing what not to know," see Taussig's *Defacement: Public Secrecy and the Labor of the Negative*, where he further defines the public secret as "*that which is generally known, but cannot be articulated*" (5).

48. Pierres Desrochers, "Market Processes and the Closing of 'Industrial Loops': A Historical Reappraisal," *Journal of Industrial Ecology* 4, no. 1 (2000): 29–43.

49. The NRA, founded in 1933, represents both U.S. and Canadian renderers. Because it represents independent North American renderers—those not incorporated into or immediately adjoined to slaughter facilities owned by megameatpackers such as ConAgra or BP Foods Ltd.—it has come to assume something of a rogue and even outlaw identity in relation to the consolidation of rendering by these giants of animal capital. One would need to go beyond the cursory industrial genealogy I offer here to unpack the significant

differences separating "classes" of rendering capital (i.e., independent renderers versus those incorporated into larger meatpackers). Suffice it to say that the rendering industry is by no means unified and is riven by its own internal differences and antagonisms.

50. Iconic for Pierre Desrochers, similarly, is "what the North American Plains Indians did with buffalo by-products" ("Market Processes," 34).

51. Philip Drucker and Robert F. Heizer, *To Make My Name Good: A Reexamination of the Southern Kwakiutl Potlatch* (Berkeley: University of California Press, 1967), quoted by Burnham in "The Rendering Industry," 6–7.

52. For a history and analysis of potlatch prohibitions and fantasies in North America, see Christopher Bracken's *Potlatch Papers: A Colonial Case History* (Chicago: University of Chicago Press, 1997).

53. If a series of statutes and prohibitions of colonial and neocolonial governments in Canada have criminalized the perceived wastefulness of West Coast potlatch economies (arguably because potlatches pose a threat to the enclosure of natural and cultural resources necessary for the hegemony of colonial and neocolonial capitalism), European intellectuals such as Marcel Mauss and George Bataille dangerously exoticize the radical laying to waste of property that they see potlatches as performing. See, for instance, Bataille's fascination with the potlatch as a figure of "excessive" or "*nonproductive expenditure*" in "The Notion of Expenditure," 117, in *Visions of Excess: Selected Writings, 1927–1939,* ed. and intro. Allan Stoekl, trans. Allan Stoekl with Carl R. Lovitt and Donald M. Leslie Jr., Theory and History of Literature, vol. 14 (Minneapolis: University of Minnesota Press, 1994).

54. In a 1999 documentary coproduced by Nimpkish Wind Productions and the National Film Board of Canada, *T'lina: The Rendering of Wealth,* 'Namgis filmmaker Barb Cranmer films the current grease making of the Kwakwaka'wakw Nation in British Columbia. The film replays archival footage of "grease potlatches" from several early ethnographic films, footage showing West Coast natives pouring buckets of eulachon oil over one another's heads. Yet the film gives proportionally more screen time to a present-day grease potlatch, so while it necessarily risks feeding into a white ethnographic imagination, it also resists the consignment of the Tsimshian's "other" culture of rendering to the past.

55. Burnham, "The Rendering Industry," 14.

56. National Renderers Association, *North American Rendering: The Source of Essential, High-Quality Products,* 2nd ed., http://www.renderers.org/ publications/index.htm (accessed June 2007).

57. Cecelia Tichi, *Shifting Gears: Technology, Literature, Culture in Modernist America* (Chapel Hill: University of North Carolina Press, 1987), 65.

58. Rudolph A. Clemen, *By-Products in the Packing Industry* (Chicago: University of Chicago Press, 1927), vii, quoted by Desrochers in "Market Processes," 39.

59. William Cronon, *Nature's Metropolis: Chicago and the Great West* (New York: W. W. Norton, 1991), 251.

60. Karl Marx, *Capital: A Critique of Political Economy,* vol. 1, trans. Ben Fowkes (London: Penguin, 1976), 1021.

61. For one example of a postcolonial deconstruction of the Marxist grand narrative framing the concepts of formal and real subsumption, see Gayatri Chakravorty Spivak's analysis of Marx's notorious reference to an "Asiatic Mode of Production" in *A Critique of Postcolonial Reason: Toward a History of the Vanishing Present* (Cambridge, Mass.: Harvard University Press, 1999), 71.

62. Spivak, *Critique of Postcolonial Reason,* 68–69.

63. Peter Lund Simmonds, *Animal Products: Their Preparation, Commercial Uses, and Value* (New York: Scribner, Welford and Armstrong, 1875), 24–25, quoted by Desrochers in "Market Processes," 40.

64. Donald S. Moore, Jake Kosek, and Anand Pandian, eds., *Race, Nature, and the Politics of Difference* (Durham, N.C.: Duke University Press, 2003), 18. Moore, Kosek, and Pandian implicate Haeckel's science of "ecology" (coined in 1866) in constructions of race.

65. Desrochers, "Market Processes," 40.

66. Simmonds, *Waste Products and Undeveloped Substances, or Hints for Enterprise in Neglected Fields* (London: Robert Hardwicke, 1862), 1–2, quoted by Desrochers in "Market Processes," 40–41.

67. Simmonds, *Animal Products,* 4, quoted by Desrochers in "Market Processes," 39.

68. Akira Mizuta Lippit, *Electric Animal: Toward a Rhetoric of Wildlife* (Minneapolis: University of Minnesota Press, 2000), 22.

69. Tichi, *Shifting Gears,* 56.

70. Ibid., 77.

71. Ibid.

72. Upton Sinclair, *The Jungle* (1905; New York: New American Library, 1960), 35. Pierre Desrochers also notes, although with none of Sinclair's dark irony, that "it has long been said that 'everything but the squeal' is being used as a productive input in the meatpacking industry" ("Market Processes," 34).

73. Sinclair, *The Jungle,* 40.

74. Burnham, "The Rendering Industry," 9.

75. As Anne McClintock writes: "At the beginning of the nineteenth century, soap was a scarce and humdrum item and washing a cursory activity at best. A few decades later, the manufacture of soap had burgeoned into an imperial commerce; Victorian cleaning rituals were peddled globally as the God-given sign of Britain's evolutionary superiority, and soap was invested with magical, fetish powers" (*Imperial Leather: Race, Gender, and Sexuality in the Colonial Contest* [New York: Routledge, 1995], 207).

76. Cary Wolfe, *Zoontologies: The Question of the Animal* (Minneapolis: University of Minnesota Press, 2003), xx.

77. It would also be reductive to equate the praxis of a politics of rendering with vegetarianism, say. A theory of rendering speaks not only to the production and consumption of animals as meat but to the countless ways animals are produced and consumed as signs and substances in cultures of capital. The impossibility of living outside the double logic of rendering resists the idea that there might be some higher moral ground from which to challenge animal capital. That said, in contexts of biopower, interrogating what and how one eats is as good a place to begin as any other.

78. Thomas Keenan, "The Point Is to (Ex)Change It: Reading Capital, Rhetorically," in *Fetishism as Cultural Discourse,* ed. Emily Apter and William Pietz (Ithaca, N.Y.: Cornell University Press, 1993), 168. This is, at least, how Keenan translates "*Gallert.*" Instead of placing the emphasis on *labor* as the element common to all commodities, Keenan makes the unusual move of focusing on the idea of the *human* as the axis of equivalence: "Before endorsing or condemning some labor theory of value, we need to ask about the status not so much of labor as of the abstraction, the abstraction that is humanity" (169). The law that establishes the "commensurable magnitudes" (170) of commodities, suggests Keenan, is the abstract law of humanism. This leads him to claim that "Marxism is the critical analysis of capitalism precisely insofar as capitalism is a humanism. Humanity, the abstraction, is the ghostly residue that names the pragmatic necessity of likeness in exchange" (171–72).

79. Keenan, "The Point Is to (Ex)Change It," 172.

80. Marx, "Economic and Philosophical Manuscripts," in *Karl Marx: Selected Writings,* ed. David McLellan (Oxford: Oxford University Press, 1977), 81. This distinction is drawn both *within* the human species and *between* human and animal, because for Marx human species life becomes human species being only through historical consciousness of its universal essence. Gayatri Spivak has examined the repercussions of the fact that Marx's distinction between

species life and species being is drawn within the category of the human as well as between human and animal, arguing that in the Marxian subtext non-Europeans are aligned with species life and only Europeans with the full humanity of species being (see *Critique of Postcolonial Reason*).

81. Michael Hardt and Antonio Negri, *Empire* (Cambridge, Mass.: Harvard University Press, 2000), 52.

82. Negri, "Constitution of Time," 26.

83. A founding precept of humanist ideology, as Cary Wolfe argues, is that language possession is what ultimately distinguishes humans from animals (*Animal Rites: American Culture, the Discourse of Species, and Posthumanist Theory* [Chicago: University of Chicago Press, 2003]).

84. Negri, "Constitution of Time," 65.

85. James O'Connor, *Natural Causes: Essays in Ecological Marxism* (New York: Guilford, 1998), 331.

86. Martin O'Connor, "On the Misadventures of Capitalist Nature," in *Is Capitalism Sustainable? Political Economy and the Politics of Ecology*, ed. Martin O'Connor (New York: Guilford, 1994), 129, 144.

87. Jean Baudrillard, "Design and Environment, or How Political Economy Escalates into Cyberblitz," in *For a Critique of the Political Economy of the Sign*, trans. Charles Levin (St. Louis: Telos, 1981), 201, quoted by M. O'Connor in "Misadventures of Capitalist Nature," 129.

88. Ibid.

89. O'Connor, "On the Misadventures of Capitalist Nature," 137. O'Connor notes that, contrary to the fantasy of participatory nature, "the enlarged system of capitalized nature is in permanent ferment, and acutely conflict-ridden" (137). Through natural disasters and "accidents," he argues, nature exceeds "instrumental control" (142).

90. Negri, "Constitution of Time," 29.

91. Ibid., 41.

92. Noel Castree provides a helpful overview of post-Marxist theorizations of "produced nature" (many of them emerging out of the discipline of cultural geography). Theories of produced nature challenge the bourgeois idea of a universal and external nature and variously contend that nature is, instead, socially produced. Yet Castree suggests that although Neil Smith's *Uneven Development,* for instance, was pivotal in theorizing the social "*production of nature*" under capitalism," it in turn lost sight of what Castree calls "the *materiality of nature*" ("The Nature of Produced Nature," *Antipode: A Radical Journal of Geography* 27, no. 1 [January 1995]: 12–48; 19, 20). "In seeking to overturn the

ideologies of external and universal nature," argues Castree, "there is the risk of reverting to a monism centered on the labor process—*the* production of nature—which tends to exaggerate the transformative powers of capitalism" (20).

93. Negri, "Constitution of Time," 41.

94. Bruno Latour elaborates a complex political philosophy around the possibility of a "collective" democratically composed of both humans and nonhumans (*Politics of Nature: How to Bring the Sciences into Democracy*, trans. Catherine Porter [Cambridge, Mass.: Harvard University Press, 2004], 82). Although Latour does not, to my mind, adequately acknowledge power asymmetries between humans and nonhumans within the heterogeneous assemblages he evokes (particularly when he privileges laboratories as spaces mediating the voices of nonhumans), he does provocatively illuminate the limits I have been arguing in relation to the work of Negri when he declares: "While the revolutionary examples have their charm, still, the constitutional upheavals of the past concerned humans alone! Now, today's counterrevolutionary upheavals also concern nonhumans" (60).

95. See David L. Meeker, ed., *Essential Rendering: All about the Animal By-Products Industry* (Arlington, Va.: National Renderers Association, 2006). The rendering industry's commitment to biosecurity in response to public health concerns has its historical precedents. The U.S. Food and Drug Administration was created, in large part, in response to the public agitation stirred by Upton Sinclair's disturbing representation, in *The Jungle* (1905), of the unknowns that fall into the rendering vat and end up in the sausages.

96. Andrew Ross, "The Ecology of Images," in *The Chicago Gangster Theory of Life: Nature's Debt to Society* (London: Verso, 1994), 165.

97. Negri, "Constitution of Time," 105.

98. O'Connor, "Misadventures of Capitalist Nature," 133.

99. Ibid., 136.

2. Automobility

1. David Harvey, *The Condition of Postmodernity: An Inquiry into the Origins of Cultural Change* (Cambridge, Mass.: Blackwell, 1990), 28. James Flink likewise claims that "the Ford Motor Company innovated modern mass-production techniques at its now Highland Park plant" (*The Automobile Age* [Cambridge, Mass.: MIT Press, 1988], 37).

2. "It is uncertain where or when the overhead assembly line origi-

nated," writes Louise Carroll Wade, "but many Cincinnati and Chicago plants had them by the late 1850s" (*Chicago's Pride: The Stockyards, Packingtown, and Environs in the Nineteenth Century* [Urbana: University of Illinois Press, 1987], 62).

3. Antonio Gramsci, *Selections from the Prison Notebooks*, ed. and trans. Quintin Hoare and Geoffrey Nowell Smith (New York: International, 1971), 235.

4. Frederick Winslow Taylor, *Principles of Scientific Management* (New York: Harper and Brothers, 1914), 40.

5. Taylor proposed to improve the inefficient motions of pig iron handlers in Pennsylvania steel mills, stating: "This work is so crude and elementary in its nature that the writer firmly believes that it would be possible to train an intelligent gorilla so as to become a more efficient pig-iron handler than any man can be" (*Scientific Management*, 40).

6. The sign of the monkey is at the same time racially overdetermined (as I examine in detail in chapter 4), suggesting that Taylorism also perpetuated a biological discourse of race.

7. Gramsci takes up Taylor's comment on the "intelligent gorilla" as the most condensed expression of the effort "to develop the worker's mechanical side to the maximum, to sever the old psychophysical nexus of skilled professional work in which the intelligence, initiative, and imagination were required to play some role, and thus to reduce the operations of production solely to the physical aspect" (*Prison Notebooks*, 214, 216).

8. Gramsci, *Prison Notebooks*, 169.

9. Bill Brown, *The Material Unconscious: American Amusement, Stephen Crane, and the Economics of Play* (Chicago: University of Chicago Press, 1996), 5.

10. In another recent reconsideration of Fredric Jameson's theory of the political unconscious, Lawrence Buell theorizes "the environmental unconscious" (*Writing for an Endangered World: Literature, Culture, and Environment in the United States and Beyond* [Cambridge, Mass.: Harvard University Press, 2001], 18). Like Brown, Buell privileges literature as a site of access to material history while arguing that material history needs to be considered more broadly as environmental history. Thus, for Buell, the environmental unconscious constitutes a literary subtext that inscribes culture's inescapable "embeddedness in spatio-physical context" (24).

11. Brown, *Material Unconscious*, 13, 14.

12. As Brown notes, "The (structuralist) Barthes of 'The Reality Effect' (1968)" reads Flaubert's barometer "as a superfluous notation, a diegetically

and symbolically nonfunctional detail of the sort that realism deploys in the effort not to denote a specific materiality but to... effect the realist illusion" (*Material Unconscious,* 15).

13. *Gelatin* will sometimes appear with an *e* and sometimes without over the course of this chapter, reflecting its inconsistent spelling in the texts I refer to.

14. Here I use *vanishing point* to name the point at which animal material is rendered perfectly nontransparent to visual culture, as well as the moment in the slaughter of animals at which, in the words of Noëlie Vialles, they become just "a substance to be processed" (*Animal to Edible,* trans. J. A. Underwood [Cambridge: Cambridge University Press, 1994], 44). In his early description of a tour of a slaughterhouse, Frederick Law Olmsted used the words "vanishing point" to name this identical moment: "We entered an immense low-ceiled room and followed a vista of dead swine, upon their backs, their paws stretched mutely toward heaven. Walking down to the vanishing point, we found there a sort of human chopping-machine where the hogs were converted into commercial pork" (*A Journey through Texas, or A Saddle-Trip on the Southwestern Frontier* [1857; reprint, Austin: University of Texas, 1978], 14, quoted by William Cronon in *Nature's Metropolis: Chicago and the Great West* [W. W. Norton, 1991], 228. *Vanishing point* also references a perspectival effect in the visual arts.

15. Brown, *Material Unconscious,* 14.

16. Akira Mizuta Lippit, *Electric Animal: Toward a Rhetoric of Wildlife* (Minneapolis: University of Minnesota Press, 2000), 104.

17. Brown, *Material Unconscious,* 5.

18. The claim that "the animal lives *unhistorically*" is Friedrich Nietzsche's, from "On the Uses and Disadvantages of History for Life," in *Untimely Meditations,* trans. R. J. Hollingdale (Cambridge: Cambridge University Press, 1983), 61, quoted by Lippit in *Electric Animal,* 68.

19. Jonathan Crary suggests that "any optical apparatus," in this instance the camera obscura, is "what Gilles Deleuze would call an assemblage... a site at which a discursive formation intersects with material practices" (*Techniques of the Observer: On Vision and Modernity in the Nineteenth Century* [Cambridge, Mass.: MIT Press, 1992], 31). Geoffrey Batchen takes a similarly nonempirical approach by locating the conditions of photography in a framework of "discursive desire" rather than in its technological determinations (*Each Wild Idea: Writing, Photography, History* [Cambridge, Mass.: MIT Press, 2001], 5).

20. Brown, *Material Unconscious*, 239.

21. Wade, *Chicago's Pride*, 32.

22. Ibid., xiv. Writes Wade: "In 1875, when the stockyard was only ten years old, a Chicago editor asserted that visitors would as soon think of leaving the city without having seen the yards and packinghouses as 'the traveler would of visiting Egypt, and not the pyramids; Rome, and not the Coliseum; Pisa, and not the Leaning-Tower'" (*Chicago's Pride*, xi).

23. Wade, *Chicago's Pride*, xiv.

24. There seems to have been a historical "window" in which slaughter enjoyed and capitalized on its visibility rather than sought invisibility, a window in which tours of abattoirs were immensely popular and the industry played a large role in publicizing the modern nation's efficiencies. This window did not remain open for long, however; although tours of slaughterhouses have continued across the twentieth century and into the twenty-first (often with the pedagogical purpose of giving schoolchildren a glimpse of industrial economy), the space of slaughter has become increasingly identified with resistance to graphic exposure, so that films of slaughterhouses circulated by animal rights organizations such as People for the Ethical Treatment of Animals in the second half of the twentieth century and the twenty-first have been seen as forced glimpses into a clandestine space barred from the public view.

25. Upton Sinclair, *The Jungle* (1905; New York: New American Library, 1960), 38.

26. Ibid., 102. While Sinclair's fictional focus on the trials of a Lithuanian family in *The Jungle* played a pivotal role in politicizing the conditions of immigrant workers in the stockyards, his text perpetuates racist stereotypes of African Americans as lazy, opportunistic "scabs" willing to replace desperate strikers. More than a trope for the predatory relations of capital, "the jungle" is a racist trope closely tied to a seminal scene in the novel that describes an orgy of black strike-breakers flooding the stockyards, a scene that portrays them as promiscuous and primitive bodies surging up from "the South" to undermine a Euro-American socialist movement. While one of the first working bodies to appear in Sinclair's fictional rendition of the slaughterhouse tour is the spectacularized body of the "Negro," then, work in the stockyards is otherwise identified with exploited but decidedly white ethnicities (suggesting that "the great burly Negro" functions aesthetically in Sinclair's text to excite the currency of slaughter as spectacle). The "Negro" in the quoted passage appears as a figure even more gratuitously inserted by Sinclair to spectacularize slaughter when read against the later description of the indolent and riotous black

strikebreakers who, Sinclair suggests, can never fill the place of labor because they are the very embodiment of unruly, disorganized nature. The labor movement depicted by Sinclair can be read as protecting the hope and essence of an "America" imperilled not only by capitalist greed but by unimprovable racial natures. See Amy Kaplan's discussion of how "the meaning of America" is constructed in its supposed distance and difference from "the jungle" in "Left Alone with America: The Absence of Empire in the Study of American Culture," in *Cultures of United States Imperialism*, ed. Amy Kaplan and Donald E. Pease (Durham, N.C.: Duke University Press, 1993), 7.

27. Brown, *Material Unconscious*, 48.

28. Sinclair, *The Jungle*, 39.

29. Ibid., 38, 35.

30. Ibid., 36. Wade writes that alongside the yards' mechanized hoisting and transporting, the "new method of slaughtering hogs impressed visitors for two other reasons. One was the spurting of blood caused by heart and muscular action during the dangling hog's death-struggle. It lasted only a minute or two but startled those who expected a slow gurgle. The other surprise was the noise. Prior to the introduction of the pig-hoist, hogs never made much noise on the killing floor. However, catching the live hog by a hind leg, clamping the pulley to that leg, and raising him to the overhead rail caused a shrill, piercing cry of alarm. By the late 1860s the frantic squealing of startled hogs was a common feature of the pork houses" (*Chicago's Pride*, 63).

31. In his history of the rendering industry, Pierre Desrochers writes, "It has long been said that 'everything but the squeal' is being used as a productive input in the meatpacking industry" ("Market Processes and the Closing of 'Industrial Loops': A Historical Reappraisal," *Journal of Industrial Ecology* 4, no. 1 [2000]: 34).

32. The Swift booklet is classified as a piece of "advertising ephemera" in a digital archive at Duke University titled *Emergence of Advertising in America: Advertising Ephemera (1850–1920)*. The guidebook is available online at http://scriptorium.lib.duke.edu/eaa/ (accessed March 1, 2005). I am indebted to Mark Simpson's scrupulous archival research into early American postcard cultures, during which he came across the Swift and Company souvenir booklet and shared it with me.

33. Lauren Berlant, *The Queen of America Goes to Washington City: Essays on Sex and Citizenship* (Durham, N.C.: Duke University Press, 1997), 28.

34. The little girl in Swift and Company's booklet helps Swift and Com-

pany to disavow, too, the pervasively masculinist discourses that construct woman as meat through the crossing of sexual and alimentary codes (theorized by Carol Adams in *The Sexual Politics of Meat: A Feminist-Vegetarian Critical Theory* [New York: Continuum International, 1990]).

35. Lynne Kirby, *Parallel Tracks: The Railroad and Silent Cinema* (Durham, N.C.: Duke University Press, 1997), 8.

36. Batchen, *Each Wild Idea*, 117.

37. Vialles, *Animal to Edible*, 53.

38. Sinclair, *The Jungle*, 36.

39. Vialles, *Animal to Edible*, 53–54.

40. The complicit logics of animal disassembly and filmic assembly are intensified when slaughter is itself the subject, or content, of film, as in Georges Franju's *Le sang des bêtes* (Forces et Voix de France, 1949).

41. Kirby, *Parallel Tracks*, 8.

42. Lippit, *Electric Animal*, 194. Lippit writes that Dziga Vertov and Sergei Eisenstein argue "for an understanding of cinema as organism" (194).

43. Brown, *Material Unconscious*, 242.

44. Michel Chion, "Quiet Revolution and Rigid Stagnation," *October* 58 (Fall 1991): 70–71.

45. Lippit, *Electric Animal*, 186.

46. Jonathan Beller, *The Cinematic Mode of Production: Attention Economy and the Society of the Spectacle* (Lebanon, N.H.: University Press of New England, 2006).

47. Ibid., 39. The notion of "kino-eye" is Dziga Vertov's, first posited in his 1929 film manifesto *Man with a Camera* (quoted by Beller in *Cinematic Mode of Production*, 39).

48. Beller, *Cinematic Mode of Production*, 283.

49. I discuss the distinction first made by Marx between the formal subsumption and the real subsumption of labor in the final section of chapter 1.

50. Lippit, *Electric Animal*, 1.

51. Samuel E. Sheppard, *Gelatin in Photography* (New York: Van Nostrand for Eastman Kodak, 1923), 25. Sheppard noted that 1873 was significant, "for during that year the preparation of a gelatin emulsion in a practical form was successfully accomplished. That gelatin was attracting much attention at this time is attested by the fact that the first advertisement of gelatin for photographic purposes to appear in the British Journal Photographic Almanac was in 1873" (14).

52. Sheppard, *Gelatin in Photography*, 25.

53. See the last section of chapter 1, where I discuss Marx's figure of "mere jelly."

54. Contrary to what some may think, the use of gelatin emulsions has not abated with the shift from photochemical to digital imaging technologies. On their Web page the Gelatine Manufacturers of Europe assure their stakeholders that "gelatine is also indispensable for digital photography. The inkjet printer paper coated with gelatine guarantees brilliant colors and clear shapes" (http://www.gelatine.org; accessed March 2004).

55. Douglas Collins, *The Story of Kodak* (New York: Harry N. Abrams, 1990), 49.

56. On its "History of Kodak" Web page today, the Kodak Company pays homage to the understated role of emulsion coatings in image production under the heading "Emulsion, the Image Recorder" (http://www.kodak.com/US/en/corp/aboutKodak/KokakHistory/filmImaging.shtml; accessed November 20, 2003). It is perhaps significant that Kodak has made transparent the until-now invisible role of emulsions only now that the business of making photochemical film stocks has ostensibly become "history" due to the digitization of image production.

57. Kodak Company, "History of Kodak" Web page.

58. Brown, *Material Unconscious*, 14.

59. Sheppard, *Gelatin in Photography*, 25.

60. Collins, *Story of Kodak*, 65.

61. Kodak Company, "History of Kodak" Web page.

62. Collins, *Story of Kodak*, 129.

63. Ibid., 359, 337.

64. Hemacite is described in an 1892 issue of the journal *Manufacture and Builder* in a story titled "Doorknobs, etc. from Blood and Sawdust" as follows: "A novel enterprise has been in successful operation in Trenton, N.J. for several years, the productions of which, consisting of a line of builder's hardware and various articles, for interior decorations, are manufactured of a substance known as 'hemacite,' which material is nothing else than the blood of slaughtered cattle and sawdust, combined with chemical compounds, under hydraulic pressure of forty thousand pounds to the square inch" (*Manufacture and Builder* 24, no. 1 [January 1892]). A digitized version of the article appears in Cornell University Library's The Making of America digital collection, http://cdl.library.cornell.edu/moa/index.html (accessed April 17, 2004).

65. Jeffrey Meikle, *American Plastic: A Cultural History* (New Brunswick, N.J.: Rutgers University Press, 1997), 11.

66. The Celluloid Manufacturing Company was founded in 1871, as Miekle notes, by the Hyatt brothers (*American Plastic,* 11).

67. Meikle, *American Plastic,* 12.

68. Ibid.

69. Ibid., 17.

70. The rhetoric of "hunting with a camera" was already in circulation in the 1890s, making one of its first appearances in Edward Augustus Samuels's "With Fly-Rod and Camera" (1890), as well as subsequent appearances in works such as Richard Tepe's "Hunting with a Camera" (1909). An article titled "Big Game Hunting with a Kodak" appeared in a 1925 issue of *Kodakery: A Journal for Amateur Photography.*

71. As Douglas Collins writes, the "barrel of Marey's 'chronophotographic gun' contained the camera's lens, behind which glass plates were arranged along the edge of a revolving metal disc. With his gun loaded with relatively fast gelatin dry plates Marey was able to make twelve exposures per second" (*Story of Kodak,* 69). The new sport of hunting with the camera as a quasi gun is also notated, as Collins shows, in the word "snapshot," formerly "a British hunting term" that "would come to signify any photograph taken quickly and casually" (72).

72. Lippit, *Electric Animal,* 187.

73. Michael Taussig, *Mimesis and Alterity: A Particular History of the Senses* (New York: Routledge, 1993), 22. See the Introduction to this book, in which I discuss Taussig's notion of a two-layered mimesis.

74. Collins, *Story of Kodak,* 46.

75. Ibid.

76. Kenneth Mees, quoted by Collins in *Story of Kodak,* 200.

77. Documents pertaining to gelatin manufacture, emulsion science, and the Eastman Gelatine Corporation are scarce in the University of Rochester Library's Eastman archives. After searching on my behalf, archivists eventually located a slim folder containing fewer than ten documents, including early press releases and news stories on Eastman Gelatine, internal reports on gelatin's manufacturing history, a manual for employees of Eastman Gelatine, and a "Commentary" on the company's dry gelatin stocks. The archivists' difficulty in locating information on gelatin reinforces my contention that it constitutes a "material unconscious" of mass image culture.

78. "Gelatin Is Simple Stuff," anonymous article, George Eastman Archives, University of Rochester Library, Rochester, N.Y., 2.

79. Ibid.

80. Ibid.

81. Jacques Derrida, "And Say the Animal Responded?" in *Zoontologies: The Question of the Animal,* ed. Cary Wolfe (Minneapolis: University of Minnesota Press, 2003), 137.

82. "Gelatin Is Simple Stuff," 2.

83. In an article of unspecified date titled "This Is Eastman Gel" (George Eastman Archives, University of Rochester Library, Rochester, N.Y.), *Kodakery* editor and author Bob Lawrence writes, "It is estimated that parts of 5,000,000 or more animals go into its gelatine making annually." In 1999, the Eastman Gelatine Corporation was still annually purchasing 80 million pounds of bovine skeleton from slaughterhouses to make into photographic gelatin (Alec Klein, "A Kodak Moment: Company Grinds Cow Bones, but Keeps Costs Close to the Bone," *Wall Street Journal,* January 18, 1999). The company's largest supplier of cow bones at that time was Monfort of Greeley, Colorado.

84. "Gelatin Is Simple Stuff," 15.

85. A. M. Kragh, "Swelling, Adsorption, and the Photographic Uses of Gelatin," in *The Science and Technology of Gelatin,* ed. A. G. Ward and A. Courts (London: Academic, 1977) 439–74. Kragh writes that because gelatin "contains the sulphur sensitizers later found essential for obtaining high sensitivity" and because the DNA in gelatin is a natural restrainer, "it might be thought that gelatin had been designed with the photographic process in mind" (471).

86. "Commentary on Dry Gelatine Raw Stocks in Storage," internal report of Eastman Kodak, Charles Eastman Archives, University of Rochester Library, Rochester, N.Y., 1969.

87. Eastman Kodak Company, *A Handbook for the Men and Women of Eastman Gelatine Corporation,* Charles Eastman Archives, University of Rochester Library, Rochester, N.Y., 1945.

88. Kristin Ross, *Fast Cars, Clean Bodies: Decolonization and the Reordering of French Culture* (Cambridge, Mass.: MIT Press, 1995), 38.

89. Andrew Loewen, "The Ford Motion Picture Department: Reel Subsumption and Intensive Taylorism," unpublished article, 1.

90. AdAge, http://www.adage.com (accessed April 2, 2002).

91. Saul A. Rubinstein and Thomas A. Kochan, *Learning from Saturn:*

Possibilities for Corporate Governance and Employee Relations (Ithaca, N.Y.: Cornell University Press, 2001), 2.

92. Mark Dery, "'Always Crashing in the Same Car': A Head-On Collision with the Technosphere," in *Against Automobility*, ed. Steffen Bohm, Campbell Jones, Chris Land, and Matthew Paterson (Oxford: Blackwell/ Sociological Review, 2005), 223.

93. Taussig, *Mimesis and Alterity*, 223.

94. As Lisa Gitelman shows, when it was not an animal it was a racialized human other who was plugged into this mimetic template to serve as the phonograph's "natural" foil. Gitelman analyzes a stereotypical Edison-era anecdote of a black man who, listening to a Buckeye Music Company phonograph recording of "The Flogging" (excerpted from *Uncle Tom's Cabin*), jumped up and declared he'd like to get that slave driver. "The man didn't hear the phonograph or the record," writes Gitelman, "he heard through them to Simon Legree whipping Uncle Tom. It is this selective hearing that the Buckeye proprietor recognizes as the highest compliment that can be paid to any communicative or inscriptive medium, including the talking machine" (*Scripts, Grooves, and Writing Machines: Representing Technology in the Edison Era* [Stanford, Calif.: Stanford University Press, 1999], 121). Gitelman notes that the "proprietor's anecdote plays off an important trope resident in Anglo-American constructions of race and class, the familiar narrative of the alien naif who mistakes mimetic representation for reality" (121).

95. Flink, *Automobile Age*, 114.

96. In 1895, the first two periodicals devoted to automobiles appeared: *Horseless Age* and *Motorcycle* (Flink, *Automobile Age*, 18).

97. Jonathan Crary, *Suspensions of Perception: Attention, Spectacle, and Modern Culture* (Cambridge, Mass.: MIT Press, 1999), 144.

98. Lippit, *Electric Animal*, 187.

99. Ibid., n. 71.

100. David Gartman, *Auto-Opium: A Social History of American Automobile Design* (New York: Routledge, 1994), 93.

101. Rubinstein and Kochan, *Learning from Saturn*, 37.

102. Ibid., 2.

103. Flink, *Automobile Age*, 44.

104. The Saturn Vue campaign ran from February to May of 2002. Alongside its print ads, television ads depicting, among other things, the Vue morphing into a rabbit as it darted behind trees were aired during CBS's *Survivor*

series, during coverage of the Salt Lake City Olympics, and during the Grammy Awards.

105. This particular ad in the Saturn campaign appeared in a 2002 issue of *Martha Stewart Magazine*.

106. As Taussig notes, "Controlled mimesis is an essential component of socialization and discipline, and in our era of world history, in which colonialism has played a dominant role, mimesis is of a piece with primitivism" (*Mimesis and Alterity*, 219).

107. Johannes Fabian, *Time and the Other: How Anthropology Makes Its Object* (New York: Columbia University Press, 1982), 31.

108. Along with Donna Haraway, I invoke the multiple connotations of "specie": "I hear in species filthy lucre, specie, gold, shit, filth, wealth. . . . Norman O. Brown taught me about the join of Marx and Freud in shit and gold, in primitive scat and civilized metal, in specie" (*The Companion Species Manifesto: Dogs, People, and Significant Otherness* [Chicago: Prickly Paradigm, 2003], 16).

109. See Fredric Jameson's *Postmodernism, or The Cultural Logic of Late Capitalism* (Durham, N.C.: Duke University Press, 1992).

110. Dorothee Brantz, "Recollecting the Slaughterhouse," *Cabinet Magazine* 4 (Fall 2001): 120.

111. Karl Marx, *Capital: A Critique of Political Economy*, vol. 1, trans. Ben Fowkes (London: Penguin, 1976), 163–64.

112. James O'Connor, *Natural Causes: Essays in Ecological Marxism* (New York: Guilford, 1998), 26.

113. Bill Brown, "Science Fiction, the World's Fair, and the Prosthetics of Empire, 1910–1915," in *Cultures of United States Imperialism*, ed. Amy Kaplan and Donald E. Pease (Durham, N.C.: Duke University Press, 1993), 136.

114. Vialles, *Animal to Edible*, 51.

115. Gayatri Chakravorty Spivak provoked sustained debate around the subaltern subject's ability to speak and to be heard within dominant systems of symbolic sense with her famous essay "Can the Subaltern Speak?" She repeats that question, with a difference, in *A Critique of Postcolonial Reason: Toward a History of the Vanishing Present* (Cambridge, Mass.: Harvard University Press, 1999).

116. Spivak, *Critique of Postcolonial Reason*, 307, 309.

117. Brown, *Material Unconscious*, 5.

118. Mark Simpson, "Immaculate Trophies," *Essays in Canadian Writing* 68 (Summer 1999): 97.

119. Friedrich Nietzsche, "On the Uses and Disadvantages of History for Life," in *Untimely Meditations*, trans. R. J. Hollingdale (Cambridge: Cambridge University Press, 1983), 61, quoted by Lippit in *Electric Animal*, 68.

3. Telemobility

1. As Robert Montraville notes in his introduction to Galvani's *Commentary*, while Galvani was the first to popularize experiments using frogs, he was not the first to study animal electricity: "A few years before, in Bologna, Floriano Caldani (1756) and Giambattista Beccaria (1758) were able to demonstrate electrical excitability in the muscles of dead frogs" (Luigi Galvani, *Commentary on the Effect of Electricity on Muscular Motion* [1791], trans. Robert Montraville [Cambridge, Mass: Elizabeth Licht, 1953], xi).

2. Walter Benjamin, "Theses on the Philosophy of History," in *Illuminations*, ed. Hannah Arendt, trans. Harry Zohn (New York: Harcourt, Brace and World, 1968).

3. See chapter 1 under the heading "First Genealogy."

4. Régis Debray, *Media Manifestos: On the Technological Transmission of Cultural Forms*, trans. Eric Rauth (London: Verso, 1996), 46.

5. Jacques Derrida, *Specters of Marx: The State of the Debt, the Work of Mourning, and the New International*, trans. Peggy Kamuf (New York: Routledge, 1994), 79.

6. Akira Mizuta Lippit, *Electric Animal: Toward a Rhetoric of Wildlife* (Minneapolis: University of Minnesota Press, 2000), 190.

7. Michel Foucault, *The Order of Things: An Archaeology of the Human Sciences* (New York: Pantheon, 1970), 277.

8. Ibid.

9. Karl Marx, *Capital: A Critique of Political Economy*, vol. 1, trans. Ben Fowkes (London: Penguin, 1976), 169.

10. Karl Marx, "The Early Writings 1837–1844," in *Karl Marx: Selected Writings*, ed. David McLellan (Oxford: Oxford University Press, 1977), 110.

11. Edward B. Tylor, *Primitive Culture: Researches into the Development of Mythology, Philosophy, Religion, Language, Art, and Custom* (1871), 7th ed. (New York: Brentano's, 1924), 160.

12. Ibid.

13. W. J. T. Mitchell, *What Do Pictures Want? The Lives and Loves of Images* (Chicago: University of Chicago Press, 2005), 7.

14. Mitchell suggests a "critical idolatry," that is, "an approach to images that does not dream of destroying them, and that recognizes every act of disfiguration or defacement as itself an act of creative destruction for which we must take responsibility" (*What Do Pictures Want?* 26). Drawing on Nietzsche, Mitchell therefore proposes "sounding out" the idols with the hammer or "tuning fork" of critical language, "playing upon them as if they were musical instruments" (26).

15. John Berger, "Why Look at Animals?" in *About Looking* (New York: Vintage, 1992), quoted by Mitchell in *What Do Pictures Want?* 30.

16. Debray, *Media Manifestos*, 46.

17. While Edison certainly oversaw its design, it was Harold Brown, working at Edison's Menlo Park laboratory, who worked out the details of the electric chair. Edison is notorious for taking credit for the inventions of his underlings and for borrowing or buying the patents of competitors to then market under his name.

18. Edison's ostensible opposition to capital punishment reversed abruptly at the species line. Edison regularly invited the local press to his laboratory in West Orange, where he electrocuted pets purchased from neighborhood children in order to disseminate news of the potential deadliness of alternating current and to boost his own system of direct current.

19. In actuality, it was the Clearnet corporation that initially developed the brand "look" that Telus decided to keep and intensify when it purchased Clearnet in 2001.

20. As noted in the Introduction to this book, the market campaigns of Canada's top telecommunications corporations have all recently deployed animals as metaphors of global wireless mobility, from the digital beavers performing in Bell Canada ads to the faithful canines representing Fido.

21. André Gaudreault, "Film, Narrative, Narration: The Cinema of the Lumiere Brothers," in *Early Cinema: Space, Frame, Narrative,* ed. Thomas Elsaesser (London: British Film Institute, 1990), 71.

22. In another essay, "Showing and Telling: Image and Word in Early Cinema," Gaudreault writes: "To tell a story one has to use one of two fundamental modes of narrative communication: narration, and what I call monstration. One must either narrate the different events which constitute the story (narration), as the lecturer does; or show them (monstration), as the glass slides attempt to do" (in *Early Cinema,* 276).

23. Lippit, *Electric Animal,* 30.

24. Jacques Derrida, "And Say the Animal Responded?" in *Zoontologies:*

The Question of the Animal, ed. Cary Wolfe (Minneapolis: University of Minnesota Press, 2003), 130.

25. Ibid., 130. As Derrida notes, Lacan refuses to say that an animal can be a "subject of the signifier" on grounds that it cannot lie, that is, because of its "incapacity with respect to the 'signifier,' to lying and deceit, to pretended pretense" (132).

26. Cary Wolfe, *Animal Rites: American Culture, the Discourse of Species, and Posthumanist Theory* (Chicago: University of Chicago Press, 2003), 109.

27. Debray, *Media Manifestos*, 46.

28. Debray critiques semiologists who privilege the code—the "*message made absolute*"—above the "mere means" of its transmission (*Media Manifestos*, 72, 80). His critique addresses this semiotic fantasy especially as it is promoted in telecommunications culture.

29. Luigi Galvani, *Commentary on the Effect of Electricity on Muscular Motion* (1791), trans. Robert Montraville (Cambridge, Mass: Elizabeth Licht, 1953), 69.

30. Robert Montraville, "Introduction," in Galvani, *Commentary on the Effect of Electricity on Muscular Motion*, xi.

31. According to the dissertation of his nephew, Giovanni Aldini, Galvani held that a subtle "electric fluid" was more abundant in "brute beasts" than in "men" ("Dissertation on the Origin and Development of the Theory of Animal Electricity," in *Commentary on the Effect of Electricity on Muscular Motion*, 3).

32. Galvani, *Commentary on the Effect of Electricity*, xxv.

33. Mary Shelley, *Frankenstein: The Original 1818 Edition*, ed. Gary Kelly, 2nd ed. (Peterborough, Ontario: Broadview, 1999), 90, 83.

34. Galvani, *Commentary on the Effect of Electricity*, 44.

35. Bernard Cohen, "Foreword," in Marcello Pera, *The Ambiguous Frog: The Galvani-Volta Controversy on Animal Electricity*, trans. Jonathon Mandelbaum (Princeton, N.J.: Princeton University Press, 1992), xi.

36. Ibid., xiii.

37. Galvani, *Commentary on the Effect of Electricity*, 79.

38. Michael Taussig, *Mimesis and Alterity: Toward a Particular History of the Senses* (New York: Routledge, 1993), 21–22.

39. Galvani, *Commentary on the Effect of Electricity*, 58.

40. Jonathan Crary, *Techniques of the Observer: On Vision and Modernity in the Nineteenth Century* (Cambridge, Mass.: MIT Press, 1992), 48. Writes Crary, "Descartes advises his reader to conduct a demonstration involving

'taking the dead eye of a newly dead person (or, failing that, the eye of an ox or some other large animal)' and using the extracted eye as the lens in the pinhole of a camera obscura. Thus for Descartes the images observed within the camera obscura are formed by means of a disembodied cyclopean eye, detached from the observer, possibly not even a human eye" (47).

41. Martin Jay, "The Disenchantment of the Eye: Surrealism and the Crisis of Ocularcentrism," in *Visualizing Theory: Selected Essays from V.A.R. 1990–1994,* ed. Lucien Taylor (New York: Routledge, 1994), 176.

42. Avita Ronell, *The Telephone Book: Technology, Schizophrenia, Electric Speech* (Lincoln: University of Nebraska Press, 1989), 296, 239.

43. Lisa Gitelman, *Scripts, Grooves, and Writing Machines: Representing Technology in the Edison Era* (Stanford, Calif.: Stanford University Press, 1999), 10. Gitelman also insists on signs' "double character, both material and semiotic" (10). "Modern technology has made some features of this doubleness seem particularly arcane," she writes. "For example, the original electric meters of the 1880s were really halves of little batteries; to 'read the meter' a technician had to remove a zinc electrode and weigh it in order to determine the amount of ion deposit.... These ion deposits, like the ion deposits on photographic plates or strips of celluloid, are the stuff of inscription" (10).

44. Jeremy Stolow, "Techno-Religious Imaginaries: On the Spiritual Telegraph and the Circum-Atlantic World of the 19th Century," a report of McMaster University's Institute on Globalization and the Human Condition, March 2006, http://globalization.mcmaster.ca/wps.htm (accessed November 2, 2007), 3.

45. Ronell, *The Telephone Book,* 7.

46. Jeffrey Sconce, *Haunted Media: Electronic Presence from Telegraphy to Television* (Durham, N.C.: Duke University Press, 2000), 61.

47. Lippit, *Electric Animal,* 187.

48. William Kennedy Laurie Dickson, working for Edison, is now widely recognized as having invented the first motion picture camera. In 1902, a court ruled that Edison did not invent the movie camera *(Edison v. American Mutoscope).* However, shortly afterward Edison purchased the patent from the American Mutoscope and Biograph Company (for which Dickson then worked) and marketed the movie camera as his own invention.

49. "Bad Elephant Killed: Topsy Meets Quick and Painless Death at Coney Island," *Commercial Advertiser,* January 5, 1903. Giorgio Agamben theorizes that an "animal voice" or cry is the negative trace or condition of lan-

guage in *Language and Death: The Place of Negativity,* trans. Karen E. Pinkus with Michael Hardt (Minneapolis: University of Minnesota Press, 1991), 45.

50. Mark Seltzer, *Bodies and Machines* (New York: Routledge, 1992), 11.

51. Lippit, *Electric Animal,* 1.

52. Michel Foucault, *Discipline and Punish: The Birth of the Prison,* 2nd ed., trans. Alan Sheridan (New York: Vintage, 1995), 16.

53. Ibid., 23.

54. Michel Foucault, *The History of Sexuality,* vol. 1, *An Introduction,* trans. Robert Hurley (New York: Vintage, 1980), 141.

55. Lippit, *Electric Animal,* 190.

56. From the back cover of *Coney Island: The Ups and Downs of America's First Amusement Park,* prod. and dir. Ric Burns, Public Broadcasting Service, 1991, videocassette.

57. The Elephant Hotel was a small hotel built in the shape of an elephant by James V. Lafferty in 1885. It burned down in 1896 in one of Coney Island's famous fires. According to Jeffrey Stanton's Coney Island History Web site, "A cigar store operated out of one front leg, and a diorama was in the other. A spiral staircase in the hind leg led visitors upstairs where a shop and several guest rooms were located. The elephant's head, facing the ocean, offered good vistas of the sea through slits where the eyes were located" (http://naid.sppsr.ucla.edu/coneyisland/articles/earlyhistory2.htm; accessed December 2004).

58. Edison must have been cognizant that the name of the elephant he filmed being electrocuted in 1903 was the same as that of the black slave girl in Harriet Beecher Stowe's *Uncle Tom's Cabin,* for he produced a full-length (fourteen-minute) silent film based on the novel the same year. *Topsy* was a stereotypical name for the infantilized, animalized black character that was a staple of minstrelsy well into the 1930s.

59. "Bad Elephant," *Commercial Advertiser,* January 5, 1903.

60. When the sympathetic magic of animal handling was broken by Montecore (the white tiger who acted out in 2003), Siegfried tried to heal the puncture in the fantasy by assuring the media that the tiger was confused (at first because Roy seemed to have tripped on stage but in a later version of the story because it sensed that Roy was having a minor stroke). On the *Today Show,* Siegfried told a U.S. television audience that "there was no injury from Montecore, it was just a little punch hole. . . . Montecore carried him 30 feet offstage to his safety. Now that's a story" (http://www.reviewjournal.com/

home/2003/Dec-02-Tue-2003/news/22706426.html; accessed April 7, 2004).
Tiger experts, however, maintain that it was an attempted mauling. Siegfried
and Roy have helped to "conserve" royal white tigers for capitalist postmodernity in a multi-million-dollar simulated habitat inside the Mirage Hotel and
Resort where they performed magic shows for thirteen years.

61. Topsy was not, however, the last elephant in North America to be
publicly executed for killing a human. In 1916, an elephant owned by the Sparks
Brothers Circus was dubbed "Murderous Mary" for killing a handler and was
hanged from a derrick car. Her lynching suggests, again, the intertwined imaginaries of race and species.

62. For a study of animal trials from the Middle Ages up to the modern
era, see E. P. Evans, *The Criminal Prosecution and Capital Punishment of Animals:
The Lost History of Europe's Animal Trials* (New York: E. P. Dutton, 1906).

63. Cary Wolfe, "*Faux* Post-humanism, or Animal Rights, Neocolonial-
ism, and Michael Crichton's *Congo*," *Arizona Quarterly* 55, no. 2 (1999): 117;
Jacques Derrida, "'Eating Well,' or the Calculation of the Subject: An Inter-
view with Jacques Derrida," trans. Peter Connor and Avita Ronell, in *Who
Comes after the Subject?* ed. Eduardo Cadava, Peter Connor, and Jean-Luc
Nancy (New York: Routledge, 1991), 112.

64. Deaths caused by animals, as Lippit notes, could not properly be
called crimes according to the modern perception because that perception
held that they were ruled by reflex and incapable of premeditation: "The animal cannot be held accountable for its crimes because, like Oedipus, it is
unaware of its actions" (*Electric Animal*, 50).

65. Lippit, *Electric Animal*, 191.

66. Derrida, "And Say the Animal Responded?" 134.

67. Mark Essig dates the creation of Europe's first humane societies
prior to Bentham and contends that they originated less out of a concern for
animal suffering than from an interest in reviving the dead: "Physicians in the
1740s had discovered that some people who appeared to be dead could be revived by forcing air into their lungs. Suddenly, the boundary between death
and life became blurred.... In the 1760s, these doubts inspired the creation of
the first 'humane societies,' organizations dedicated not to the welfare of animals
but to reviving the apparently dead" (*Edison and the Electric Chair: A Story of
Light and Death* [Toronto, Ontario: McLelland and Stewart, 2003], 43).

68. Jeremy Bentham, *An Introduction to the Principles of Morals and Leg-
islation* (1789), ed. J. H. Burns (New York: Oxford University Press, 1996), 7.

69. Jacques Derrida, "The Animal That Therefore I Am (More to Follow)," trans. David Wills, *Critical Inquiry* 28 (2002): 395.

70. Joanne Zurlo, Deborah Rudacille, and Alan M. Golderd, "Appendix D: United States Animal Welfare Timeline," Johns Hopkins University Center for Alternatives to Animal Testing, http://caat.jhsph.edu/publications/animal_alternatives/appendices/d.htm (accessed October 3, 2008).

71. Ernesto Laclau and Chantal Mouffe, *Hegemony and Socialist Strategy: Towards a Radical Democratic Politics,* 2nd ed. (London: Verso, 2001), xvii. It is in the context of contemporary neoliberal discourse that Laclau and Mouffe argue that the point is not to "manage [capitalism] in a more humane way" but to contest its seemingly inevitable hegemony (xvii).

72. Noëlie Vialles, *Animal to Edible,* trans. J. A. Underwood (Cambridge: Cambridge University Press, 1994), 32.

73. Ibid., 45.

74. Benjamin Franklin, quoted by Essig in *Edison and the Electric Chair,* 10.

75. John R. Romans, William J. Costello, Kevin W. James, C. Wendell Carlson, and P. Thomas Zeigler, eds., *The Meat We Eat,* 12th ed. (Danville, Ill.: Interstate Printers and Publishers, 1985), 94.

76. "Bad Elephant."

77. Ronell, *The Telephone Book,* 256.

78. J. Hillis Miller, "Virtual Automobility: Two Ways to Get a Life," in *Against Automobility,* ed. Steffen Bohm, Campbell Jones, Chris Land, and Matthew Paterson (Oxford: Blackwell, 2006), 201.

79. Lippit, *Electric Animal,* 101.

80. Debray, *Media Manifestos,* 44. In Debray's sustained critique of the model and semiotics of "communication," he challenges "the notion of 'act of communication' understood as a dual and punctual relation between a sending pole and receiving pole, with only a code common to the line's two extremities" (44).

81. Derrida, "The Animal That I Am," 372.

82. See Telus's assurance of its respectful handling of its "spokescritters" on its Web page: http://www.telusmobility.com/about/company_background_ff.shtml (accessed January 2004).

83. Telus Web page.

84. Jean and John Comaroff identify neoliberal culture at the millennium, or what they term "millennial capitalism," with cultures that speculate

in the promise of wealth without work, consumption without production. See their "Millennial Capitalism: First Thoughts on a Second Coming," in *Millenial Capitalism and the Culture of Neoliberalism*, ed. Jean Comaroff and John L. Comaroff (Durham, N.C.: Duke University Press, 2001).

85. http://www.taxi.ca (accessed January 2004).

86. Marx, *Capital*, 163.

87. Derrida, *Specters of Marx*, 152.

88. For Nicolas Abraham and Mario Torok, writes Lippit, "metaphors end where they begin—in the mouth" (*Electric Animal*, 244). See Nicolas Abraham and Mario Torok, "Mourning *or* Melancholia: Introjection *versus* Incorporation," in *The Shell and the Kernel*, ed. and trans. Nicholas Rand (Chicago: University of Chicago Press, 1994), 125–38.

89. Mark Simpson theorizes "liveness" in relation to turn-of-the-century practices of collection and conservation in North American culture and, more specifically, to "the supposed immediacy or liveness" of the taxidermic specimen ("Immaculate Trophies," *Essays in Canadian Writing* 68 [Summer 1999]: 93).

90. The hedgehog ad can be viewed online at http://www.strategymag .com/aoy/2001/taxi/telus/ (accessed December 2007).

91. Wolfe, "*Faux* Post-humanism," 145.

92. Taussig, *Mimesis and Alterity*, xv.

93. Henry Louis Gates nevertheless works to recuperate a black critical praxis from the racist currency of the sign of the simian by theorizing "the Signifying Monkey" as an "ironic reversal of a received racist image in the Western imagination" (*Figures in Black: Words, Signs, and the 'Racial' Self* [Oxford: Oxford University Press, 1987], 236).

94. As Marshall McLuhan argues in his analysis of an electronic age, "The 'content' of this new environment is the old mechanized environment of the industrial age" (*Understanding Media: The Extensions of Man* [Toronto, Ontario: McGraw-Hill, 1966], vii).

95. Evoking other popular texts (*Charlotte's Web*, the *Babe* movies) in which pigs, far from wallowing in filth and stupidity, are portrayed as intellectually razor sharp and affectively acute, the Telus ad also suggests that the piglet is the incarnation of smart technology.

96. The slaughter numbers for 2003 are posted by the government of Canada on its Department of Agriculture and Agri-Food Web site, under "Hog Statistics at a Glance" (http://www.agr.gc.ca; accessed November 2007).

97. Roger Caillois, "Mimicry and Legendary Psychasthenia (1938)," trans. John Shepley, *October* 31 (Winter 1984): 17.

98. Ibid., 25.

99. Earlier in this chapter I expressed wariness toward W. J. T. Mitchell's invitation to entertain animistic belief in things and, more particularly, toward his suggestion that pictures may embody the subaltern "desires of animals." Here Mitchell's suggestion can be seen in its uncanny similarity to that posed by the animal pictures of Telus Mobility Inc.

100. Debray, *Media Manifestos*, 45.

101. For an acute analysis of Heidegger's efforts to distinguish the "prehensile" grasp of the animal from the human hand, see Eleanor Byrne and Martin McQuillan, "Walt Disney's Ape-Man: Race, Writing, and Humanism," *New Formations* 43 (Spring 2001): 103–16.

102. Seltzer, *Bodies and Machines*, 122. As Seltzer notes: "One of the most evident paradoxes of the insistently paradoxical notion of a 'culture of consumption' is the manner in which a style of life characterized by its excessiveness or gratuitousness—by its exceeding or disavowing material and natural and bodily needs—is yet understood on the model of the natural body and its needs, that is, on the model of hunger and eating" (121).

103. Donna Haraway, *Primate Visions: Gender, Race, and Nature in the World of Modern Science* (New York: Routledge, 1989), 139.

104. Debray, *Media Manifestos*, 46.

105. United Nations Security Council (UNSC), *Final Report of the Panel of Experts on the Illegal Exploitation of Natural Resources and Other Forms of Wealth of the Democratic Republic of the Congo* (New York: United Nations, October 2002).

106. A 2002 report of the International Peace Information Service (IPIS) helped to organize lobbies against some of these corporations: "Leading international corporations using tantalum capacitors such as *Alcatel, Compaq, Dell, IBM Ericsson, Nokia* and *Siemens* are called upon to immediately refrain from buying components containing tantalum originating from occupied Congo and its neighbours" ("Supporting the War Economy in the DRC: European Companies and the Coltan Trade," IPIS Report, IPIS, Antwerp, Belgium, January 9, 2002, 7). Although Nokia and Motorola publicly pledged to stop buying from suppliers that could not certify that their coltan did not come from the Congo, the commercial supply chain is so convoluted and murky that few take their statements as more than lip service to the problem.

107. UNSC, *Final Report,* 15. The Rwandan Patriotic Army and the Ugandan People's Defense Forces were showing signs of withdrawing from the eastern Congo when the 2002 UNSC *Final Report* was submitted. Yet, as the report states, "The necessary networks have already become deeply embedded to ensure that the illegal exploitation continues, independent of the physical presence of the foreign armies" (28).

108. IPIS, "Supporting the War Economy," 9.

109. Chris McGreal, "The Cost of a Call," *Guardian,* August 20, 2001.

110. UNSC, *Final Report,* 5.

111. The "blood" invoked in the "no blood on my mobile!" campaigns took on new value and meaning with the participation of the Dian Fossey Gorilla Fund. Media coverage in the West, particularly, recited the slogan in relation to the tragedy of the lowland gorillas. The blood of the Congo's threatened lowland gorillas arguably provoked more sympathy than the blood of the estimated 3.5 million Congolese killed in three years of civil war.

112. "Gorillas under Threat," produced by Carol Albertyn Christie for Carte Blanche, a South African broadcasting network, available at http:// www.durbanprocess.net/en/resources.html (accessed April 13, 2003).

113. Motorola's statement has been formalized as "Motorola Position on Illegally Mined Coltan," available at the Motorola Web site, http://www .motorola.com/mot/doc/1/1444_MotDoc.pdf (accessed October 3, 2008).

114. Haraway, *Primate Visions,* 11. As Haraway writes: "Simian orientalism means that western primatology has been about the construction of the self from the raw material of the other, the appropriation of nature in the production of culture, the ripening of the human from the soil of the animal, the clarity of white from the obscurity of color, the issue of man from the body of woman, the elaboration of gender from the resource of sex, the emergence of mind by the activation of body. To effect these transformative operations, simian 'orientalist' discourse must first construct the terms: animal, nature, body, primitive, female" (11).

115. Donna Haraway, "The Promises of Monsters: A Regenerative Politics for Inappropriate/d Others," in *Cultural Studies,* ed. Lawrence Grossberg, Cary Nelson, and Paula A. Treichler (New York: Routledge, 1992), 308.

116. Haraway, *Primate Visions,* 140.

117. Nature in the Congo is split, again, between two contradictory discourses: those that seek to help the Congo regain "national" order and state control over its natural resources and those that continue to view certain nat-

ural resources (particularly lowland gorillas in national parks such as Kahuzi-Biega, which is a World Heritage site) as international birthrights. In the case of the Dian Fossey Gorilla Fund, both discourses are operative at once, concealing a highly interested division of nature. While the Fund would like to see Congolese coltan production nationalized and regulated under state environmental controls, it has no intention of relinquishing the international claims it makes on other portions of African nature, portions whose anthropological and genetic as well as touristic and symbolic capital is safeguarded by Western culture under the assumption that it is the property of universal "man."

118. Tamara Gignac, "Telus and Its Union in Battle over Ads," *Calgary Herald,* January 29, 2004, A1.

119. Debray, *Media Manifestos,* 45.

120. After the court injunction was delivered, traces of the three union ads, which aired only in Canada's two westernmost provinces (Alberta and British Columbia), were virtually erased from electronic media memory. The injunction prohibited them not only from being aired on television but from being posted on the union's Web site, where they had briefly been available for viewing.

121. Slavoj Žižek, "Multiculturalism, or the Logic of Multinational Capitalism," *New Left Review* 225 (1997): 30.

4. Biomobility

1. Akira Mizuta Lippit, *Electric Animal: Toward a Rhetoric of Wildlife* (Minneapolis: University of Minnesota Press, 2000), 186.

2. Régis Debray, *Media Manifestos: On the Technological Transmission of Cultural Forms,* trans. Eric Rauth (London: Verso, 1996), 46.

3. Arturo Escobar, "Cultural Politics and Biological Diversity: State, Capital, and Social Movements in the Pacific Coast of Colombia," in *The Politics of Culture in the Shadow of Capital,* ed. Lisa Lowe and David Lloyd (Durham, N.C.: Duke University Press, 1997), 210.

4. Ibid.

5. Michel Foucault, *The History of Sexuality,* vol. 1, *An Introduction,* trans. Robert Hurley (New York: Vintage Books, 1980), 142.

6. For a view of the biopolitical dark side of modern biopolitics, see Mike Davis, *Late Victorian Holocausts: El Nino Famines and the Making of the Third World* (London: Verso, 2001). Davis argues that the climactic causes

of devastating famines in the late nineteenth century in India, China, and Brazil were inextricable from their political causes in European (primarily British) empire and in the institutionalized racism of capitalism's imperialist expansion.

7. Glen Elder, Jennifer Wolch, and Jody Emel, "Le Pratique Sauvage: Race, Place, and the Human-Animal Divide," in *Animal Geographies: Place, Politics, and Identity in the Nature-Culture Borderlands,* ed. Wolch and Emel (New York: Verso, 1998), 81.

8. I am referring to one of Mike Davis's many influential books, *Ecology of Fear: Los Angeles and the Imagination of Disaster* (New York: Vintage, 1999).

9. Jean and John Comaroff, "Millennial Capitalism: First Thoughts on a Second Coming," in *Millennial Capitalism and the Culture of Neoliberalism,* ed. Jean Comaroff and John L. Comaroff (Durham, N.C.: Duke University Press, 2001), 7, 10.

10. Gambling "also expresses itself in a fascination with 'futures' and their downmarket counterpart, the lottery" (Comaroff, "Millennial Capitalism," 5).

11. Rebecca Tuhus-Dubrow, "Crying Fowl: A Talk with 'City of Quartz' Author Davis on Another Disaster in the Making,' *Village Voice,* September 9, 2005, http://www.villagevoice.com/books/053,tuhusdubr,67713,10.html (accessed September 24, 2007).

12. Marshall McLuhan, who first put the expression into circulation in his study of the effects of electronic media, held a much darker view of the "global village" than the term popularly connoted in the latter half of the twentieth century. He wrote of "the tribal consequences" of the small world created by the aural or oral (versus print) media of electronic communication: "We shall at once move into a phase of panic terrors, exactly befitting a small world of tribal drums, total interdependence, and superimposed co-existence.... Terror is the normal state of any oral society, for in it everything affects everything all the time" (*The Gutenberg Galaxy: The Making of Typographic Man* [1962], reprint, Routledge, 2001, 30). While McLuhan's vision of tribalism hinges on primitivizing stereotypes, his evocation of "panic terrors" is prescient.

13. Brian Massumi, "Preface," in *The Politics of Everyday Fear,* ed. Brian Massumi (Minneapolis: University of Minnesota Press, 1993), vii.

14. Ibid., viii.

15. Brian Massumi, "Everywhere You Want to Be," in *The Politics of Everyday Fear,* ed. Brian Massumi (Minneapolis: University of Minnesota Press, 1993), 12.

16. In the latter half of this chapter I look more closely at how pandemic speculation has spurred individual states around the world (not to mention private citizens) to purchase and, as far as supplies permit, stockpile treatments of the antiviral drug Tamiflu, whose patent is owned by the Swiss pharmaceutical company Hoffman–La Roche.

17. Donald S. Moore, Jake Kosek, and Anand Pandian, eds., "The Cultural Politics of Race and Nature: Terrains of Power and Practice," in *Race, Nature, and the Politics of Difference* (Durham, N.C.: Duke University Press, 2003), 42, 1, 5.

18. I use Giorgio Agamben's notion of "bare life" in the broadest sense, as that domain of *zoé* or natural life that is no longer situated "at the margins of the political order... [but] gradually begins to coincide with the political realm" (*Homo Sacer: Sovereign Power and Bare Life*, trans. Daniel Heller-Roazen [Stanford, Calif.: Stanford University Press, 1998], 9).

19. Roger Keil and Harris Ali, "Multiculturalism, Racism, and Infectious Disease in the Global City: The Experience of the 2003 SARS Outbreak in Toronto," *Topia* 16 (Fall 2006): 42, 30.

20. Mei Zhan, "Civet Cats, Fried Grasshoppers, and David Beckham's Pajamas: Unruly Bodies after SARS," *American Anthropologist* 107, no. 1 (2005): 38.

21. Williams describes a "structure of feeling" as "the distilled residue of the organization of the lived experience of a community over and above the institutional and ideological organization of the society" (Raymond Williams, *Marxism and Literature* (Oxford: Oxford University Press, 1977), 130.

22. Judith Butler, *Precarious Life: The Power of Mourning and Violence* (London: Verso, 2004), 42.

23. See the *Ashes and Snow* Web site, http://www.ashesandsnow.org (accessed August 4, 2006). The text that appears on the Web site has been revised more than once since I first visited it. All subsequent citations from the Web site are as they appeared on the site between June 1, 2006, and July 30, 2007.

24. Alexander Jung, "The Box That Makes the World Go Round," *Spiegel Online,* November 25, 2005, http://www.spiegel.de/international/spiegel/0,1518,386799,00.html. See also Marc Levinson, *The Box: How the Shipping Container Made the World Smaller and the World Economy Bigger* (Princeton, N.J.: Princeton University Press, 2006).

25. *Ashes and Snow* Web site.

26. The biography of Shigeru Ban posted on the *Ashes and Snow* Web site makes reference to Ban's humanitarian design of "paper houses" for refugees and victims of natural disasters: "As a consultant for the United Nations High Commissioner for Refugees, Ban created paper shelters made of plastic sheets and paper tubes for refugees in Rwanda. He also designed emergency housing in Kobe, Japan, after the 1995 earthquake. More recently, his paper houses provided shelter for people in Turkey and India after earthquakes destroyed their homes." Beyond the affiliation of Colbert's project, through the architect bio, with Ban's humanitarian design, there is the more insidious implication of an aesthetic affinity or resemblance between the nomadicity of his traveling museum and the temporariness of the refugee or disaster shelter. Far more than the voiding of the economic content of shipping containers, this suggested resemblance allowed for in the Colbert-Ban collaboration bespeaks a profound aestheticization of the material politics of mobility.

27. Both the economics (not to mention carbon politics) of international travel and the ideological implications of buying into the phonocentrism of the "museum experience" itself, particularly when the fetishistic idea of an immersive, unmediated experience of animal nature is integral to the discourse of *Ashes and Snow,* informed my decision to approach the exhibit through the more visibly mediated discourse of the Web site, interviews, and so on. This does not, however, absolve me, through some assertion of critical distance, of participation in and susceptibility to the experience. As Donna Haraway says in relation to her critical reading of Edward Steichen's midcentury photodocumentary *The Family of Man,* "It is a rule for me not to turn a dissolving eye onto straw problems, not to 'deconstruct' that to which I am not also emotionally, epistemologically, and politically vulnerable" ("Universal Donors in a Vampire Culture: It's All in the Family; Biological Kinship Categories in the Twentieth-Century United States," in *Modest_Witness@Second_Millennium: FemaleMan©_Meets_OncoMouse™: Feminism and Technoscience* [New York: Routledge, 1997], 243).

28. The nomadic museum, while generally garnering rave reviews in the mainstream and alternative presses, has also been subject to sharp criticism. It has been a heated topic of debate on Weblogs and Internet discussion lists. Amardeep Singh, professor of English at Lehigh University in Philadelphia, posted a critical review of the exhibit on his blog, including a retort to the mantra of ashes and snow recited in the nomadic museum that is not unrelated to the materialist criticism this section will bring to bear on the exhibit. Writes Singh: "'Flesh to fire, fire to blood, blood to bone, bone to marrow,

marrow to ashes, ashes to . . . snow.' To which my response is: 'Cow to beef, beef to burger, burger to mouth, mouth to stomach, stomach to shit, shit to . . . snow'" (http://www.lehigh.edu/~amsp/2005/05/ashes-snow-traveling-circus .html; accessed July 23, 2007).

29. *Ashes and Snow* Web site.

30. From the title of Rosaldo's article "Imperialist Nostalgia," *Representations* 26 (Spring 1989).

31. Interview with John Canning, in "Gregory Colbert's *Ashes and Snow*," March 28, 2006, http://www.travel.news.yahoo.com/b/rba_daily/20060328/ rba_daily3223 (accessed May 4, 2006).

32. Ibid.

33. Rapturous reviews far outnumber critical ones in media coverage of the show. Snippets of the exhibit's glowing reviews are routinely posted on the *Ashes and Snow* Web site. One clip, from a review in the *New York Times,* rhapsodized, "They are simply windows to a world in which silence and patience govern time." A review in Canada's *Globe and Mail* claimed that "Colbert's work operates in a parallel universe to ours, an earnest, refreshing, post-ironic world where pure wonder and awe still reside" (http://www.ashesandsnow.org). Roberta Smith, writing in the *New York Times,* is one of the few reviewers to apprehend the "imperialist nostalgia" that Colbert's show dangerously excites. As well as describing *Ashes and Snow* as "an exercise in conspicuous narcissism that is off the charts, even by today's standards," Smith notes that "Mr. Colbert's sepia-toned images prove once again that while colonialism may be dead or dying, its tropes are ever with us" ("When Nature Becomes a Looking Glass: A Tour through the Exotic Elsewhere," *New York Times,* March 12, 2005).

34. Description from the TED Web site, http://www.ted.com (accessed July 2007).

35. Ibid.

36. Ibid.

37. I discuss animal capital as a literal "species of fetish" in the Introduction to this book under the heading "The Ring of Tautology."

38. *Ashes and Snow* Web site.

39. Divya Watal, "Nomadic Elephant Exhibit Opens on Pier," *Villager* 74, no. 44 (March 9).

40. Edward Steichen, introduction to *The Family of Man,* prologue by Carl Sandburg (New York: Museum of Modern Art, 1955), 4.

41. Roland Barthes, *Mythologies,* trans. Annette Lavers (London: Jonathan Cape, 1972), 101.

42. *Ashes and Snow* Web site.

43. Haraway, "Universal Donors," 240. Haraway offers an acute reading of Steichen's *The Family of Man* photodocumentary in this chapter.

44. Anne McClintock, *Imperial Leather: Race, Gender, and Sexuality in the Colonial Contest* (New York: Routledge, 1995), 40.

45. *Ashes and Snow* Web site.

46. Slavoj Žižek, "Multiculturalism, or the Cultural Logic of Multinational Capitalism," *New Left Review* 225 (1997): 28–51.

47. Ibid., 37.

48. Quoted by Donna Haraway in *Primate Visions: Gender, Race, and Nature in the World of Modern Science* (New York: Routledge, 1989), 134.

49. Michael Hardt and Antonio Negri, *Empire* (Cambridge, Mass.: Harvard University Press, 2000), 22. Hardt and Negri argue that "the formation of Empire is a *response* to proletarian internationalism," including anticolonial struggles (51). In other words, "The multitude is the real productive force of our social world, whereas Empire is a mere apparatus of capture that lives only off the vitality of the multitude—as Marx would say, a vampire regime of accumulated dead labor that survives only by sucking off the blood of the living" (62).

50. Renato Rosaldo, "Imperialist Nostalgia," *Representations* 26 (Spring 1989): 107.

51. Rosaldo notes that the object of imperialist nostalgia is not only another culture but also Nature. Imperialist nostalgia encompasses an "attitude of reverence toward the natural [that] developed at the same time that North Americans intensified the destruction of their human and natural environment" ("Imperialist Nostalgia," 109).

52. From Laura McCandish's article for Columbia University's news service, "Marrying Art and Science: Nomadic Museum Prepares to Travel the World," March 1, 2005, http://www.jscms.jrn.columbia.edu/cns/2005-03-01/mccandish-nomadart.

53. *BusinessWeek*, August 5, 2007, http://images.businessweek.com/ss/06/07/top_brands/source/72.htm (accessed August 6, 2007).

54. On the Web site of the Rolex Institute, supplied as a link on the *Ashes and Snow* Web site, appears a commodity timeline that inadvertently traces the role Rolex watches have played in the microcapture of once extrinsic time. In 1955, according to the timeline, "the Oyster Perpetual GMT Master is launched, making it possible to read the time in any two time zones." That was also the year that "the first atomic clock, accurate to within one

second in 300 years, is invented." In 1956, "The Oyster Perpetual Day-Date is created and features a display which spells out the day of the week in full. Today it is available in 26 languages." And so on and so forth, along a series of dates marking time's commodification, standardization, and globalization (http://www.rolex.com).

55. Found on the Rolex Web site, http://www.rolex.com.

56. Alan and Nancy Colchester, "The Origin of Bovine Spongiform Encephalopathy: The Human Prion Disease Hypothesis," *Lancet* 366, no. 9488 (September 3, 2005): 859.

57. Indeed, the Colchesters' article did not pass without comment. Susaria Shankar, head of neurology at the National Institute of Mental Health and Neuroscience in Bangalore, India, cautioned that their hypothesis was not based on evidence. The Hindu Human Rights Organization responded to the potential "anti-Hindu sentiment" suggested by the Colchesters' hypothesis, arguing that Hindu funerary practices are a "convenient scapegoat" that displaces blame from the practice of animal cannibalism, or what they describe as the "unnatural form of feeding and rearing domesticated animals" ("The Anti-Hindu 'Mis-Steak' in CJD Research," http://www.hinduhumanrights.org/articles/mis_steak.html [accessed May 28, 2006]).

58. Elizabeth Povinelli, *The Cunning of Recognition: Indigenous Alterities and the Making of Australian Multiculturalism* (Durham, N.C.: Duke University Press, 2002), 5.

59. Ibid., 27.

60. Mike Davis, *The Monster at Our Door: The Global Threat of Avian Flu* (New York: New Press, 2005), 47.

61. For instance, H5N1-infected birds were discovered in 2003 in the province of British Columbia, Canada, resulting in the mass culling of approximately 19 million poultry and fowl.

62. Davis, *Monster at Our Door,* 123.

63. Ibid., 177.

64. This and other director's speeches and WHO media releases related to avian flu can be accessed through its online media center at http://www.who.int/csr/disease/avian_influenza/mediacentre/en/index.html.

65. Charles L. Briggs, "Communicability, Racial Discourse, and Disease," *Annual Review of Anthropology* (first published online as Review in Advance [anthro.annualreview.org]) (June 14, 2005): 279. As Briggs says of "biocommunicability": "The term puns on various senses of the word. Communicability suggests volubility, the ability to be readily communicated and

understood transparently, and microbes' capacity to spread from body to body. I add a new sense to the word in which communicability is infectious—the ability of messages and the ideologies in which they are embedded to find audiences and locate them socially and politically" (274).

66. Melinda Liu, "The Flimsy Wall of China," *Newsweek,* October 31, 2005, 41.

67. Davis, *Monster at Our Door,* 60.

68. In a news article about SARS in China, Briggs notes that "the *New York Times* featured images of cooks cutting up animals not found on U.S. plates and customers selecting live, seemingly exotic animals for their meal" (Briggs, "Communicability," 276).

69. Zhan, "Civet Cats," 33.

70. Hardt and Negri, *Empire,* 136.

71. The Chinese government is known to have concealed incidences of avian flu and to have threatened that "any physician or journalist who reported on the disease would risk being persecuted for leaking state secrets" (Davis, *Monster at Our Door,* 70).

72. Davis, *Monster at Our Door,* 4.

73. "On October 18, 2005, H5N1 made its first known appearance in Europe, when a Thai man was stopped at Zaventem Airport, in Brussels, for a random drug check. Within his hand luggage, packed into plastic tubes, customs officers found two small, crested hawk eagles" (Vincent Lam, M.D., and Colin Lee, M.D., *The Pandemic Flu and You: A Canadian Guide,* foreword by Margaret Atwood [Toronto: Doubleday Canada, 2006], 216).

74. The news story was posted online at http://www.bloomberg.com/apps/news?pid=10000080&sid=aiu7Xi_3TZEY&refer=asia.

75. Ibid.

76. Ibid.

77. Davis, *Monster at Our Door,* 81.

78. The Retort Collective is a group of dissenting intellectuals in San Francisco who analyze the politics of spectacle in relation to new contexts of military neo-liberalism.

79. Iain Boal, T. J. Clark, Joseph Matthews, and Michael Watts, *Afflicted Powers: Capital and Spectacle in a New Age of War* (London: Verso, 2005), 75. Hardt and Negri argue a similar point: "Primitive accumulation is not a process that happens once and then is done with; rather, capitalist relations of production and social classes have to be reproduced continually" (*Empire,* 258).

80. Lam and Lee, *Pandemic Flu and You*, 221.

81. Carly Weeks, *CanWest News Service*, November 30, 2006.

82. Ibid.

83. Jia-Rui Chong, "Tamiflu Linked to Abnormal Behavior: Delirium and Suicide," *Los Angeles Times*, November 14, 2006.

84. "Sales of Tamiflu Soar amid Pandemic Worries," CTV News, August 22, 2005, http://www.ctv.ca/servlet/ArticleNews/story/CTVNews/1124715724150_1201249241?hub=Health (accessed October 8, 2008).

85. "The WHO has a stockpile of 3 million courses of Tamiflu in Switzerland and the United States that can be rushed to the first affected areas to treat everyone in a geographic area" (Lam and Lee, *Pandemic Flu and You*, 80).

86. That said, Tamiflu is not Hoffman–La Roche's first drug to be linked to adverse, even fatal, side effects. "Roche is also the manufacturer of the drug *Lariam* (Mefloquine), an anti-malarial prescription medication. Larium is linked to severe psychotic episodes, panic attacks, convulsions, epilepsy, headaches, hallucinations, paranoia, suicide attempts and homicidal rage." Hoffman–La Roche is also "the target of several human rights campaigns and some government officials who claim that the company deliberately withheld and overpriced AIDS drugs in Africa. The controversy in the AIDS/Africa scandal also included allegations that the company refused to allow cheaper, generic versions of their AIDS drugs to be made" (http://www.onlinelawyersource.com/drug_company/hoffman_la_roche.html; accessed July 13, 2007).

87. Davis, *Monster at Our Door*, 55.

88. WHO Web site, http://www.who.int/csr/alertresponse/ (accessed January 2007).

89. This war is not just a matter of surveillance, of flu-testing networks and rationalized poultry and livestock production, but has also involved the slaughter of tens of millions of birds since the deadly strain of H5N1 emerged in China in 2003.

90. TED Web site, http://www.ted.com (accessed June 1, 2008).

91. Martin O'Connor, "On the Misadventures of Capitalist Nature," in *Is Capitalism Sustainable: Political Economy and the Politics of Ecology*, ed. Martin O'Connor (New York: Guilford, 1994), 131.

92. TED Web site.

93. Rosaldo, "Imperialist Nostalgia," 110.

94. Jacques Derrida, "The Animal That Therefore I Am (More to Follow)," trans. David Wills, *Critical Inquiry* 28 (Winter 2002): 415.

95. Ibid.
96. Jacques Derrida, "Autoimmunity: Real and Symbolic Suicides; A Dialogue with Jacques Derrida," In *Philosophy in a Time of Terror: Dialogues with Jurgen Habermas and Jacques Derrida* (Chicago: University of Chicago Press, 2007), 94.
97. Butler, *Precarious Life,* 149.
98. Derrida, "The Animal That Therefore I Am," 405.

Postscript

1. Fredric Jameson, *Postmodernism, or The Cultural Logic of Late Capitalism* (Durham, N.C.: Duke University Press, 1992), x. I take it that Jameson has some idea of a "first nature" in mind when he writes, "Postmodernism is what you have when the modernization process is complete and nature is gone for good" (x).
2. Jacques Derrida, "The Animal That Therefore I Am (More to Follow)," trans. David Wills, *Critical Inquiry* 28 (Winter 2002): 394.
3. Michael Taussig, *Mimesis and Alterity: A Particular History of the Senses* (New York: Routledge, 1993), 252.
4. Benedict Anderson, *Imagined Communities: Reflections on the Origin and Spread of Nationalism* (London: Verso, 1983).
5. Jacques Derrida, "'Eating Well,' or The Calculation of the Subject: An Interview with Jacques Derrida," trans. Peter Connor and Avita Ronell, in *Who Comes after the Subject?* ed. Eduardo Cadava, Peter Connor, and Jean-Luc Nancy (New York: Routledge, 1991), 113.
6. Lorne Gunter, "Eat Beef for the Sake of Our Farmers, and Our Province: Latest Mad Cow Case Will Hit Alberta Harder than Anywhere Else," *Edmonton Journal,* December 31, 2003, A13. John Peck, in an article titled "The Mad Cows Finally Come Home" (*Z Magazine* 17, no. 3), notes that British politicians had likewise modeled a commitment to faithful meat eating during the BSE epidemic in the United Kingdom in the 1980s and 1990s: "In one of the more bizarre public relations attempts to boost consumer morale, British agriculture secretary, John Gummer, fed a hamburger to his four-year-old daughter before television cameras in 1990. Three months later British health minister, Stephen Dorrell, was before Parliament telling the world that mad cow could also sicken humans. Six years later, the first victims emerged. Over 140 people have now died in Europe" (online posting, March 2004, http://zmagsite.zmag.Mar2004/pecko304.org/html; accessed May 2, 2004).

7. According to a Canadian government report, two U.S.-owned multi-nationals, Cargill and Tyson, "control 80 per cent of [Canadian beef packing] capacity." The report, *Empowering Canadian Farmers in the Marketplace*, was written by the Honourable Wayne Easter, MP for Malpeque, parliamentary secretary to the minister of agriculture and agrifood, in July 2005 (http://www.agr.gc.ca/farmincomee.phtml; accessed November 26, 2007).

8. Dr. Stanley Prusiner won the 1997 Nobel Prize in medicine for his discovery of prions.

9. Throughout this book I have made reference to Marx's visceral metaphor of "mere jelly" in describing labor time as the abstract measure of exchange value. See the Introduction to this book, where I suggest that in Marx's metaphor we can glimpse the "real subsumption" of nature as well as of labor.

10. Taussig, *Mimesis and Alterity*, 246.

11. Jean and John Comaroff, "Millennial Capitalism: First Thoughts on a Second Coming," in *Millennial Capitalism and the Culture of Neoliberalism*, ed. Jean Comaroff and John L. Comaroff (Durham, N.C.: Duke University Press, 2001), 3–4.

12. Antonio Negri, "The Constitution of Time," in *Time for Revolution*, trans. Matteo Mandarini (New York: Continuum, 2003), 27.

13. Bruno Latour, *The Politics of Nature: How to Bring the Sciences into Democracy*, trans. Catherine Porter (Cambridge, Mass.: Harvard University Press, 2004), 112, 114.

14. Jürgen A. Richt, Poothappillai Kasinathan, Amir N. Hamir, et al., "Production of Cattle Lacking Prion Protein," in *Nature Biotechnology*, published online December 31, 2006, on the *Nature Biotechnology* Web site, http://www.nature.com/nbt (accessed November 22, 2007).

15. Fred J. Dunn, auditor general of Alberta, *Report of the Auditor General on the Alberta government's BSE-related Assistance Programs* (July 27, 2004), http://www.oag.ab.ca/?V_DOC_ID=846.

16. Bill Brown, *The Material Unconscious: American Amusement, Stephen Crane, and the Economics of Play* (Chicago: University of Chicago Press, 1996), 11–12.

17. Jean Baudrillard, *Simulacra and Simulations*, trans. Sheila Faria Glaser (Ann Arbor: University of Michigan Press, 1994), 1.

18. Ibid., 22.

Index

Spivak, Gayatri Chakravorty, 69, 129, 137, 249n61, 250n80, 262n115; as postcolonial theorist, 25

spokescritters in ad campaigns, 42, 161, 165–66, 178, 269n82

Stanton, Jeffrey, 267n57

Steichen, Edward: *Family of Man*, 197–99, 276n27, 278n43

stereotypes, 4–6, 154, 196, 210, 234n7, 255n26, 261n94, 267n58, 274n12. *See also* racism

stock: biological, 14, 24, 74; and film stock, 104–14; markets, 126; market speculation, 14; and rendering, 24; as virtual and carnal capital, 126

stockyards, 92–96, 106, 126, 255–56nn. *See also* meatpacking industry; slaughter

Stowe, Harriet Beecher: *Uncle Tom's Cabin*, 154, 261n94, 267n58

strikes, labor: sitdown and wildcat strikes, 128–29; stockyards, 255–56. *See also* protest

subaltern: and alterity of animal desire, 138; and animal protest, 129–30; and peasant farmers, 213; and Spivak, 129; and women, 129

subjectivity: and animal, 156, 197; and cinema, 153; loss of, 57; and subject-form of capital, 189

substance: animal and ethnic alterity, 200, 220; of animal life, 17; of communication, 182; fetishism of, 6; of interspecies intimacy, 203; pathological, 142, 200, 204; perishable, 63; and Saussure, 26; of the sign, 143

subsumption, 55, 69–70, 76–80, 86, 249n61, 283n9; and biopower, 7;

formal, 69, 75, 77, 83; and globalization, 225; of labor, 257n49, 283n9; of mimesis, 59; of nature, 76–86; real, 16, 69–70, 75–86; and rendering, 59, 70, 75–76, 82; tautological time of, 17–18, 77–78, 81, 203, 228

survival: and biopower, 39, 226; and Derrida, 242–43n131; of the fittest, 125; of life itself, 182–83; and *mimetisme*, 57; pandemic fear of, 207

Swift and Company, 95–100, 256n32, 256–57n34

symbolic capital, 3, 7, 14, 20, 190, 236–37n40, 272–73n117

sympathetic magic, 22. *See also* mimesis; Taussig, Michael

Tamiflu, 212, 215–16, 221, 275n16, 28nn83–86

tannery city (Peabody, Mass.), 110

Taussig, Michael: *Mimesis and Alterity*, 22–23, 49–59, 118–19, 124–25, 136, 226, 228, 244n3, 259n73, 262n106

tautological time, 16–18, 45, 52, 59, 75–78, 81–83, 86, 203, 220, 228

tautology: of animal cannibalism, 47; of animal capital, 138; of Animal Copyright Foundation, 219; and fetishism, 14–20, 229; and rendering, 232; and subsumption, 17–18, 77–78, 81, 203, 228

taxidermy, 130, 270n89

taxonomies: of animal anatomy, 3; of colonial kinship, 198; of gelatin dry stock, 111; of species classification, 122–25

Taylor, Edward B.: *Primitive Culture*, 135–36, 238–39n59
Taylor, Frederick Winslow, 72–74, 88–89, 113, 119, 253nn4–7
Taylorism, 73–74, 88–89, 113, 128, 253n6
techno-tele-discursivity, 39
TED (Technology, Entertainment, Design) conference, 194, 196, 219
telecommunication. *See* communication; telemobility
Telecommunications Workers Union, 178
telemobility: and animal currencies, 45–46, 131–79, 263–73nn; and biomobility, 182; and biopolitics, 143, 158, 161, 164, 169, 179; and biopower, 138, 153, 155–56; and capitalism, 132–33, 136–38, 149, 154–55, 158, 164–65, 169, 176, 179; and cinema, 139–44, 150–53, 156, 158, 160; and fantasy of "painless transmission," 143, 182; and fetishism, 42–45, 132, 134–39, 148–49, 153, 161–79; and globalization, 161, 225; and labor, 162, 171–73, 178; and metaphor, 132–33, 135, 137, 139–41, 144, 148, 153–54, 178; and mimesis, 164; and monstration, 139–43, 146, 150, 153, 161, 164, 179, 264n22; and pathology, 142–50, 158–63, 169, 172; and protests, 177; and rendering, 132–52, 156–58, 162, 165, 178; as telecommunication, 27, 42–46, 131–79, 225, 263–73nn, 264n20, 265n28. *See also* automobility; biomobility; communication; electric animals

Telus Mobility Inc. ad campaigns, 42, 46, 51, 140–43, 161–79, 264n19, 269n82, 270n90, 270n95, 271n99
Tepe, Richard, 259n70
terrorism, 10; and extreme rendering, 23, 229; and terrorizing times, 227. *See also* bioterrorism
Tesla, Nikola, 160
Theory of the Leisure Class, The (Veblen), 71
Thompson, Frederick, 154–57
Tichi, Cecelia: *Shifting Gears*, 71–73
time-motion studies, 72–73, 90–91, 93, 101–5, 116, 119, 123, 128, 144
Topsy (elephant), 46, 93, 107–8, 139–43, 149–61, 171–72, 261n94, 264nn17–18, 266n48, 266–67n49, 267n58, 268n61
transnationalism, 6–8, 13, 32, 111–12, 175, 190, 210, 243n145
Tsing, Anna Lowenhaupt, 238n56
tuberculosis, 228. *See also* diseases, wasting
28 Days Later (film), 181–82, 188

Uncle Tom's Cabin (Stowe), 154, 261n94, 267n58
United Nations, 172, 173, 174, 175
universality, 4, 60, 65–66, 199–200
U.S. Central Intelligence Agency (CIA), 23
U.S. Food and Drug Administration (FDA), 214–15, 227, 252n95
U.S. Forest Service, 73
U.S. Homeland Security Advisory System, 219

Nicole Shukin is assistant professor of English at the University of Victoria in British Columbia, Canada.